Bahawalpur

ANABEL LOYD

Bahawalpur

The Kingdom That Vanished

VINTAGE
An imprint of Penguin Random House

VINTAGE

USA | Canada | UK | Ireland | Australia
New Zealand | India | South Africa | China

Vintage is part of the Penguin Random House group of companies whose addresses can be found at global.penguinrandomhouse.com

Published by Penguin Random House India Pvt. Ltd
4th Floor, Capital Tower 1, MG Road,
Gurugram 122 002, Haryana, India

First published in Vintage by Penguin Random House India 2020

10 9 8 7 6 5 4 3 2

ISBN 9780670093779

Typeset in Bembo by Manipal Technologies Limited, Manipal
Printed at Replika Press Pvt. Ltd, India

www.penguin.co.in

For Aneeza and Bahawal

'What's past is prologue'

CONTENTS

FOREWORD

It all began with a description of the Coronation Durbar of the King Emperor, George V, and Queen Mary at Delhi in December 1911. At the military review on 14 December, the Indian chiefs led their state troops in person, and it was the youngest of those princes who held all eyes. He was the nawab of Bahawalpur, aged seven, who:

> led his camel-corps past, himself riding a camel in front of a grave and trusty trooper. Dressed in full uniform of khaki with gold-embroidered skirts, the little fellow boldly faced the King-Emperor at the saluting point, threw out a baby's right arm to its full length, and with perfect correctness and time in every motion brought down his tiny sword to the salute. Seventy or eighty years hence, it may be, he will be conspicuous as the only survivor of the many gallant gentlemen who rode past King George on that day.[1]

Seventy years later, that shining child, General Jalalat ul-Mulk, Rukn ud-Daula, Saif ud-Daula, Hafiz ul-Mulk, Mukhlis ud-Daula wa Muin ud-Daula, Al-Haji Nawab Sir Sadiq Muhammad Khan Bahadur Abbasi V, Nusrat-i-Jung, Amir of the God-gifted Kingdom of Bahawalpur, GCSI, GCIE, KCVO, ruler of a state the size of Denmark, where the five life-giving rivers of the Punjab combine as the Panjnad, had died five years earlier at his English home. By then, he was no longer a ruling prince; his country had divided and his state had disappeared into the united entity of West Pakistan. His body had been carried back to Bahawalpur, to the palace of Sadiqgarh and thence by gun carriage into the desert to his final resting place in the family mausoleum.

I had never heard of Bahawalpur. John Fortescue, eyewitness chronicler of the 1911 Durbar, wrote truthfully of the Indian people: 'No one man has ever seen, nor will ever see, in spite of motor cars, and aeroplanes and railways, one hundredth of the eighteen hundred thousand square miles over which they are spread. No one man has ever visited, nor will ever visit all the cities, living and dead, which they have builded.' Nevertheless, like all visitors to India who have read their South Asian histories and their travellers' tales, I had some idea that I had at least heard the names at one time or another of most of the former princely states.

Quite wrong, as I discovered when I tackled the list of all 565 states in existence at Independence. They ranged from the twenty-one-gun-salute states, remembered by one British viceroy with the mnemonic 'hot kippers make a good breakfast', of Hyderabad, Kashmir, Mysore, Gwalior and Baroda, to the tiny non-salute slip of a village in Gujarat called Vejanoness, with an area of 0.76 sq. km and a population of 206. Bahawalpur was much closer to the kippers. Slightly smaller in land area than Bikaner in Rajasthan, with which it marched, and larger than Jaipur, it was, like them, a seventeen-gun-salute state.

Since then, unlike its neighbours in tourist-friendly Rajasthan, Bahawalpur had vanished from the map so far at least as foreigners were concerned, behind the borders of an unexplored and potentially perilous Pakistan. My lack of recognition of the name showed my ignorance of the geography and literature of Partition, when Bahawalpur had been on the front line of the rift with India. In Delhi, vague memories were stirred in the minds of older generations, of family homes in Lahore or Karachi, of the lives of their parents and grandparents before Partition and, of Bahawalpur, of notions of a wealthy Punjab state, glamorous nawabs, fleets of Rolls-Royces and remarkable palaces lost to view.

As the state was absorbed into the Punjab, it became a less-favoured backwater, marginalized by the upper-Punjab power base, with little of the wealth and few people or businesses flowing south. Even in Lahore and Islamabad, few people had been to Bahawalpur. They knew of, and could sometimes name, palaces 'saved' by the army; they remembered family quarrels propagated in public and through the courts, and slippery tales of secret tunnels and buried treasure. Beyond the tittle-tattle, most knew of the respected and very private 'Nawab Sahib', Salahuddin Abbasi, grandson of Sadiq Muhammad Khan V, who kept his own counsel except in the matter of promises made and broken by successive governments on behalf of his people in Bahawalpur.

Ubiquitous Google provided photographs of nineteenth-century palaces, sketchy Abbasi family trees that stretched back beyond the birth of Islam and, the greatest initial lure to me, images of the spectacular Derawar Fort, its massive brick bastions rooted in the sand of the Cholistan Desert. I had been to Derawar's close cousin, the Bhatner Fort (otherwise known as Hanumangarh), only a few months earlier. Part of the same chain of defensive forts along the invasion route from Central Asia into India, it had once been the seat of the same Bhati Rajputs who held Derawar.

In century-old photographs, Hanumangarh stood like Derawar alone in the desert, an outpost of Bikaner state. Now it is in the centre of an eponymous market town, more busily Punjabi than Rajasthani. Dwellings are built almost into the monumental bastions; a good view of the extent of the ramparts requires invasion of someone's roof space, tea and a community photography sitting. The interior of the fort is ruined but the rusted signs bearing the hopeful protective mantra of the Archaeological Survey of India (ASI) are matched by some essential restoration to the walls.

Now I imagined a desert quest. An expedition, possibly involving camels, in search of Derawar and the further crumbling links of fortifications once intended to protect India's wealth. I spoke to Pakistani friends in London. How to get to Derawar? And straightaway it all became simple. Everyone has a cousin or a sister, brother, uncle, a whole extended family spread across the world in the Pakistani diaspora. I am inclined to believe that it is possible to get almost anywhere through the web of Pakistani relationships. The home country is the easiest of all and the most hospitable. The traveller is delivered from hand to hand along the family line like a precious parcel, looked after, entertained, feasted, fattened, carried hither and thither according to her interests and desires, and so it was for me to Derawar.

Only, slightly sadly, in the end there were no camels. It was a more prosaic twenty-first-century day trip in 4WD comfort and a banquet of a picnic with the Abbasi family, guardians of the fort since 1733. Magnificent Derawar lived up to all expectations, shadowed only by the sorrows of its relatively recent internal ruination and fears for its future care in a country careless of its antique treasures. For nearly 300 years, the great fort has been at the centre of the story of the princes who are buried there in gilded marble halls and turquoise-tiled sarcophagi. It is where the last ruler was finally brought to lie in perpetuity in a long, cool room, surrounded by his forefathers. For me, the towering walls of Derawar and those quiet and beautiful tombs were a goal reached but, as things turned out, also the beginning of a family story to be told.

Later, in the garden of his great-, or it may have been several more greats, grandmother's bungalow, he is not sure, behind ruinous Sadiqgarh Palace, at Dera Nawab Sahib outside Bahawalpur city, I swapped outdated reminiscences of old-fashioned English nannies with Salahuddin Abbasi, who retains the religious title of amir of Bahawalpur. The house itself is reputedly haunted. Certainly, it is one of those, when the electricity flickers and dims on a chilly February evening and the gas fire dies on the dot at 9 p.m., where thoughts turn to former inhabitants. It has the same atmosphere as a Viennese palace, the feeling of someone, his photograph there on a nearby table, just gone from the room, or standing out of sight in the shadow of a bookcase, watching present generations play an improbable but hard-fought game of whist.

Moving on from childhood afflictions like being fed sago pudding for breakfast by an English nanny, which I still don't believe possible, Salahuddin, with Coco the Pekingese preening on his knee, began to tell the long history of his family. His birth on 29 July 1946, the first son of the heir to a royal *gaddi*, had to be announced formally by telegram to the viceroy, Lord Wavell. Just over a year later, India became independent, and Bahawalpur acceded to the new independent country of Pakistan.

This book is based upon further conversations with Salahuddin in Islamabad and Lahore over several weeks in 2016. He hoped, by telling his story to a foreigner who started with an open mind and scant knowledge of Pakistan, let alone of the Abbasi family, to avoid the whole spectrum of shades of truth and points of view that colour and reinterpret any Pakistani tale and may make 'Good Morning' a political statement, a promise or a threat. The story is, as far as possible, Salahuddin's view of his family history, his country and his particular interpretation of Pakistan since Independence and Partition. Like me, he studied *The Tempest* at school. There have been times enough during the past seventy years when he has had reason to believe, 'Hell is empty, all the devils are here.'

INTRODUCTION

History is to a nation or community what memory is to an individual. History enables the members of a nation or community to recognise their identity with previous generations from whom they have inherited their religious beliefs, their moral ideals, their social and legal institutions, in short, their whole culture.[1]

At a meeting in Bombay between 27 and 29 July 1946, the council of the All-India Muslim League (AIML) withdrew their previous acceptance of the Cabinet Mission's constitutional proposals for independent India and agreed on a programme of Direct Action for 'the immediate achievement of an independent and fully sovereign state of Pakistan'. The travails of the Partition of India and the difficult emergence of a new country had begun.

On 29 July that year, Salahuddin Abbasi was born in the western Himalayas at Al-Hilal,[2] the summer house among the tea gardens of Palampur built by his grandfather in the 1930s. His fifteen-year-old mother, his father's much-loved only wife, was the granddaughter of his grandfather's former tutor and éminence grise, Maulvi Ghulam Hussain. She had been chosen for his father, Nawabzada Muhammad Abbas Khan, the nawab's favourite English consort. She has been a quiet witness to the whole capricious lifetime of Pakistan, the perversity in practice of the country's successive leaders, the misery of her husband in the public roles forced on him and the battles of her eldest son to right or mitigate the wrongs to Bahawalpur implemented by those leaders.

In his presidential address to the new Constituent Assembly of Pakistan on 11 August 1947, three days before Independence, Muhammad Ali Jinnah reiterated his vision for his country. First, he reminded the assembly that power brings great responsibility. Its first duty would be to maintain law and order; corruption should be put down 'with an iron hand'; nepotism not countenanced; and the well-being of the people, especially of the poor, should be of primary consideration; that there should be no discrimination between any community, caste or creed; religious affiliation should be down to the personal faith of the individual but all would be citizens, and equal citizens, of the state. He pointed out that the endless 'angularities' of the various communities of India had been the 'biggest hindrance in the way of India to attain freedom and independence and but for this we would have been free people long ago'. Jinnah also said:

> As you know, history shows that in England, conditions, some time ago, were much worse than those prevailing in India today. The Roman Catholics and the Protestants persecuted each other. Even now there are some States in existence where there are discriminations made and bars imposed against a particular class. Thank God, we are not starting in those days. We are starting in the days where there is no discrimination, no distinction between one community and another, no discrimination between one caste or creed and another. We are starting with this fundamental principle that we are all citizens and equal citizens of one State.

So much of that dream had already been bloodied and reduced by the violence that had further precipitated the moment of Partition during the first year of Salahuddin Abbasi's life. In the decades since, he has watched as Jinnah's image of Pakistan has been buried. Not only under the flow of patronage and corruption that oils the cogs of state institutions at all levels but under the illusion and imperative, the 'mirage', of the Islamic state.[3] The sheer one-upmanship of the everyday, increasingly archaic, public practice of religion in Pakistan hinders the running of a contemporary progressive state and argues an almost impossible case for reinstatement of Jinnah's aspirations for nationality rather than communality. Basic good governance and state machinery operating for the benefit of the nation, not the individual, remains a simpler, more tangible ambition from which new understanding might grow, but the Hercules who will clean out the present Augean stable at the heart of government has not yet arrived.

It is hard for a visitor to Pakistan, harder still for those in the country whose spirit has been consumed by the endless forced engagement with dishonesty and corruption, to see beyond the losses and failures. Easier by far to take comfort in a longer view of life based on religious belief and better things to come. The nation suffers from seventy years of broken promises, the loss of honour, respect, history and heritage, and yet many of the generation who remember Independence remain alive to memories of the high expectation at the birth of their nation and believe they may yet come to pass, Inshallah.

Salahuddin Abbasi's mother-in-law, Suraiya Aslam, a biochemist and his mother's younger sister, continues to engage in the political battle for governance of her country that might come closer to the image conjured by the Quaid-i-Azam.[4] More optimistic for the future than her nephew, she sees the circle beginning to turn again through the agency of the PTI, the Pakistan Tehreek-i-Insaf party[5] founded by Imran Khan in 1996. Unfortunately, the PTI's centrist, populist and anti-corruption vision of an egalitarian, democratic, modern Islamic welfare state, secure in its sovereignty against outside interference and based on principles laid down by Jinnah, is easier to pursue in theory than in practice. In spite of electoral gains in 2013, the all-important tacit approval of the Pakistan Army and the ability to motivate the hopeful to turn out in large numbers at anti–status quo protest rallies, Imran Khan has not yet found the success he seeks. As the purity of his message is further diluted by expedient orthodoxy on religious matters and the double-edged sword of affiliation with well-known older-style politicians, it remains to be seen if his light waxes or wanes. A further obstacle to his progress against longer-established parties is the ubiquity of a level of corruption in the system that discourages even his supporters from the ordinary populace from voting for a man unlikely ever to have favours to distribute.[6]

The divisions in Pakistani society are wider than ever. The old may clearly remember the birth pangs of their country, but they are already history to the selfie generation. For them, a residual and well-stocked hatred of their Indian neighbours is the most prevalent continuing reminder of Pakistan's violent nativity. En masse, the young are less interested than before in history and heritage. Their tragedy in the long run, but it is the privilege of the old and the wealthy to conserve the treasures of the past, and youth must first look forward. Pakistan is more than ever girt with the restraints of caste, creed and class, but young people continue to dream of something better and of levelling the ground. Those living in extreme poverty may be easily seduced or coerced by the promises of extreme Islam: a glorious life to come after death providing some sort of solace or reward for the lack of any uplift through education or public services during the only earthly existence available to them.

For the privileged, those who have inherited status or have gained it through the acquisition of vast new wealth, education abroad has become standard. Not all are lured for long by migration for the sake of further fortune and life with fewer complications elsewhere in the world. Those graduates who return are entrepreneurial, creative and determined to find ways to circumvent or rise above endemic corruption in order to move forward. They may already be enmeshed in the threads of nepotism and corruption by virtue of the endless unbreakable network of familial connections at the top of Pakistani politics and society. Some will accept the easy pickings, but there are others who resent the implicit dishonesty and endless circularity of the faces and families who hold power, strangle progress and continue to impoverish their country, for their personal enrichment.

In geopolitical terms, Pakistan is young but the world has changed dramatically in the last seventy years. The new generation has reached adulthood in a different millennium. Pakistan looks backwards for religious authenticity, backwards to a dream of national identity and unity never fulfilled after Partition tore the country from its past. But Pakistan no longer looks back far enough to its extraordinary history as part of a greater whole. That past was cast into the deep chasm of Partition. Nowadays the country often appears neither to look back nor forwards beyond the trappings of new infrastructure in transport systems, shopping malls and increased urbanization. Such changes leave the poor exactly where they have always been, with nothing, and, regardless of the blandishments of government, does little to encourage outsiders to come in. Perhaps the next generation can bring change and break through the layers of the nepotism and corruption ruining their country to take a long view of their history, towards a future where some of the dreams of Independence are extant.

The narrative of Bahawalpur and its rulers also takes the armchair time traveller far back through the long past of the subcontinent.

Further again, to Muhammad and the early spread of Islam. The choice of Nawab Sadiq Muhammad V to follow Muhammad Ali Jinnah towards his vision of a Muslim homeland in 1947 created no less of a divide between the past and the future of his family and of Bahawalpur than that between the history, presents and futures of India and Pakistan. The author of a 1959 history of Bahawalpur wrote of the moment when the amir signed away the last remnants of state sovereignty to Pakistan on 20 December 1954,[7] asking 'Was it surrender or sacrifice?'[8]

There are two sides to the story of the last nawab—no, this is Pakistan, there are truths and near-truths, myths, legends, rumour and lies—but his sometimes-colourful life did not exclude him from the ranks of the modernizing rulers of princely states of the late nineteenth and early twentieth centuries in terms of education and public health. They included his co-religionists in Bhopal and Rampur, but Bahawalpur was the only state of any size with both a Muslim ruler and a principally Muslim population. Beyond majority religion, Bahawalpur had far more in common with its neighbouring states in Rajasthan than with the small, habitually warring tribal states spread across the rest of what is now Pakistan.

The debt on the Sutlej Valley canal and irrigation project imposed by the paramount power during the nawab's minority hung over his head and curtailed his powers for much of his reign. World War II brought relief, with a monumental rise in agricultural values and land prices. By Partition, relatively well managed to avoid loss of life in Bahawalpur, there was free healthcare, primary and secondary education, and Bahawalpur had delivered a five-year plan. According to Sir Richard Marsh Crofton, British prime minister of Bahawalpur during 1942–47, expenditure on the army, the nawab's always most-favoured institution, had been trebled during his tenure. In addition, in 1951 he had founded the Sadiq Public School, still maintained today on a 500-acre campus.

Bahawalpur acceded first to Pakistan and, through supplementary instruments of succession and the final Merger Agreement implemented in 1955, became fully integrated. By then, the former nawab had handed over an operational welfare state, his well-resourced army, vast funding from his treasury to keep the institutions of the new country afloat, agricultural wealth, plans and potential for new industry in the Bahawalpur region. On top of that, he was delivering, unknowingly, his lands, palaces, forts, movable chattels, records and long history into the maw of a careless state uninterested in saving an important heritage for the nation or from the squabbles of the large family that was Sadiq Muhammad Khan's most destructive legacy.

Surrender or sacrifice? By 1955, his powers steadily reduced since 1947, Sadiq Muhammad Khan lived mainly in England. Perhaps he simply tried to forget, but his son and heir, Amir Muhammad Abbas Khan Abbasi, was forced to suffer for his inheritance under the socialist stick of Zulfikar Ali Bhutto and the Islamization of Zia ul-Haq. Abbas Khan's daughter-in-law, Salahuddin's wife Moniba, says that he was a good and gentle man. His early death from inherited diabetes seems likely to have been hastened by the strains of family warfare and political stress, and the rulers of his country did their best to recreate the dream of Pakistan, each in his own image, and his family to tear itself limb from limb. His eldest son, Salahuddin, has proved himself a determined fighter and the strong man he has needed to be as he has battled throughout his adult life to save or reinstate what is left of the past in Bahawalpur, to take back what has been stolen by the government or by the army in more recent times and to demand the provincial status promised to his state at Independence, when so much was given willingly and without ties to make reality from Jinnah's dream. Salahuddin's efforts to salvage a share of that dream for Bahawalpur have been as central to his life as his wife and children.

Salahuddin's family story begins with a shadowy view of the far-distant past in Arabia. It comes into sharper focus in the documented lives of princes, admired, disinherited, imprisoned, embattled or poisoned over the past 200 years, embellished with rumours of buried treasure, ghosts and holy men. As for the present, it is not possible to write or recount the wholly unexpurgated version of a life in progress, or even of one already past, if the perceived sins of a sharp mind and quick tongue may be visited by vengeful authority on later generations, or if the fear of such eventuality exists. Salahuddin Abbasi is a forthright man. He is well aware that not all his views are likely to be palatable to the endlessly mutating powers in Pakistan.

Beyond that, the years of loss and destruction of his family's heritage at the hands of Pakistan's rulers have left few records in Pakistan to support his personal memories and account of his family history. Family quarrels, since his grandfather's death and before, have created trails of different truths in recent times and encouraged further destruction that cannot be blamed on the ravages of natural or national agencies. In addition to the loss of facts and artefacts, there are questions in any long family story of received and diluted memory, not only of a family itself but of its chroniclers; axe grinders; sycophants; or genuine reporters of first-hand truth and experience.

The vast archives of the India Office Records in the British Library have provided details of the lives of some of the Bahawalpur princes from the British point of view. The older nineteenth-century records, in the fading looping hand of nameless writers, are also slowly disappearing from sight, but enough decipherable records remain to give at least a partial picture of relatively recent Bahawalpur and the ruling nawabs through the eyes of the paramount power. The servants of the British Empire were rarely seduced by images of beautiful ringletted young men in embroidered coats and diamond crowns if their accounts were in the red or their conduct found wanting. A level of sympathy from a close observer or adviser to a young prince sometimes trumped puritanical teeth-sucking in the corridors of power. Those records and occasional published books such as Sir Penderel Moon's eyewitness account of Bahawalpur during Partition[9] are nevertheless often at odds with accepted family memory.

During Salahuddin Abbasi's lifetime and that of his country, the determination to give a new country a new history to match contemporary development and the ideal of the Islamic state has allowed or encouraged the past to disappear. Lack of care or interest, as well as outright wilful destruction has meant the loss of everything. Papers and records have been shredded or lost to fire, water or insect damage, and there has been widespread despoliation or ruination of the built heritage palaces, historic buildings and national monuments. There is no respect for ancient crafts and skills. A 200-strong team of experienced stonemasons working to restore Emperor Jehangir's tomb in Lahore has been reduced in the space of twelve years to eight ill-paid and disgruntled individuals. Most of them will encourage their sons, the heirs to their craft, to go and work instead on new roads and new housing developments. Those are needed too but not at the cost of Pakistan's history.

In Salahuddin's case, there have been other losses through death or family rift, through the imperatives of service to his state and his country, the personal compulsion to remain independent of established political networks and to be silent in the face of so much surrounding pain and noise. Old friends from university days in London fell by the wayside long ago; old friends in Pakistan have their own loyalties and are compelled to follow their own paths through the maze of economic, political and familial life in Pakistan. Others still, so many, have given up the unequal struggle and joined the worldwide Pakistani diaspora, often with notable success. A huge and spreading family in Bahawalpur 100 years ago has diminished to a handful of aunts, uncles, warring cousins of closer or more distant kinship, all claiming some part of the broken Bahawalpur estate.

Meanwhile, Salahuddin continues to piece the past together, literally as he mends broken art works or creates a mosaic ceiling in Islamabad from wood salvaged from another demolished family house where he lived as a child in Karachi. In a different life he says he would have been a carpenter. His son, Bahawal, returned from university in London, is following his own vision of regeneration through heritage tourism, planting trees and new gardens among the Bahawalpur ruins and hoping one day, with outside help, to recreate an image of the past in palace museums and, best of all, within the bastions of the Derawar Fort.

Who knows what is possible? Pakistan is a country of dishonest government, broken promises and loss, where superstition and religion pour in to fill the voids of disappointment and poverty. The powerful dance their endless pavane, changing partners for temporary expediency. The steps of the dance, laid down on recognized patterns of kinship and patronage, are unchanging. Occasionally, there is a glimmer of something else, possibly an anachronistic harking back to a princely past or maybe a rare sign of respect for integrity and a man of principle who has tried to do his best for his country. In the centre of Islamabad, a policeman manning a security post flagged down Salahuddin Abbasi's car with its recognizable diplomatic plates, stuck his head through the window and asked for 'Nawab Sahib'. No, there was nothing wrong. No, he did not want anything material. He was not a Bahawalpuri but he knew all about Salahuddin. He said he was sorry to stop the car but he would just like the opportunity of shaking the Nawab Sahib's hand.

Part 1

The Wide Sweep of History

1

DYNASTY

Salahuddin Abbasi, amir of Bahawalpur, grandson of the last ruling nawab, is the sixty-second in a line of descent traced back through the Abbasid caliphs of Cairo and Baghdad to Al Abbas Ibn Abdul al Muttalib, uncle of Prophet Muhammad. The Rajput ruling princes of the states of Bikaner and Jaisalmer, in Rajputana, Bahawalpur's near neighbours around the Great Indian Desert until Partition, claimed descent respectively from the sun and the moon. Such are the received and recited genealogies of the past that have added lustre and legitimacy to the names of princes, reiterated through family and folk tradition and notoriously romanticized by James Tod, author of the fabulous *Annals and Antiquities of Rajasthan.*

Whether the Abbasi of Bahawalpur are descended from the uncle of the Prophet via a branch of the Abbasid dynasty can be disputed ad infinitum. Whether the Abbasid dynasty was likewise descended is as lost in the great gaps of unrecorded histories—the who begat whom among the warring Islamic tribes—as the recorded modern history of the rulers of Bahawalpur has been hollowed out by recent forces of destruction. In *The History of Bahawalpur*, published in 1848,[1] Shahamet Ali[2] traces the early history of Islamic conquests of Sindh and the eventual arrival of descendants of the last Abbasid caliph of Baghdad, via five generations of rulers in Egypt, in the person of Sultan Ahmed II sometime between 1366 and 1370. Invading from the coast into Mekran (Makran), Ahmed was faced by Raja Rai Dhorang Sahta, who, on the strength of a terrible dream, sued for peace at the cost of a third of his territory and married his daughter to his former foe to seal the deal.

Thereafter, *The History of Bahawalpur* hurtles down through the generations, pointing out to its readers individuals of particular interest or importance. Here we find Amir Muhammad Chani Khan Abbasi was made a Panjhazari, commander of 5000, by Prince Murad Bukht, the son of Akbar the Great. It is said that when Prince Murad was visiting the governor of Multan, the local chiefs, including Amir Chani Khan were summoned to pay homage to the emperor's son. Why Chani Khan should have been seen by his peers as particularly likely to reap rewards from Prince Murad is not recorded. Perhaps it was all a ruse to rid themselves of an upstart rival.

When the time came for his presentation, Chani Khan discovered that the other chiefs had replaced the rich jewels and offerings he had brought as gifts for the prince with clods of earth and rubbish. Horrified, Chani Khan held his nerve and turned events to his advantage. Standing in front of the prince, he delivered a long and eloquent speech pointing out that he and his tribe were poor refugees with nothing of material value to offer to a great prince. Instead, he said, the had gathered together '*tabruquat*'[3] from the soil of the Holy Kaaba, from Karbala and from other sacred places and carried these relics with them on their migration. Now they offered to Prince Murad that which they held of greater value than all the treasures of the world. Much moved, the prince accepted the sacred relics and rewarded Chani Khan with a royal decree that bestowed tracts of land on him, along the Indus River near Hyderabad, and the governorship of a taluka or district stretching from Makran in Sindh to Marwar (now in Rajasthan). He was also given the title of Hamie Din or Supporter of the Faith. He retired, presumably well satisfied with his deception, to Savistan, now probably Sehwan Sharif[4] in northern Sindh and a town or village then called Jhanker Bazar.

According to *The History,* Chani Khan died in a freak accident when his boat was kicked by a horse and sank. The author further states that the date of his death is unknown but his age—and longevity is used to fill several awkward gaps in *The History*—was 150. Although he was a man of peace, keen to ally himself with other chiefs through negotiation and the exchange of valuable presents, such amity did not survive into the next generation. Of his two sons by a possible Hindu wife, the younger, Daud Khan, survived him long enough to seize the succession, hotly disputed by his deceased elder brother's son, Kalhora Khan. *Sadiqnamah*, a 1959 history of Bahawalpur by Brigadier Nazeer Ali Shah[5] in honour of Nawab Sadiq Muhammad Khan V, notes that the two sections of the Abbasi tribes, Kalhora and Daudputra, quarrelled violently after Chani Khan's death, the Arab tribes siding with the Daudputra.

The reader senses that Brigadier Shah arrives with considerable relief at the moment, sometime at the end of the seventeenth century, that he describes the emergence of the modern history of Bahawalpur state and the Abbasi family. Enough of mythologizing. *The History,* meanwhile, continues to weave taller tales as Daud Khan is forced to retire from civil war with his nephew to found a village and take up agricultural pursuits. His son and grandson are dismissed as dull farmers and the story picks up with Daud

Khan's beautiful great-grandson. He had enough sons and grandsons to beget most of the known tribes and lived to an age of more than 200 years which certainly brings him well on into recorded history. He is known as the great-grandfather or possibly the great-great-grandfather.

It is not hard to understand why, in the face of so much relatively local and recent historical confusion over individual, name, generation, time and place, claiming descent from the family of the Prophet is so disputatious. V.S. Naipaul, whose wife was previously married to a Bahawalpuri landowner, argues that the Abbas of Bahawalpur is not the Abbas of the Abbasids.[6] As Naipaul points out, he is supported in this claim in an article on Bahawalpur in the *Encyclopaedia of Islam* by Shaikh Inayatullah[7] which states that the 'Abbasiyya' of Bahawalpur are named after a local ancestor called Abbas and have nothing to do with the Abbasids of Baghdad or Egypt. They became chiefs independent of the Durrani Afghan kings towards the end of the eighteenth century, thereafter making treaty with the British in 1838 as Mughal power broke down. One of the references for the article is, yet again, Shahamet Ali's complicated and contradictory *History*. Whatever he understood or believed, the historian took considerable care to promote the 'Arab' legitimacy of the rulers of Bahawalpur by suggesting that their ancestors were supported in their endeavours by 'the Arab tribes'. Truth is in the eye of the beholder. The last nawab in particular, Sadiq Muhammad Khan V, continued visibly to validate his Arab origins through the 'Iraqisation of Bahawalpur',[8] renaming his capital Baghdad-ul-Jadid, New Baghdad, and adopting the fez or Rumi topi as courtly headgear to express his family loyalty to the Ottoman Caliphate. It is still worn by Salahuddin Abbasi, his son and their servants today, although the antique hats wear thin in days when their traditional makers in Egypt are few and hard to find. The first stamps issued by the state of Bahawalpur on 1 January 1945 carried both Arabic and English inscriptions.[9]

Naipaul considers claims to Arab ancestry to be 'the primary neurosis of the converted'. The multitudes of subcontinental Sayeds treasure their tattered shajras, the family trees that tie them to the roots of Islam through descent from the family of the Prophet through his grandsons Hussain and, arguably, Hasan. Naipaul contends that such families were instead descended from the Hindu converts of successive Islamic invasions. In Pakistan today, as much as such ancestry in the past added religious authority to the temporal power of Islamic rulers and weight to their imperial ambitions in the eyes of their supporters, so claims to Arab blood add a religious mystique to family names in the only country that was specifically created as an Islamic state. Pakistan has turned its face increasingly towards a medieval Arab religious ideal. It attempts to destroy or envelop the diverse culture, individualism, liberality, education and colour of this part of the subcontinent in the burka of religious conformity according to the most puritanical interpretations of sharia. There is competition to practise religion better, be more Islamic and, ideally, more Arab.

We should beware of the 'obsession with origins'. While discussing the mythical underpinnings of the Islamic state of Pakistan in the earliest conquest of Sindh by Umayyad troops in 711 CE, Manan Ahmed Asif quotes historian Marc Bloch,[10] author of *The Historian's Craft*, 'an origin is a beginning which explains. Worse still, a beginning which is a complete explanation'. The foundations of Pakistan go back to the earliest history of Arab Muslim arrival in India, first through trade into Sindh and then through the conquest in 712 CE, by Muhammad bin Qasim. In spite of somewhat radical methods of conquest against those who opposed him, bin Qasim was said to be a more benevolent ruler than the local Hindu rajas who were highly unpopular with their predominantly Buddhist population. His involvement of Hindus and Buddhists, however, in his administration and considerable freedom of religion, did not have them flocking to convert as some might suggest. This 'originary myth' involves freedom of religious practice at the same time as showing the obvious advantages of Islam, jumping on as it does to the glories of the Mughals and rising above any ruler or period that failed to fulfil the ideal. It has very little to do with historical fact; the reality is that Islam took hold over long centuries.

For ruling princes, the myth of illustrious origin, the closer to the preternatural the better, was once important, if not essential, to raise a man or woman above the common weal and make him or her unique. Dieu et mon droit, The divine right of kings. Origin was a complete explanation and, as Asif Ali explains, originary narratives metamorphose to fit the narrator's purpose. Salahuddin Abbasi accepts the tradition of his origin. It is not impossible. Aside from descent from celestial bodies, there are plenty of families around the world who claim antique corporeal figures as progenitor. In the case of the Massimo family of Rome, putatively descended from Quintus Fabius Maximus Verrucosus who lived during 275–203 BCE, the story is told of the then Principe Massimo being questioned by Napoleon as to the veracity of his ancestry. The prince answered, '*Je ne saurais en effet le prouver, c'est un bruit qui ne court que depuis douze cents ans dans notre famille*' ['I cannot actually prove it, it's a rumour that only runs for twelve hundred years in our family.'] The Massimo family more recently has traced its ancestry back only as far as 950 CE, not far-distant in time from innumerable British families descending from knight invaders in the train of William of Normandy, from the conqueror himself or sometimes long before any such opportunistic and bastard parvenu. Arab records, especially those pertaining to descent from the family of the Prophet, are both too valuable to have been neglected and too valuable not to have been counterclaimed by other opportunistic parvenus over the generations.

For Salahuddin Abbasi, his descent has, in part, informed his life, in particular his public and political life, which has always been one of service. The veracity of where it all began in the years before records and the confusion of tribal family existence, conquest, migration and power struggles, hardly matters. So far as he is concerned his forefathers, sons of the sons of Al-Abbas and so on through caliphs and sons of caliphs, inscribed in the endless revisions of long-lost family trees, came once upon a time from Mecca through long years and generations in Baghdad, to Egypt, to Sindh and thence at last, through luck, good leadership and strength, to found and build Bahawalpur in the aeolian sands of the Cholistan Desert. He is an orthodox but generally privately observing Sunni Muslim, dismissive of the present requirement for public displays of faith, loving the great story of the Prophet and the traditions of Islam as part of a contemporary life and appalled like most of his generation by extremes bred of ignorance, poverty and misinterpretation.

The origins that were so important to earlier rulers seeking religious and temporal authenticity and to Salahuddin's grandfather, Sadiq Muhammad Khan V, as a ruler in thrall to the paramount power, as an Islamic prince and as a seeker of religious truth, required observance, of course, of the five pillars of Islam: faith, prayer, charity, fasting and the Hajj. More than that, they required close association with the roots of Islam in Mecca and the wider ummah through grand gestures befitting the nawab at home and abroad. Schools were founded, orphanages, the Jamia Abbasia University in

Bahawalpur, renamed the Islamia University by Zulfikar Ali Bhutto, and other new foundations and institutions, supported long after Independence by the Sadiq Muhammad Khan Hamas Trust drawn up in 1957.

In the wider Islamic world, the great Islamic royal dynasties, including Bahawalpur, Hyderabad and Bhopal, acquired land in the holy cities of Mecca and Medina at various times and built *rubat*, charitable accommodation for pilgrims. In the case of Bahawalpur, these were right up against the Kaaba and dated from the 1880s and the days of the unusual builder of palaces and embellisher of modern Bahawalpur, Sadiq Muhammad Khan IV. These holy properties, dedicated to Allah, were generally founded through their sons by the women of ruling families who were unable themselves to make the difficult pilgrimage and sought other means of fulfilling the requirements of their faith. There were gifts of chandeliers, to light the interior of the Kaaba, and of *kiswah*, its traditional embroidered covering. An antique kiswah, a return gift from the Saudi royal family, hangs now in Salahuddin Abbasi's Islamabad house. All this has been absorbed by him into a life following a tradition of responsibility to the governed and to the faith of the Koran. In his case, encouraged by his wife, he laid aside a jaundiced view of public religion and actually travelled to Saudi Arabia for the Hajj. He unwillingly admits to feeling 'lighter' for the experience.

Like his father, no longer a ruling prince but still holding the title of Amir, the religious leader, Salahuddin has worked for his country under the same Pakistan flag and the basic precepts of his religious belief to uphold the standing of his family and Bahawalpur long after the days of princely rule. He has engaged and been engaged in the endlessly byzantine political life of Pakistan to try to mitigate the worst excesses of the country's leaders. He has watched since childhood the political disasters visited on his country by presidents and prime ministers accredited, they believe, by an ever more prescriptive Islam to which their people must pay homage and by the flag of Pakistan borne by the ghost of the Quaid-i-Azam under which they rule as if anointed. He has been sorely disappointed as the mullah and the military establishment have rolled over the culture, history, heritage and the civilization of the country.[11] The military, in the case of Bahawalpur, has fraudulently sequestered his family's property and denied the promises for the provincial status of Bahawalpur made at Independence. So much of the origins of this part of the subcontinent have been destroyed or lost as Pakistan's leaders have been party to or proponents of oppressive and confused government even as, in the manner of tyrants, they have feathered their own nests through unimaginable levels of corruption.

The trappings of princely life that have been increasingly preserved and valued across the border in India for the enrichment of that country and its regions through tourism have been lost, looted and destroyed in Pakistan. Where history is undervalued, its treasures are viewed as wealth alone, as bargaining chips or with reductive envy. Salahuddin Abbasi has lived up to his own exacting expectations within the framework of a history and tradition of origin and the role he inherited. In present-day Pakistan it is easy for deprived populations to take a rosy view of the past, but the rulers of Bahawalpur nevertheless made their state one of the richest in the subcontinent during their tenure. Figures 1.1 and 1.2 below show the ancestry of the nawabs of Bahawalpur and the genealogy of Abbasi sahibzadas of Bahawalpur, respectively:

Figures 1.1: Genealogy of Abbasi sahibzadas of Bahawalpur

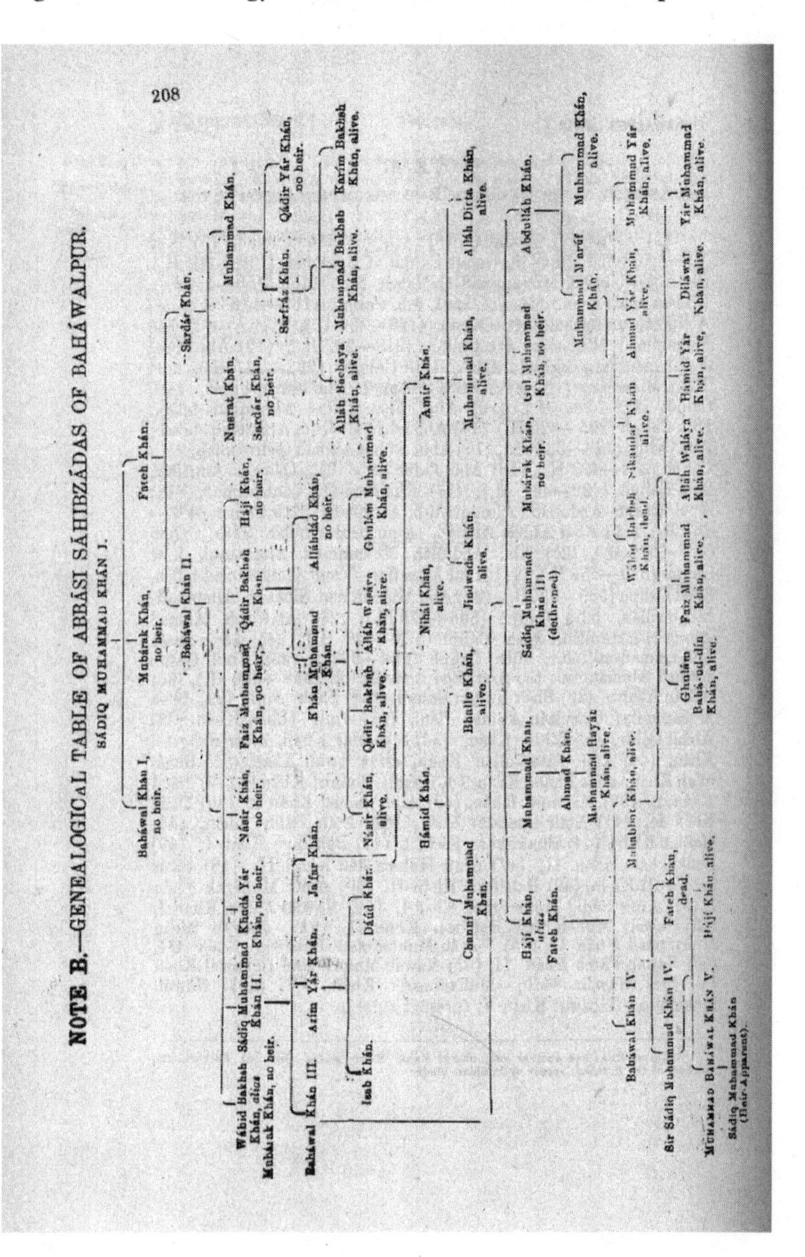

Figures 1.2: Ancestry of the nawabs of Bahawalpur from father to son

(1) Abbás, (2) Abdulláh, (3) Alí, (4) Muhammad, (5) Abú J'afar Abdulláh Mansúr, second Caliph of Baghdád, (136—158 H.), (6) Abú Abdulláh Muhammad-al-Mahdí, 3rd Caliph (158—169 H.), (7)Abú Muhammad Músa Alhádí, 4th Caliph (169—170 H.), (8) Al-Hárún-ur-Rashíd, 5th Caliph, (170—193 H.), (9) Abú Is-háq Muhammad M'utasim, 8th Caliph, (218—227 H.), (10) Abul Fazl J'afar Almutawakkil-ala-Alláh, 10th Caliph, (232—247 H.), (11) Talha Muwaffaq, (12) Abul Abbás Ahmad Alm'utazid-billáh, 16th Caliph (279—289 H.), (13) Abul Fazl J'afar Almuqtadá-billáh, 18th Caliph (295—320 H.), (14) Abú Isháq Ibráhím Almuttaqí-billáh, 21st Caliph (329—333 H.), (15) Abul Abbás Ahmad Qádir-billáh, 25th Caliph (381—422 H.), (16) Abú J'afar Abdulláh, Qáim-bi-Amrilláh, 26th Caliph (422—467 H.), (17) Khair-ud-Dín Muhammad, (18) Abul Qásim Abdulláh Almuqtadí-bi-Amrilláh, 27th Caliph (467—487 H.), (19) Abul Abbás Ahmad, Almustazhir-billáh, 28th Caliph (487—512 H.), (20) Abú Abdulláh Muhammad Almuttaqí, 31st Caliph (530—555 H.), (21) Abul Muzaffar Yúsuf Almustanjid-billáh, 32nd Caliph (555—566H.), (22) Abú Muhammad Alhasan, Almustafí-bi-Amrilláh, 33rd Caliph (566—575 H.), (23) Al-Abbás Ahmad Annásiri-li-dínilláh, 34th Caliph (575—622 H.), (24) Abun-nasar Muhammad-ut-Táhir, 35th Caliph (622—623), (25) Abul Qásim Ahmad Almustansir, the first Egyptian Caliph (659—660 H.), (26) Sultán Yásín, (27) Sháh Sultán Suhail, (28) Sháh Aqíl, (29) Sháh Muzammil, (30) Sultán Ahmad Sání, (31) Amír Ibban Khán, (32) Abdul Qáhir, or Káhír Khán, (33) Sikandar Khán, *alias* Sangrási Khán, (34) Amír Fateh-ulláh Khán, *alias* Thull Khán, (35) Bahá-ullah Khán, *alias* Bhallá Khán, (36) Amír Channí Khán,[1] (37) Dáúd Khán I, (38) Mahmúd Khán, (39) Muhammad Khán I, (40) Dáúd Khán II, (41) Amír Chandar Khán, (42) Amír Sálih Khán, (43) Haibut Khán, (44) Bhakhkhar Khán I, (45) Bahádur Khán I, (46) Bhakhkhar Khán II, (47) Amír Muhammad Khán II, (48) Fíroz (or Piruj) Khán, (49) Bahádur Khán II, (50) Amír Mubárak Khán I, (51) Amír Sádiq Muhammad Khán I, (52) Nawáb Fateh Khán I, (53) Nawáb Muhammad Baháwal Khán II, (54) Nawáb Sádiq Muhammad Khán II, (55) Nawáb Muhammad Baháwal Khán III, (56) Nawáb Fateh Khán II, (57) Nawáb Muhammad Baháwal Khán IV, (58) Nawáb Sádiq Muhammad Khán IV, (59) Nawáb Muhammad Baháwal Khán V, (present ruler).

[1] Channi Khán had another son, named Mahdi Khán, whose son was Kalhora, the founder of the *Kalhora* dynasty of Sindhian kings.

2

THE FAMILY LINE

It is as difficult to find romance in a skeletal list of names, be they of princes or peasants, as it is to imagine the lives once led among the worn stones of ancient ruins. In the case of the thirteen official rulers of Bahawalpur state between 1702 and 1955, the more recent, often photographed in spectacular finery, come alive while the earliest tribal chiefs sometimes appear as little more than dusty labels noting dates, battles, campaigns and conquests. To add meat to their bones, they will, where possible, be placed in the context of their proper page in history. This becomes much easier from the time when India Office Records and inveterate English nineteenth-century visitors and recorders of adventurous travels began to document one view, however biased, of their story. Sometimes, however, earlier rulers of Bahawalpur will remain little more than names of tribal leaders involved in local rivalries, however qualified with small final sentences in old books that briefly memorialize their qualities.

First, let us go back a little into the tapestry of descent from the 200-year-old great-great-grandfather and the warring branches of the Abbasi tribes. The separate lines of the Daudputras and Kalhoras further tangle the threads but begin to unravel with the death of Muhammad

Khan II during the reign of Emperor Jehangir, the withdrawal to a religious life of his eldest son and his passing of the *dastar-i-amarat*, turban of state, to his younger brother, Feroz Khan. It is to him the Daudputras paid homage and, from him, all the Abbasi rulers are descended. His son, Bahadur Khan, 'remarkable for his conciliatory and engaging manners', according to the *Sadiqnamah*, settled in Bhakkar, now in the Punjab. He acquired a large area of land on the banks of the Indus from Mirza Khan, governor of Sindh, under the emperor and founded the town of Shikarpur. Thereafter, Shahamet Ali has Bahadur Khan turning to agriculture for his livelihood 'which he carried on with much care and prudence by artificial means of irrigation'.

The careful husbandry version of the ongoing story is less credible than the one in which the Kalhoras continued to attack Bhakkar in force until Prince Muhammad Muizz ud-din, governor of Multan, marched against them, with a large army, on Emperor Aurangzeb's orders. Their leader, Nasir Muhammad Kalhora, was sent as a prisoner to Delhi but escaped. Surprisingly, he sought refuge with his former enemy, Bahadur Khan, who was then successfully fighting off another branch of the Abbasi tribes. Bahadur Khan died suddenly, to be succeeded by his son Muhammad Mubarik Khan I, who was forced to take up arms against Bakhtiyar Khan, a former refugee in his court and son of his father's old friend, Mirza Khan, governor of Sindh. Prince Muizz ud-din's initial refusal to intercede was reversed when the amir came to his aid after a revolt was raised by the governor of Dera Ghazi Khan.

It is said that the enemy had attacked the private tents of the prince but his women were bravely rescued by the Abbasi hero Sanjar Khan, and the prince's heart was won over, once again, to the amir's cause. Now the prince, accompanied by Muhammad Mubarik Khan, led his army against Bakhtiyar Khan, invading Shikarpur where Sanjar Khan, rising once more to the occasion, killed Bakhtiyar Khan. On Prince Muizz ud-din's orders, 'to satiate his brutal revenge',[1] Bakhtiyar Khan's body was quartered, with one piece sent to each of the towns of Khanpur, Shikarpur, Bhakkar and Bakhtiyarpur. The prince entered Shikarpur to bestow rewards on the amir and his Abbasis, granting them *jagir*, landholdings, in all four towns and the superintendency of the fort and the district of Bhakkar. Not that that was the end of the story, for another Kalhora leader rose from his lair in the Cholistan Desert to fight yet another battle at Shikarpur before a brief period of peace. This ended with the feast to mark the abdication of Amir Muhammad Mubarik in favour of his son Sadiq Muhammad Khan I, to which all the Abbasi clans were invited. The latest Kalhora leader, Nur Muhammad, arrived with a 60,000-strong army, to lay siege to Shikarpur and invest the city for six months until he was granted half the revenue of the town and of Khanpur.

Thus, the pattern continued and the *Sadiqnamah* records, 'this period in the history of India is full of upheavals', as the Mughal Empire began to collapse after the death of the last of the great Mughals, Aurangzeb, in 1707. Nur Muhammad attacked Shikarpur for the fifth time in 1726 with so large a force that Sadiq Muhammad Khan retreated to Bet Dabli, then a fertile island in the Indus in the Dera Ghazi Khan district. Thereafter, Sadiq Muhammad Khan seems to have gone from strength to strength, invited to the holy city of Uch, receiving landholdings there, founding the town of Allahabad in Sindh, and slowly consolidating his fiefdom into that all-important 'united kingdom'. In 1733 he took the ninth-century fort of Derawar from Rawal Akhai Singh of Jaisalmer to make it the almost literal bedrock of his state and, eventually, its most famous landmark.

When Nader Shah made his lightning invasion of India to storm Delhi through the Derajat region of Pakistan in January 1739, Sadiq Muhammad Khan managed again to be in the right place at the right time. Sensibly, he rode out, meeting the cruel and irascible conqueror at Dera Ghazi Khan, to pledge his allegiance. Despite Nader Shah's well-known propensity for taking offence, Sadiq Muhammad must have made a favourable impression and Salahuddin Abbasi believes gifts were exchanged. It seems likely that some of the extraordinary Mughal jewels that were part of the treasure of Bahawalpur, and now of the Al-Thani collection, came from Nader Shah's largesse on his return journey. The staggering booty from his looting and destruction of Delhi included the Peacock Throne, embedded with the Koh-i-Noor and the Timur Ruby.[2] Most important of all, Nader Shah conferred the title of nawab on the amir, setting the seal on his leadership of his tribe and his right to rule. A year later, in 1740, Nader Shah partitioned Sindh, confirming Nawab Sadiq Muhammad Khan's landholdings as Shikarpur, Larkana, Siwistan, now Sehwan Sharif, Chhatar (Ratar Chhatar, Indian Punjab) and the *ilaqa*s or estates of Chaudhari (Chaudhary Charagh Din) and Derawar.

An irritating 'etc' follows this list in the *Sadiqnamah* but the area covered appears to be considerable, a tract of about 200 miles from Goth Johra, now in Sadiqabad, Rahim Yar Khan district, to Shahr Farid, which is now between the modern cities of Bahawalnagar and Bahawalpur. Unfortunately for the new nawab, no sooner had Nader Shah left Sindh than his Kalhora cousins once again decided to attack Shikarpur, laying siege to the city and finally killing Sadiq Muhammad in 1746. Of his three sons, the eldest Muhammad Bahawal Khan I was elected by the tribe and ascended the throne to reign, busily but with mixed success, for three years until his death in 1749. Derawar was lost once more to Jaisalmer through an alliance of the nawab's enemies but his own alliance with the diwan of Multan resulted in further rewards in land. Among other towns, he founded Hasilpur and, most importantly, Bahawalpur. Following in the family footsteps, he 'always had the welfare of the cultivators at heart', improving agriculture in the state and building canals.

Muhammad Bahawal Khan died childless and was succeeded by his second brother, Muhammad Mubarik Khan II, with the support of the Daudputra chiefs who were carving out their own territories by seizing land and forts, founding and building towns and more canals. Muhammad Mubarik Khan's lands appear to have prospered under his rule. He defeated an Afghan invasion, repulsed the Sikhs at Multan, built forts and canals, and won a victory against Bikaner that forced the return of Derawar with further new territory from Rawal Rai Singh. The 'state', however, remained, for now, 'a confederation of petty principalities' under the purely nominal rule of the nawab. Muhammad Mubarik Khan died on 2 June 1772. Like his eldest brother, he left no son to inherit.

The throne instead passed to his nephew, son of the youngest of Sadiq Muhammad Khan I's three known sons, who ruled as Muhammad Bahawal Khan II. His birth, on the day in 1752 when news of the death of Nur Muhammad Kalhora, greatest of the enemy and rival clan's leaders, reached the state, had been seen as so auspicious that he was adopted by his uncle, the nawab, and elected to rule by the Daudputras although his father was still alive. It sounds as if Bahawal Khan started with a more secure seat on his throne than his predecessors and certainly his reign was to be longer, but he lived in turbulent times. The 'country of the Ameers'[3] was both on the path of conquest and relied on the support of a conglomeration of the same jealous and quarrelsome feudal landlords whose descendants have filled the ranks of the ruling class of the invented nation of Pakistan.

The Sikhs returned to wrest Multan from the subedar, Haji Sharif Beg Tuglu, in 1772. Five years later, the governor of Shujabad enlisted the nawab's aid in a successful attack on the city. Multan was plundered and the occupying Sikhs put to the sword. In 1780, the king of Delhi, Shah Alam II, sent a firman authorizing Bahawal Khan to administer the Kachhi (Kutch) and conferred upon him the titles Rukn ud-Daula, Nusrat-i-Jang and Hafiz ul-Mulk,[4] with the gift of valuable *khillat*s or robes of state. Bahawalpur was being noticed and the nawab was now in a position to add to his territory through suitable marriages, gaining land by dowry in Khairpur Nauranga and Ahmedpur East, where Sadiqgarh Palace was later built by Sadiq Muhammad Khan IV and, lately, the area of Salahuddin Abbasi's parliamentary constituency. Bahawal Khan took advantage of a change in course of the Indus River that opened up areas of the Muzaffargarh district to conquest, seizing land in Jatoi and several other villages and talukas. He also repaired the eighth-century Bijnot Fort and built another at Khangarh. Both are in ruins today.

Bahawalpur both suffered and gained from its position in a land of rivers, on the path of migration, conquest and trade, between acquisitive dynastic rulers. The state also had its own local share of tribal warfare and acquisition-hungry petty leaders whose loyalties and swords were for sale to the highest bidder. Timur Shah Durrani, successor to Ahmad Shah as king of Afghanistan, continued to fight the increasingly well-established Sikhs for control of the Punjab and to bring the bellicose amirs under his control. His commander, the Ishakzai chief, Sardar Madad Khan,[5] was sent to retake Multan in 1788 and was encouraged by an alliance of amirs to attack Bahawalpur, which he plundered and burnt. The nawab had meanwhile garrisoned Derawar and, when his troops met the enemy, Madad Khan was defeated and retreated into Sindh. Three years later, the king himself, Timur Shah, took Derawar, leaving it in the charge of Shah Muhammad Khan Badozai. Setting out for Kabul to put down an uprising, he got no farther than Dera Ghazi Khan when news came that the nawab had retaken Bahawalpur and captured the women and children of the Afghan troops garrisoning Derawar, threatening to kill them if the garrison did not surrender. The soldiers were permitted to evacuate the fort and returned home.

Timur Shah had carried the nawab's eldest son, Sahibzada Mubarik Khan, back with him to Kabul as a hostage and now proceeded to give him titles, gifts and Bahawalpur itself by firman, hoping to turn him against his father. On the sahibzada's return home, the prodigal son was promptly imprisoned by his father, who, with the bit firmly between his teeth, went on to attack Dera Ghazi Khan, free the Daudputras who had been imprisoned there, seize a large part of the land held by the subedar of Multan and liberate the cannon that had been taken from Bahawalpur. At this point, Makhdoom Baksh of Uch, a previous ally of the Kalhoras, whose 'subsequent acts showed him to be insane',[6] plotted with other chiefs to raid Ahmedpur East. He was finally captured by the nawab and placed under house arrest, which required, according to the *Sadiqnamah*, the consent of the other *makhdooms* in the 'noble traditions of the Arabs', because, 'however reasonable, taking such a step amounted to placing a Lord Bishop under house arrest'. The makhdoom escaped shortly thereafter and continued to pursue his nefarious activities into Ahmedpur East.

A further revolt was raised against Bahawal Khan by the Kehrani, Jamani and Arbani Daudputras who enlisted the support of Maharaja Surat Singh of Bikaner. He was a somewhat Caligula-like figure who gained his throne by getting his mother to poison his brother and personally strangling the latter's infant son. He was also unable to resist a good local fight and severely impoverished his state by his military excursions. He entered into a treaty of perpetual friendship with the Honourable East India Company in 1818 after seeking their protection since the beginning of the century. In 1799, as Ranjit Singh and the Khalsa marched on Lahore and Tipu Sultan made his last stand at Seringapatam, the mad makhdoom rescued Mubarik Khan from Derawar. He proclaimed him ruler of Bahawalpur, meanwhile gathering more rebels to his cause to attack Mubarik Khan's father, the nawab. They were defeated by his army, led by the second of his seven sons, Sahibzada Abdulla Khan, later Nawab Sadiq Muhammad Khan II, and fled to Bikaner only to return the following year when several of the Cholistan forts fell briefly to the invaders. Peace was finally negotiated in 1800 when Surat Singh returned home after he had been paid off for his expenses during the war.

By 1802 Bahawal Khan was being courted for his support by Mahmud Shah of Afghanistan, Timur's son, ruling after deposing his brother Zeman during the turbulent years of civil strife after Timur's death. The nawab, on the other hand, was feeling secure enough in his own state to set the public seal on his rule with the opening of a mint that struck gold, silver and copper coins inscribed Humayun Mahmud Shah, for the Afghan overlords, and, on the reverse, *Dar-us-surur* Bahawalpur, Abode of Joy Bahawalpur. Nevertheless, Bahawalpur continued to be threatened by enemies from various expedient alliances during the early years of the century as the Afghan Durrani Empire ebbed. Sikh power grew and the stretch and influence of the Honourable East India Company expanded, usually to the nawab's advantage as he conquered further enemy territory and drew it into Bahawalpur state.

The History, written only a generation after these events, at this point gives the most colourful blow-by-blow accounts of plots and counterplots, the vanquishing of enemies and the almost unbelievable magnanimity of the nawab towards his enemies. These were days, after all, when Shah Shuja Durrani was practising medieval cruelties on those of his followers who displeased him, cutting off their body parts for the slightest misdemeanour, and, as a result, giving his court the sort of generally mutilated appearance imaginable in Europe during the Hundred Years War. Bahawalpur, in contrast, was becoming a modern kingdom, attracting noble families from Lahore, Delhi, Dera Ghazi Khan, Multan and other cities to settle in the state and fill the high offices of the nawab's durbar. Several of the trans-Indus tribes crossed into the state at about this time and settled. In following reigns, some of the major Afghan families, notably Khakwani, Saddozai, the same clan as the Durrani emperors, Babar and Mallezai, also migrated and settled in Bahawalpur.

Nawab Bahawal Khan had ruled for long enough to see his enemies fail, fall or die off. He had avoided confrontation with Ranjit Singh through judicious advice to the Sikh leader during his siege of Multan, being rewarded with gifts of an elephant and a shawl, added to several instalments of 'friendly messages'.[7] Bahawal Khan's most inveterate enemy, the makhdoom of Uch, died and was succeeded by his son, Makhdoom Shams ud-din and his brother who was recognized by the nawab when he rode to Uch in person to perform the ceremony of placing the 'Turban of Recognition' on his head.

In 1808, Mountstuart Elphinstone came to Bahawalpur en route to Kabul on the exploratory journey he described in *An Account of The Kingdom of Caubul and Its Dependencies in Persia, Tartary and India.* The Treaty of Tilsit in 1807 between Napoleon and Tsar Alexander I had raised, for the first time, the fear of overland invasion of India by Russia in alliance with the French bogeyman, and the governor general, Lord Minto, sent Elphinstone to Afghanistan, with other envoys to Persia and to Ranjit Singh, to gain promises of cooperation in the event of French incursions.

It is unsurprising that Elphinstone was impressed by Bahawal Khan. He must have been impressive to have successfully manoeuvred a path through the hurdles, both of the tribal enmities of his times and greater invading powers. Before 'we enter on the narrative of the passage of an embassy from the British Government',[8] it is too irresistible not to digress to Shahamet Ali's rose-tinted description of England, where the roads of London are 'paved with stones of various colours', the town always kept in 'clean order' while the suburbs 'are said to be covered with delightful gardens and noble buildings' and 'it is a fixed rule with every citizen, rich or poor, to whitewash his dwelling once a year'. That cloudless image might have surprised those breathing in the Great Stink and living through the cholera pandemic of the time.

Elphinstone described Bahawal Khan when he first met him on 1 December 1808 as a 'plain, open, pleasant man, about forty-five or fifty years of age, he had on white tunic, with small gold buttons, over which was a white mantle of a very rich and beautiful gold brocade and over it a loongee. About six of his attendants sat; the rest stood round and were all well dressed and respectable'. The following day, 'the Khan received us in a handsome room with attic windows and 'conversed freely on all subjects'. He 'praised the King of Caubul' but had never seen him and 'please God he never would'. He was a 'desert dweller and feared the snows of Caubul'. Instead, 'he could live in his desert, hunt his deer, and he had no desire to follow courts'. The nawab then demonstrated the skills of his people with a 'curious clock' made in Bahawalpur and gave Elphinstone parting gifts of greyhounds, two horses, 'one with gold and one with enamelled trappings' and a very beautiful matchlock 'with a powder flask in the English fashion'.

Elphinstone added, the nawab 'has been liberal and kind to us without over-civility or ceremony', with 'an appearance of sincerity in everything he said' and had shown 'a spirit of kindness and hospitality which could not be surpassed'. Elphinstone was astonished that, unlike other princes he had encountered, they did not have to 'struggle against the rapacity of the Nawab', who, on the contrary, 'would take nothing without negotiation' and was himself almost embarrassingly generous in his gifts, sending a profusion of sweetmeats, flour, nuts and raisins, 'a vast number of baskets of oranges' and, most difficult to accept, five bags of rupees to be divided amongst the servants.[9]

It appears the ambassador and the nawab were pleased with each other—certainly this meeting and the first treaty of friendship between Bahawalpur and the British was the start of a remarkably close relationship. It maintained even through the paternalism and officiousness of the colonial power, and the last nawab looked upon England as an alternative home. He died there, in his house in Sussex in the English countryside, a few years after the last vestiges of his former state were absorbed into Pakistan. Elphinstone also took a favourable view of the Bahawalpuris who were 'strong, dark, harsh-featured', although he commented that the people spoke a 'language entirely unintelligible to our Hindustanee attendants'. Saraiki, the linguistic catalyst for several more recent minority political movements, the language of the desert, Bahawalpur and other areas of Sindh and the Punjab, is proudly spoken by the Abbasis today. Interestingly, Elphinstone also noticed the preponderance of Hindus in Bahawalpur compared with adjacent areas. A large and prosperous Hindu population remained in Bahawalpur right into Partition when Nawab Sadiq Muhammad Khan V did his best to guarantee their safety and keep them in the state.

Later in his *Account,* Elphinstone wrote of the situation in Bahawalpur four years later, three years after the death of Bahawal Khan, when the second of his seven sons, Prince Abdulla Khan, had become Nawab Sadiq Muhammad Khan II. Elphinstone suggested that the story of the origins of the rulers of Bahawalpur may have begun in a former reign when the 'Dawood-pooter', a family of 'low-station' from Shikarpur, added trappings of Arab descent to suit their new royal status. Not that he cared; he describes Bahawal Khan as little less than a model prince and does nothing but praise him. His only regret is that Sadiq Muhammad Khan is far from being his father's 'equal in prudence and management' and instead 'is exposed to great uneasiness and danger from the increasing power of his neighbours the Sikhs'.[10]

3

ANGLOPHILE PRINCES

The earliest remaining official records of British involvement in the affairs of Bahawalpur in the India Office Records at the British Library date to 1832, as East India Company interests expanded in tandem with fears of Russian invasion of India. Young officers, players in 'the Great Game', between the Russian and British Empires, for domination in Afghanistan and Central Asia, passed through Bahawalpur, in Elphinstone's footsteps, and were entertained by the ruling nawab. James Tod, notorious for his mythologizing admiration of the Rajputs, also gave his seal of approval to the ruler of Bahawalpur. According to Tod, when Sadiq Muhammad Khan was faced with a desperate choice either to surrender or to sacrifice the families in his baggage train to the enemy, the nawab 'acted the Rajput', and faced his foes. The enemy, duly 'appalled at this desperate act, deemed it unwise to attack him and retreated'.

Bahawal Khan died in 1809, aged fifty-seven, regrettably leaving seven sons who might dispute claims to the throne. Prince Abdulla Khan was proclaimed the fifth nawab, as Sadiq Muhammad Khan II, on the stone throne at Derawar, and, after appointing his new ministers and officers of state, promptly had his eldest brother,

Mubarik Khan, put to death 'in accordance with Oriental custom'. It was the beginning of a tumultuous reign where the nawab was exposed to 'great uneasiness and danger', as much, in reality, from his neighbouring amirs and rebellious subjects, as from the Sikhs. At this stage, customary congratulations were received from Maharaja Ranjit Singh, Muzaffar Khan, the subedar of Multan, and various other nawabs and *mirs*. The king of Kabul, Mahmud Shah, who had recently been restored to his throne in Kabul, sent gifts and a letter which marked the end of Bahawalpur's vassal ties to the Durranis.

The *Bahawalpur Gazetteer* notes that the power of the dissenting Daudputras had been weakened by annexation of most of their territory during the reign of the late nawab, but they were still in a position to cause problems by intriguing with foreign powers or disloyal officers of the state, and the 'prevailing anarchy' in the country encouraged the ambitions of every petty tribal leader. Uprisings in support of Daudputra demands for restoration of territories by the amirs were led by Ghulam Ali of Hyderabad and Sorab Khan of Khairpur in Sindh. In 1811, Prince Ahmed Baksh, another of the nawab's brothers, was crowned at Derawar by disloyal Sardars while the nawab was on a hunting trip in the desert. After a bombardment of the fort by the nawab's men, the rebels surrendered and the usurper was executed with other leaders of the insurrection. Peace was temporarily restored with a treaty that involved Sadiq Muhammad Khan handing over his eldest son and heir, Sahibzada Rahim Yar Khan, as hostage for assurances given by his father. He was detained for a year and four months in Hyderabad before being freed in 1812.

After this, records suggest an extraordinary cavalcade of the powerful men of the time and region passed through the purview of Nawab Sadiq Muhammad Khan, or he through theirs, as the dynasties and tribes of the region and the times waxed and waned. If British visitors, agents of the Honourable Company, have no spoken part on the Bahawalpur stage in this reign, they were waiting in the wings. They turned acquisitive eyes on the Punjab after the Second Maratha War brought the cis-Sutlej states under their protection. Indeed, protection began to be part of the Company's peacetime armoury as chiefs and rulers briefly courted British interference in their affairs to remit the alternative depletions of running local warfare. Maharaja Ranjit Singh, short, illiterate and blind in one eye 'though he may have been, came to stand centre stage as the heroic ruler of the conquering Sikh Empire. Others, such as the Durrani vizier, Fateh Khan, and his twenty-one powerful brothers, also carried history on their shoulders. Afghan kings came and went, as the Company increasingly pulled the strings, and, impotent figures, the last remnants of the Mughal rulers, were hidden extras, out of view in the backdrop of the Red Fort at Delhi. These are all men whose images in portraits and miniatures are part of the picture show of the past, still freely to be examined by idle passers-by for their character and quality.[1]

In 1812, the governor of Dera Ghazi Khan, Asad Khan, attacked Bahawalpur but was defeated and forced to pay Rs 50,000 war indemnity. In 1818, Shah Shuja, exiled from Afghanistan, turned up in Bahawalpur with a request for help from Sadiq Muhammad Khan in the subjugation of Dera Ghazi Khan, which he then took with an army provided by the nawab, only to lose it again shortly thereafter to Maharaja Ranjit Singh. In the meantime, Kanwar Kharak Singh, Ranjit Singh's son, had laid siege and taken Multan from Muzaffar Khan, using the famous Zamzama, Kim's gun that stands now on the busy road outside the Lahore Museum, to breach the walls of the fort. Muzaffar was another of the twenty-one brothers of Vizier Fateh Khan, who held powerful posts all over the Durrani Afghan Empire, the youngest, Dost Muhammad, becoming amir of Afghanistan. Muzaffar Khan's youngest son, Mir Baz Khan, aged fourteen, escaped to Bahawalpur where the nawab took him in and gave him a monthly pension of 196 'English' rupees and a gift of nine wells.

When Maharaja Ranjit Singh took Dera Ghazi Khan back, while plundering the lands of the amirs, he made the town over to Sadiq Muhammad Khan for an annual payment of Rs 2,50,000. Other towns in the same area belonging to the Khosa tribe were subjugated by the nawab in 1820 when the chief of the tribe fell in battle. His younger brothers submitted, giving their daughters in marriage to the nawab. Finally, in 1824, the year before Sadiq Muhammad Khan's death from consumption, Prince Ahsan Bakht, brother of Akbar Shah II, penultimate king of Delhi, returning to Delhi himself from exile, was entertained at Bahawalpur by Sahibzada Rahim Yar Khan. His father may not have been the man his own father had been, but he had somehow negotiated a route through a tumultuous period in the Punjab and India for his own and his state's survival.

Sahibzada Rahim Yar Khan acceded to the titles and estates of Bahawalpur on 16 April 1825 as Muhammad Bahawal Khan III, 'the Generous'. An exchange of presents with Maharaja Ranjit Singh brought him a *chogha* or embroidered coat; a tikka, or head ornament; *kangan* bangles and *bazubands*, arm guards; all studded with jewels; with forty silver-and-gold brocaded turban cloths and two horses with silver and gold trappings. The romance did not last. Due mainly to the ineptitude of his wazir, Muhammad Yaqub, former *bakshi* or paymaster of his army, the new nawab's Pashtun Rohilla troops mutinied for increased pay. The mutineers occupied the thirteenth-century tomb of Jalal ud-din Syed, the saint who reputedly converted Chinghiz Khan among others, at Uch Sharif. The building was severely damaged in the bombardment by the nawab that resulted in the troops suing for peace, whereupon they were paid off and disbanded. Simultaneously, and, no doubt picking his moment, Ranjit Singh made demands for payment on the lease of Dera Ghazi Khan and sent a force under General Ventura, his mercenary leader, to occupy lands that included Dera Ghazi Khan, Multan and Muzaffargarh, which were permanently lost to Bahawalpur.

Nawab Bahawal Khan must have been distinctly aggrieved. He now found himself surrounded by all his state's old enemies at the point he most needed allies. Sindh, Bikaner and Jaisalmer were hostile and, when Ranjit Singh sent an invading army, Bahawal Khan applied to Lord William Bentinck, the British governor general, for British intervention. In 1826, Charles Masson, East India Company soldier, explorer and adventurer, had passed through Bahawalpur on his *Various Journeys in Balochistan, Afghanistan and the Panjab*.[2] He stayed with Rahmat Khan, one of the Rohilla commanders, like most of his men, a mercenary, from the state of Rampur, and heard a financial tale of woe. This involved a personal debt of Rs 6000, due to Rohilla inability to 'forget or forgo' the gaieties to which they had become accustomed when they were in service of the Mahrattas and Rahmat Khan's continuing fondness for 'nautches'. So great a sum was unlikely to be paid off on a per diem wage of Rs 2. The commander aimed to get Rs 5 a day through false muster and other practices, to which a blind eye was turned, but he and his men considered they had been in 'more honourable and lucrative employ' than at Bahawalpur.

However, just as Elphinstone had viewed Bahawal Khan's father with favour, Masson liked what he saw when he met Bahawal Khan, this young and 'remarkably handsome' prince, and found himself 'gratified with the civility of all classes of the people' in Bahawalpur. According to Masson's account, the nawab and several of his senior officers attempted to enlist him to command their troops. Masson was no General Ventura and if they had known more of his true history they might have thought twice but, after a bout of fever, the adventurer declared the climate of Bahawalpur unhealthy to live in and in any case he had other things to do.[3]

Captain Arthur Conolly's account of his *Journey to the North of India, through Russia, Persia and Afghanistan*[4] does not suggest that similar offers of command were made to him; instead he wrote, 'knowing Buhawul Khan's respect for the English, I declared myself a British officer'. The nawab was absent, hunting in the desert at Derawar, where great treasure was rumoured to be held, but he sent messages and gifts and, 'his people loaded us with civility'. Conolly goes on to describe Bahawalpur as 'not now the city that Mr. Elphinstone described it to be: the walls have fallen, and there is a general appearance of decay in the town. This is owing to the Khan's preferring to reside at Ahmudpore, where he is further from his hated neighbours the Sikhs, and nearer to his fancied stronghold in the desert.'

The following year, Bahawal Khan wrote to the governor general, Lord William Bentinck, with 'professions of attachment to the British Government'.[5] He received a politely condescending reply, in which he was assured, 'this disposition will always be remembered to your advantage. May the almighty extend his protection to you while you remain in the profession of similar sentiments', and, 'I shall always be happy to hear of your health and welfare'. Nevertheless, more earthly protection was forthcoming in due course. Bahawal Khan had become a known quantity and someone in the Company must have considered him, if not a worthwhile ally, at least a useful piece on the chessboard. Charles Trevelyan, author of *On the Education of the People of India,* might have considered Bahawal Khan particularly promising when further correspondence arrived on his desk. The young nawab's request for books to 'enable him to commence the study of the English language' was viewed with satisfaction. Manuals on English spelling, Murrays Abridgement Grammar, prose readers and a Compendium of Geography, all reeking, even at a distance of nearly 200 years, of dreary schoolrooms, were dispatched.[6]

Alexander Burnes arrived at Bahawalpur hot on Conolly's heels in 1831, on his way to deliver King William IV's whimsical goodwill gift of six dapple-grey dray horses to the Sikh maharaja at Lahore. When Burnes's fleet of eighteen boats arrived at Uch Sharif earlier than expected, Bahawal Khan's troops were encamped on the banks and the fleet was fired on when it was mistaken for the Sikh army.[7] Burnes wrote, 'I thought the apologies and regrets would never have ceased, which 'afforded us some amusement.' Bahawal Khan yet again demonstrated his generosity with gifts of food and money to be distributed for charity and, 'dilated at length on the honour which Runjeet Singh had conferred upon him in receiving presents from the King of Great Britain; nor did he, in any way, betray his feelings towards the Lahore chief, though they are far from friendly'. The nawab told Burnes that Mr Elphinstone had 'been the means of raising up a sincere and lasting friendship between his family and the British government'. So the mutual stock of admiration rose further. Burnes wrote, 'I felt equal satisfaction to find the English character stand so high in this remote corner of India' and, a nod to Elphinstone, now back in Britain, 'and the just appreciation of the high-minded individual who had been the means of fixing it maintained'.

Burnes remarked that the great tomb of Bibi Jawindi and the mound on which it sits in Uch above the shrine of Jalal ud-din Syed had been severely damaged by an 'inundation' of the Chenab in 1817 and that the people had 'failed to testify their gratitude' to the saint by making repairs. At the time of writing, there is some scaffolding on the front of the tomb which, like other historic buildings in Pakistan, is on the tentative list of UNESCO World Heritage Sites. It is hard to know if any work is actually taking place. Burnes also noticed that the principal merchants who called on him were mainly Hindus 'whose disposition peculiarly adapts them for the patient and painstaking vocation of a foreign merchant', and who, with other Jewish colleagues, were astonishingly well travelled and knowledgeable as to Afghanistan, Bokhara and the activities of Russian merchants in those parts. Burnes himself would shortly travel on an intelligence-gathering mission in those same directions.

Bahawal Khan not only begged the governor general for his assistance in stopping the Sikhs from crossing the Sutlej River to invade the heart of Bahawalpur but also requested the appointment of a British agent to the state. Claude Martin Wade, the political agent at Ludhiana, who was deputed to negotiate a treaty of friendship and alliance with Bahawal Khan, had been most responsible for establishing the good relationship between the British and Maharaja Ranjit Singh. He arrived in Bahawalpur in 1833 to negotiate, and a treaty of friendship and alliance was agreed on 22 February. With him, Wade brought Lieutenant Mackeson who had already accompanied Burnes to Kabul. Mackeson became political agent in Bahawalpur and agent for the navigation of the Indus, unofficially reporting on the situation in the Punjab and rendering 'valuable services in connection with the lines of communication of the army of the Indus'. Sir Sydney Cotton is quoted describing Mackeson in his entry in the *Dictionary of National Biography*,[8] as 'a bold and efficient officer, who well knew the character of the people with whom he had to deal, and that pusillanimous measures were not measures of humanity, tending always in the end to disaster and destruction'.

There were further Supplementary Treaties between Bahawalpur and the British in 1835, 1839, 1840 and 1843 followed by others reducing tolls on merchandise transported on the Indus and fixed duties on goods carried by land. Finally, in 1847, the nawab agreed to abolish all duties without compensation. This was generous indeed and part of a pattern of political expediency followed by Bahawal Khan to retain powerful friends. It was not entirely one-way traffic. In 1843 the villages and lands of Kot Sabzal and Bhung Bhara, lost in 1807 and one of the most fertile areas of the state, were conquered from the amirs by Sir Charles Napier, during his controversial annexation of Sindh, and restored to Bahawalpur 'as a special mark of the favour of the British Government'.[9]

In late 1838, Shah Shuja-ul-Mulk arrived once again in Bahawalpur, en route to Kabul to reclaim his throne by British determination. He was accompanied by Sir William Macnaghten on his way to become political agent in Kabul, a posting that would end with his assassination after the disaster of the withdrawal of the British from the city in 1841. The nawab sent a force of cavalry 100-strong to Kabul with the army, and news of the city's occupation was celebrated with illuminations in Ahmedpur and Bahawalpur. In July 1842, a letter to Bahawal Khan came from Amir Ali Khan, son of Amir Dost Muhammad of Afghanistan, who had retaken the throne of Kabul after the assassination of Shah Shuja the April before.

> *We have murdered Sir Alexander Burnes and all the baggage belonging to the British Government has come into our possession. The beggars of this country have been enriched at the expense of the British treasury. You should now be ready to advance the cause of friendship between the two Muhammadan States.*

This, and a second letter from Ali Khan, was immediately forwarded to the British by Bahawal Khan, gaining thanks from the governor general, Lord Ellenborough. Interestingly, the *Sadiqnamah,* possibly viewing this scenario in the light of the dream of the Islamic state of Pakistan, suggests that the Bahawalpur durbar declined the 'offer' from Kabul, not due to any loyalty to the British but to the unsettled situation in the Punjab between the Sikhs, the amirs and the hostility of neighbouring Hindu states. In 1844, following the Supplementary Treaty of 1843, the governor general's agent, Colonel Hamilton, arrived in Bahawalpur to obtain the nawab's consent for his cession of a major landholding, along the Sutlej towards Multan, that, if granted, would extend the British-held region of Abohar, now in the Indian state of Punjab, to the banks of the river.

Ranjit Singh had died in 1839 and his kingdom had very rapidly begun to disintegrate. Had Lord Ellenborough remained governor general, he would have certainly pushed for immediate annexation of the Punjab to follow Sindh. His more thoughtful successor, Viscount Hardinge, his covetous eyes still focused on the Punjab, was able to feel himself ultimately forced into action in what became the First Anglo-Sikh War through fear of the Khalsa, the powerful and well-organized Sikh army, now without an equally powerful leader to moderate its ambition. The Khalsa was perceived to be an immediate threat to British India, not least through its attraction to the disaffected and anti-British from elsewhere. Continuing rivalry among Sikh leaders assisted the British to victory, after a series of hard-won battles, and the victors entered Lahore as the band played 'See the Conquering Hero Come'[10] to sign the Treaty of Lahore with eight-year-old Maharaja Duleep Singh, Ranjit Singh's youngest son.

The Punjab paid heavily for defeat. By April 1848, Sikhs who had suffered losses, others who resented British rules, if not yet the overt British rule of the Punjab, and those like the Rohillas who considered fighting to be their trade, gathered around Diwan Mulraj, Hindu governor of Multan, whom the British were attempting to depose in favour of their own Sikh appointee. The situation was badly handled and when the Second Anglo-Sikh War began with the murder of the two young British officers who had been sent to take the keys of the Multan Fort from Mulraj, assistance was requested from the nawab of Bahawalpur by the British. Bahawal Khan supplied 23,000 men and, with additional Sikh support, Mulraj was defeated in two pitched battles and Multan besieged. The *Sadiqnamah* says 'as a result of Bahawalpur-British military alliance, Multan fell and was made part of the British Indian territory'. The Second Anglo-Sikh War, which finally buried the Sikh kingdom of Ranjit Singh and ended with British annexation of the Punjab, did not end until the whole Sikh army laid down its arms on 13 March 1849. In April that year, Maharaja Duleep Singh was exiled to England. His greatest treasure, the Koh-i-Noor diamond, wrested by his father from Shah Shuja to become the icon of Sikh power, was confiscated by the new power in India.

As a reward for his prompt action and support of the British against Mulraj, Bahawal Khan was granted a life pension of Rs 1 lakh (1,00,000). He was ceremonially received by the governor general to express the British government's gratitude, whereupon, according to Lord Dalhousie, now governor general, 'he stretched out his hands before him and asked, "What had he done to deserve such words? He was but a small Zamindar, not capable of showing the power of a Nawab!" With such like compliments from me, and deprecatory replies breathing humility and humbug from him, we discoursed awhile.'[11] It sounds as if the nawab's courtly manners owed more to Persian traditions than dull English prose readers. Every Bahawalpuri gunner was given a reward of Rs 100.

The nawab also took the opportunity to make four requests of the governor general; that his second son, Saadatyar Khan, should be recognized as his heir instead of his eldest brother Haji Khan; that instead of the pension of Rs 1 lakh, he should receive a grant of land in jagir;[12] that land seized previously owned by Bahawalpur and seized by and from Ranjit Singh should be granted to him on lease; and that an extension, as promised by General Napier, should be made to the lands restored to Bahawalpur after the annexation of Sindh. The records relate only that Saadatyar Khan was acknowledged as Bahawal Khan's heir as of January 1850. Thereafter, the nawab seems to have been badly affected by the death of his spiritual guide, Khwaja Suleman of Taunsa Sharif, and 'from that date applied no dye to his beard'[13] but went on pilgrimage to the famous Chishti shrines at Delhi and Ajmer. Between 1850 and 1852, his native political agent travelled to England but there are regrettably no records tracing his possible activities in further warming the relationship of Bahawalpur state with the British government. It became somewhat less smooth and more intrusive during the following reigns. Nawab Muhammad Bahawal Khan III died at Derawar on 19 October 1852.

The last words on this favoured prince may go to Sir Henry Havelock, the 'Hero of the Mutiny', when he visited Bahawalpur as a mere captain in the 1840s, 'disgusted in the character of most of the petty rulers of India'. In comparison, his mind rested 'with something like complacency on that of the Nawab Bahawal Khan'.

4

FAMILY MATTERS

The dastar-*bandi*, turban-tying ceremony, investing Saadatyar Khan as Nawab Sadiq Muhammad Khan III, in accordance with his father's wishes, took place on 11 November 1852. A few days later Lord Dalhousie announced the annexation of lower Burma and increased the tally of states swallowed by the British during his tenure as governor general, through war or the Doctrine of Lapse in circumstances where there was no male heir to a throne.[1] Bahawal Khan III had six sons, which created a different domestic issue that had also to be resolved. Nawab Sadiq Muhammad Khan III immediately incarcerated his eldest brother, Haji Khan, in the fort of Fatehgarh, where he was very badly treated, and his remaining brothers in other Bahawalpur fortresses. Officials, including one Captain John Hole were dismissed, and Jamadar Ahmad Khan Mallezai, subsequently wazir to Bahawal Khan IV, was banished. Other officials hurried out of the state to avoid imprisonment. The row that blew up between factions loyal to Sadiq Muhammad or to Haji Khan, and culminated in the latter's assuming his father's title, might easily have become an excuse for British intervention and resulted in another annexation.

John Lawrence, of later Mutiny fame, had been appointed one of the three members of the Board of Administration of the Punjab after annexation, with his brother Henry as president. John 'the saviour of the Punjab', was of the new, fashionably hawkish, colonizing breed who declared, 'The masses of the people, are incontestably more prosperous and far more happy in British territory than they are under Native rulers.' As he proved during his tenure as viceroy from 1864 to 1869, the interests of the 'masses of the people' were close to his heart but he mistrusted the landed aristocracy and believed that the foundations of British power in India rested on the many, not on 'the interested approval of the few'.

Lord Dalhousie was nothing loathe to acquire states by conquest or through the Doctrine of Lapse, thus 'extending the uniform application or our system of government to those whose best interests, we sincerely believe will be promoted thereby', but he resisted pressure from Lawrence, informing the commissioner that he considered himself bound by the terms of treaties between states. The first five articles of the first treaty of 1833 between the East India Company and Bahawal Khan state are as under:

- There shall be eternal friendship and alliance between the Honourable East India Company and Nawab Muhammad Bahawal Khan, his heirs and successors.
- The Honourable East India Company engage never to interfere with the hereditary or other possessions of the Bahawalpur government.
- As regards the internal administration of his government, and the exercise of his sovereign right over his subjects, the Nawab shall be entirely independent as heretofore.
- The officer who may be appointed on the part of the British Government to reside in the Bahawalpur state shall,

> in conformity with the preceding article, abstain from all interference with the Nawab's government, and shall respect the preservation of the friendly relations of the two contracting parties.

These articles are repeated in the Supplementary Treaties of the years following, mentioned in the last chapter, on the tolls on merchandise transported through Bahawalpur. Latterly, they acquire a more prescriptive and inclusive tone, 'the friends and enemies of one party shall be the friends and enemies of both parties'; 'the British Government engages to protect the principality and territory of Bahawalpur'; the nawab 'and his heirs and successors, will act in subordinate co-operation with the British Government and acknowledge its supremacy and will not have any connections with any other chiefs or states'; or 'enter negotiation with any chief or state, without the knowledge and sanction of the British Government but the usual amicable correspondence with friends and relations shall continue'; that the nawab and his heirs 'shall not commit aggressions on any one', and if any such dispute arises, 'it shall be submitted to the arbitration and award of the British Government'; the nawab 'will furnish troops at the requisition of the British Government'; and, or perhaps but, the nawab and his heirs 'shall be absolute rulers of their country, and the British jurisdiction shall not be introduced into that principality'. The 'until' or 'unless' is unwritten.

In Bahawalpur, the difficulties for the new nawab had been exacerbated by advice from Sir Henry Lawrence to cut expenditure. This resulted in the demobilization of much of the Bahawalpur army and diminution of the usual grants and gifts expected by the nawab's Daudputra clan on his accession. Captain Hole and other refugees from Bahawalpur swiftly gathered together the malcontents, taking an oath on the Koran to rescue Haji Khan and breaking into

Fatehgarh to carry him off to Khanpur. There the prince collected a force of 5000 loyal men, with supplies of arms and ammunition. The nawab's clumsy efforts to buy guarantees of allegiance from his own men and bribe his brother's followers failed. On 17 February the nawab's infantry went over in a body to Haji Khan who, two days later, entered Ahmedpur as salutes were fired, and assumed the title of Nawab Fateh Khan.

On 20 February, the garrison at Derawar tendered their submission, and Sadiq Muhammad Khan's wazir, Munshi Chaukas Rai, was captured with his family attempting to leave the fort with 10,000 gold mohurs, jewels and the draft of a treaty intended to solicit support for Sadiq Muhammad Khan III with the British. Judging by later examples of the British sticking to their no interference policy in Bahawalpur, that initiative stood no chance of succeeding. Nevertheless, the British appear to have felt some responsibility towards the former nawab on the basis of his earlier recognition by Lord Dalhousie as the legal heir to Bahawalpur. Now John Lawrence requested that, newly reduced, Prince Saadatyar Khan and his family be dispatched to British protection in Multan. Multan may have been too close for comfort for the new nawab, Fateh Khan. After signing a formal deed of abdication, Saadatyar Khan was moved on to Lahore under escort from Michael Edgeworth,[2] the commissioner of Multan, with a pension from his brother of Rs 1600.

In an unexpected postscript to the story of Sadiq Muhammad Khan III's removal, while he was imprisoned 'in a comfortable place', he sent the crown and jewels, which he had in his possession, to the new nawab, Fateh Khan. Fateh Khan, 'with great generosity', returned them, with additional valuable gifts and a large number of servants to attend him. He released his other brothers and sensibly distributed Rs 2 lakh among loyal officials and nobles and to Daudputra leaders, and 'thereby conciliated his servants and chiefs'.

Munshi Chaukas Rai, however, seen as a continuing danger, was sent to the fort at Islamgarh with orders to his escort to kill him on the journey. His body was buried under a heap of sand.

The histories only briefly note the small successes of Fateh Khan's short reign. The Daudputras continued to plot but with no effect on the administration of the state. A 146-mile road was built from Bahawalpur to Kot Sabzal; friendly relations were established with the nearby Sikh-ruled state of Patiala; and, in 1855, the nawab's official salute was fixed at seventeen guns. The merest hint of the catastrophic events of 1857 appears only in the recording of a request from Mr Oliver, superintendent of Sirsa in the present-day state of Haryana, that May for troops from Bahawalpur to help maintain law and order. Sirsa was a secondary military station where the local Bhatti Rajput nawab had been removed by the British as early as 1818 and Company policies were highly unpopular. In all, about 3000 troops were sent by Bahawalpur. As it turned out, after the news of revolt in the Haryana Light Infantry and the killing of British officers at Hisar and Hansar had arrived in Sirsa, the station's British civilian population had escaped without loss. Fateh Khan did not live long to reap greater rewards for his loyalty to the British. It was rumoured that his health had been affected by the death of a waterman who had been punished for unintentional intrusion on his privacy and he died on 3 October 1858.

Sir Penderel Moon[3] wrote of his heir, Muhammad Bahawal Khan IV, 'profiting by experience, the next Nawab of Bahawalpur, on his succession, executed his three uncles in case they should try to supplant him'. This action failed to secure the throne for long in a reign marked by disturbance, insurrection and plot, with rumour and counter-rumour reported to the British. They found the 'personal character of the Nawab despicable', oppressive, suspicious and mean, and prematurely aged by debauchery. In June 1864, Thomas

Forsyth, secretary to the Government of the Punjab, wrote 'the Nawab is a bad and unpopular ruler and it is not improbable that he may be deposed by his subjects'. He was 'menaced with displeasure' over the murder of his uncles but the lieutenant governor of Punjab had written to him, on behalf of the viceroy, to little effect.

Bahawal Khan insisted, almost certainly with complete truth, that his uncles were inciting rebellion to gain power.[4] The British indeed appear to have known exactly what was going on, while keeping events at arm's length, and maintaining hopes of one of the uncles succeeding his appalling nephew had any been allowed to live.[5] The reign ended with the nawab's murder by poison on 26 March 1866. He is said to have been discussing the political situation with his maternal grandfather when he was given news of some of his courtiers intriguing to join rebels who had taken refuge in British territory. Saying that he would deal with them in the morning, Bahawal Khan retired to his palace and asked for food which was brought by a maid called Sultana. 'On eating this he lost all self-control and soon expired.' Bahawalpur was reported to be in an anarchical condition.[6]

It is hardly surprising, following these events, that the accession to the throne of the four-and-a-half-year-old son of an unpopular ruler did little to close the door on rebellion. A letter of 21 April 1866, signed by John Lawrence and other members of the Punjab government, to Lord de Grey and Ripon, the Secretary of State for India in London, reported, 'the succession was forcibly disputed by a party under Jaffar Khan', and, 'the whole country is in a state of anarchy'. Prince Jaffar Khan was a brother of Bahawal Khan III and had also been imprisoned by his successors, probably at Derawar. It appears that when the dead nawab's body was carried to Derawar for burial, Jaffar Khan was released, installed on the throne, promptly threw all the important mourners into prison, and named his own government.

The child ruler, or, more credibly, his *durbaris*, courtiers, and his mother, 'implored the interference of the British Government', in the somewhat optimistically premature regnal name, of Amir Sir Sadiq Muhammad Khan IV GCSI. The lieutenant governor, Sir Donald McLeod, nicknamed *cunctator*, delayer, by John Lawrence, was inclined to give assistance but, 'after careful consideration' and probably some tough talking by Lawrence, the administration decided instead to follow the policy of non-interference, and merely extend 'the benefit of our moral support' to the nawab. On 30 June, the same government correspondents reported to the Secretary of State on the 'further progress of events regarding the mutiny of the Bahawalpur army, which it seems may not prove entirely unfavourable to the minor Nawab'.[7]

By that time, the commissioner of Multan, William Ford, had been to Bahawalpur, arriving in Ahmedpur East on 1 June, as the troops there were planning a riot in favour of the 'usurper'. The durbar acted quickly, deporting Jaffar Khan and the leader of the mutiny to British territory. The rebels, who had barricaded the mosque at Derawar, surrendered, and their suspected ringleader, Ghulam Muhammad Chaki, was arrested and imprisoned in the fort at Bahawalgarh by the young nawab's wazir. There, in due course, he was put to death, while the remaining rebels were amnestied and allowed to return home.

When a second request was sent to Multan by the begum dowager requesting intervention by the British, there was a change of heart and Mr Ford returned to Bahawalpur in August 1866 as political agent. He set about reforming the administration, with considerable energy from all accounts, before he returned to Multan and Captain Charles Cherry Minchin was appointed political superintendent of the state to continue the good work.[8] 'The Agency' or *Mudakhalat*, otherwise translated as encroachment or interference, from 1866 to 1879, during the minority of Sadiq Muhammad Khan IV, was a time of remarkable modernization of the state machine. It was also the beginning of a British presence in Bahawalpur that maintained until its absorption into Pakistan.

In 1872, the duke of Argyll, Secretary of State for India, exercising his view that 'the final control and direction of the affairs of India rest with the home government, and not with the authorities appointed and established by the Crown, under Parliamentary enactment in India itself', sent Major Minchin the benefit of his opinions on the form of administration in Bahawalpur. In particular, he focused on the introduction of civil and criminal laws in use in British India. A change to the confusion and abuse of a previous part-religious and part-secular rule of law, where the only certainty was the amputation of a hand for theft applied to both Hindus and Muslims, or payment of a heavy fine. The duke wrote: 'The affairs of the Bahawalpur State should be so conducted as to involve no needless break in the continuity of the administration when handed over to its future native rulers. There is a tendency to assimilate not the substance only, but forms of administration too closely to those which prevail in districts which have all along been under our direct Government and in which there is of course no probability of any change occurring.'

Judging by the great swathe of reforms carried out during Minchin's tenure—his name was permanently memorialized in the town of Minchinabad, now in the Punjab—he had the courage of his convictions for good or ill and replied: 'We have divided the administration into two distinct branches, the judicial and executive, which is nowhere enforced in British India. The Indian Penal, Procedure and Civil Codes have been introduced because of the immense advantages gained to the Administration by having written Laws and Regulations which can be applied to all classes and where the duties of each officer are clearly defined. The judicial system has been entirely carried out through Native Agency and is partly modelled on the Travancore State in the Madras Presidency.'

Government departments were formalized under a cabinet council and a general council both appointed by the nawab. The cabinet council would consist of the foreign minister, chief judge, revenue minister, and the Mushir-i-Ala or wazir of the durbar, to deliberate and advise the nawab on matters of particular importance to the state. The general council included the cabinet members with the addition of the commander-in-chief of state forces, the accountant general, the minister of public works, irrigation minister; the nawab's private secretary, and the general secretary to the council. Meetings of the general council were held at least once a week, four members forming a quorum; all orders passed in the nawab's name to be subject to revision by His Highness in council.

The state was divided into three Nizamats or districts, administered by collectors, each subdivided into tehsils, under *tehsildars*, and so on through various levels of petty officialdom. A tax system, land revenues, ownership and uses of land were regulated and the boundaries of villages demarcated as far as possible. Local custom was followed as to inheritance and the portion of widows. The hugely important questions of river access, use, ferry tolls and demarcation of fixed state boundaries, were not fully answered even by the beginning of the next century. Three district judges were appointed, extradition rules established with Jaisalmer whose people were continually raiding Bahawalpur territory, and the civil, revenue and criminal powers of public servants laid down. So far as crime went, the most reported offences in the state were cattle theft and the abduction of women.

The first hospital in Bahawalpur was established in 1867, the female Jubilee Hospital in 1898, and a Daulatkhana dispensary, overseen by a private medical adviser, opened for the nawab's zenana in 1883. Vaccinators travelled the state in the cold weather and from the list of 416 curious-sounding surgical operations carried out in the state at the beginning of the twentieth century, only seven resulted in death. Deaths and births were registered by village chowkidars and reported by them to the police. The nawab funded scholarships for Bahawalpuri students to the Lahore Medical College, and, at the close of the agency, the handful of madrasas providing education in the state had been replaced by thirty-five primary schools. Middle schools, high schools and colleges followed during the rule of Bahawal Khan IV who sent his own son and heir to Aitchison College in Lahore, where a mosque and a house were built for the boy's personal use.

In March 1871, Captain Leopold Grey took over from Major Minchin until the nawab finally attained his majority. In his letters to his grandsons, Grey wrote, 'it is a mistake to judge a native prince by our standards' but, regarding his 'first Nawab of Bahawalpur', he was 'in many respects a very fine fellow and liked by his people', although, he wrote, 'I almost despair of the problem of training Indian chiefs on English methods'. Grey was rather shocked by the changes of the last fifty years, comparing the days of 'a stately raja in his flowing robes' to 'the modern Indian noble emulating the British subaltern' in breeches and boots, or in flannels playing cricket. Enough, he thought to make that young man's 'grandsire turn in his grave'. He preferred, 'the native state system' for India, because it suited the people, even when it was bad, and 'when good it is the best possible for Orientals'. 'Having abolished the ancient remedy of revolt, which kept bad rulers in check, we must substitute supervision', not meaning 'meddlesome interference' but proper checks and balances under the authority of the emperor, which, he advocated, could be better carried out by 'native political agents' than the British, who were usually, 'too much in evidence', except in supervising the administration during a minority.

Sadiq Muhammad Khan IV was installed to his full powers by Sir Robert Egerton, lieutenant governor of Punjab, on 28 November 1879, as General Roberts occupied Kabul during the Second Anglo-Afghan War and Bahawalpur forces were gathered to support the British once again. In this case, they were not used in the theatre of war but to man frontier posts vacated by the Punjab Frontier Force which was now engaged in Kabul. It was as reward for this act of loyalty that the nawab properly received his GCSI from the hands of Lord Ripon, successor to Lord Lytton, who had himself visited Bahawalpur when on tour between November and December 1876. Lytton had resigned in June 1880 after an ill-starred viceroyalty when the first great, glittering fanfare of British imperialism, the Delhi Durbar in 1877, to proclaim Queen Victoria empress of India, coincided with the outbreak and mismanagement of a horrific famine which killed millions of people. This was followed by an unnecessary and hugely costly Afghan war that 'brought Britain no credit militarily or as a humane civilised power', and encouraged Lytton to resign to the safety of the House of Lords in Westminster and ultimately to become ambassador in Paris.

None of this is more than distant background to the history of Bahawalpur. There is no remaining written record of the young nawab attending the 1877 Durbar or 'Imperial Assemblage' but witness to his presence exists in the shredded silk banner, framed and hanging from its gilded staff in Salahuddin Abbasi's study in Dera Nawab Sahib. It bears two gilded plaques with the inscriptions Nawab Sadeq Mahammad Khan Bahadur, Nawab of Bahawalpur, From Victoria, Empress of India, 1 January 1877. As the Indian princes' symbolic act of submission, similar to the acceptance of a khillat from the Mughal emperor at one of his durbars in the past, in

1877 they now accepted the banners, made with their coats of arms in the British heraldic style, from the new empress.

After Lord Lytton, most of his viceregal successors visited Bahawalpur and are remembered in stone inscriptions for opening this or that new building or institution and in a handful of fading photographs peopled by nameless Bahawalpur courtiers and civil and military British officers. Bahawalpur was very much on the viceroys' visiting list, with a loyal ruler, valuable armed forces and, importantly, excellent shooting in the desert around Derawar. Lytton's visit coincided with Sadiq Muhammad Khan IV's construction of Noor Mahal Palace, now confiscated by the army. High under the coffered ceiling of the vast entrance hall, there used to be a glorious demilune stained-glass window. It portrayed Lytton, in undeservedly heroic style, as an almost pre-Raphaelite knightly figure, tiger-shooting from an elephant, the scarf about his sola topi billowing in the wind. Next to him the young, jewelled and turbaned nawab fired at a snarling tiger. Like so much of the Bahawalpur treasure in buildings and works of art, it has now been destroyed or lost.

5

TRAPPINGS OF MODERNITY

If Pakistan had taken a different path; if Bahawalpur had become a province, as promised by Muhammad Ali Jinnah; if Zulfikar Ali Bhutto had not determined to stamp on former rulers or anyone who commanded traditional loyalties, so reducing all to subservience on the excuse of socialist principle; if the army had not been all-powerful; if Pakistan had grown outwards instead of retreating inwards; if there had been less corruption, less adherence to the impossible dream of the true Islamic state; if there had been less terror and less fear, more celebration of the past, a greater desire to preserve and understand history and to promote and share it with others, Bahawalpur would be one of the major tourist destinations of the world. It would have become a point on the travel/business map, with Lahore and Multan, of another so-called golden triangle like Delhi, Agra and Jaipur in India, a part of tours that would include Mohenjo-Daro, Harappa, Taxila, the remnants of the Indus Valley Civilization. Then on again, north perhaps, to the beautiful Swat Valley, Gilgit and Hunza, names that have long since echoed in British ears, or on the lost hippie trail to Afghanistan. In this parallel universe, the tourist would have other choices; the beaches and seafood restaurants of Karachi; the shrines of Sindh; or marvellous Cholistan, its stupendous forts, some restored as unique 'heritage' hotels, and all the colourful traditions and music of nomadic desert tribes. Before pampered and government-courted Arab princes hunted down their scant remaining populations, there would also have been all the furred and feathered life of the desert lands. If things had been different.

It is less than 150 years since Sadiq Khan IV instituted a dramatic building programme to add to his ancient heritage. He transformed Bahawalpur into a modern city adorned with splendid palaces of eccentrically mixed architecture and public buildings intended to embellish the dignity and style of a young, glamorous, wealthy and apparently cultivated prince. Other towns were founded, industries created, ancient buildings added to and modernized; the momentum of The Agency and Major Minchin in developing the mechanisms of the state were added to by an ambitious, and, one suspects from photographic evidence, vain ruler, to make Bahawalpur shine among its peers and become a fitting setting for his own magnificence. Burning the candle at both ends brought his life to a premature end, and his personal life was not entirely smooth; but that cannot reduce his achievements and an intent to modernize and improve his state. The baton was picked up by his grandson, Sadiq Muhammad V, and carried until the end of the state of Bahawalpur and the passing of its diamond-crowned princes into history.

If the aura of the Pax Britannica did not extend to expensive little local difficulties that were often exacerbated by the arrogant certitude of British imperial officialdom in India, the last thirty years of the nineteenth century brought an end to the regular warring between most of the princely states. If Indian nationalism rose after the first meeting of Indian National Congress was held in 1885, there was still a breathing space as the Bengal Renaissance flowered and rulers used their wealth to add dignity and substance to royal images that were no longer dependent on success in battle. New trappings of royalty were no insurance against family and court quarrels and jealousies, or against the self-destructive foibles of spoilt princes, but their monuments, palaces and treasures, expanded and enriched in this period, have become the draw and delight of modern tourism. They are the image of the colour and the grandeur of princely India.

Some of the princes were already travelling to Europe by the time of Queen Victoria's golden jubilee in 1887, but her undoubtedly glamorized vision of India was fully realized with the huge influx of glittering princes on that occasion. The door to different influences was opened wider to Indians who were also beginning, like Sadiq Muhammad Khan IV, to educate their sons in schools run by British masters on British public-school models. British tutors had already become a regular feature of princely courts. An article from the *Spectator* in 1887, notes, 'It is the usual English opinion that the habit of travel must for Indian Princes be a most beneficial one.' It goes on to point out that the princes 'are often not nearly so much "impressed" as is imagined, especially in England' and 'intercourse with Europeans does not always produce liking for Europeans'.[1] And who could blame the princes? But exposure to other styles and cultures did broaden their tastes and they or their agents patronized the great European purveyors of the arts and works of art over the next fifty years as they added new, contemporary and more European elements, from chandeliers to motor cars, to their palaces and collections.

Sadiq Muhammad Khan's construction programme in Bahawalpur, perhaps influenced by the modernizing Major Minchin and his cohorts, began earlier than some of his neighbours and peers. Construction of the Lalgarh Palace in Bikaner, in the Indo-Saracenic style favoured by British architects for grand Indian buildings, did not start until 1896—likewise the Lakshmi Vilas Palace in Baroda and the palaces in Mysore and Kapurthala. Others came later; art deco masterpieces like Manik Bagh in Indore and the monumental Umaid Bhavan in Jodhpur. Princes like Maharaja Jayaji Rao Scindia rejected the Indo-Saracenic style as a British imposition in favour of the mixed metaphor of European styles of his Jai Vilas Palace in Gwalior, finished in 1875. Noor Mahal, in Bahawalpur, completed the same year, is likewise a European, Italianate palace, designed by a Mr Heenan, the state engineer, with mixed inspiration. It was intended to be the principal residence of the nawab and his current favourite wife, but neither the architect nor his client appeared to have noticed the proximity of the Maluk Shah graveyard to the palace outlook. The wife, glimpsing this ill omen from a window, refused to spend another night in the palace and it became instead a guest house and venue for ceremonial occasions.

The Bahawalgarh Mahal, built in 1876, the Daulat Khana with its beautiful garden and 400-foot pool in 1886, and the Gulzar Mahal during the reign of Sadiq Khan's son in 1902, have all but disappeared from view. The original high walls round the grounds of Daulat Khana have been further reinforced by army directives and entry forbidden to all except military familiars. Only Sadiqgarh, unfortunately described by George Birdwood, expert on and proponent of Indian vernacular arts, as 'the ghastliest piece of bare classicism', remains in more or less plain sight. It was designed by an unknown Italian architect, photographed with the nawab during construction, at Dera Nawab Sahib outside Ahmedpur as the replacement residence for Noor Mahal. Finished in 1896, Sadiqgarh was decorated by the traditional woodcarvers of Chiniot and glittered with crystal embellishments by Christofle of Paris, including a 12-metre-high fountain, huge mirrors and a crystal throne. Now largely ruined, the palace remains, in name at least, in the private ownership of Salahuddin Abbasi. All his unending efforts have been unable to save the palace and its treasures from encroachment of the army cantonment almost into the garden and from the fallout from the eternal wrangling between the military, the government and disputatious relatives.

According to R.D. Mackenzie, writing a highly coloured portrait of an exotic oriental prince, in 1899, for an American publication, *Century Magazine*, Muhammad Sadiq Khan IV preferred to live in a smaller 'palace', a 'square, low, flat-topped building'[2] in the grounds, one of several now in various stages of decay. Mackenzie's breathless description of Sadiq Khan is indicative of the fascination with the lives of Indian rulers, that grew with their higher profiles abroad and the growing number of visitors from other countries to India after the opening of the Suez Canal in 1869 made travel to South Asia easier and more fashionable. The article plays to the imagination of its readers with accounts of shikar, a nautch, pig-sticking, pockets full of gold, a jewelled sword and the famous diamond crown. It also offers a pointer to the staggering energy of the nawab, fuelled however much by the alcoholism and drug use that seems to have been most responsible for his early death. Mackenzie hardly knows where to begin with his description of Sadiqgarh:

> This palace is one of the magnificent incongruities that now and then startle the European visitor to the native states. It might be the Palais du Luxembourg. The dust and glare of the desert are so great that you are apt to fear that your head and eyes are playing you false.

At the same time not so false that he did not notice 'the cast iron fountains that never play and when you look at the dry, cracked desert sand on which you are standing, you wonder that anybody ever thought they would'.

The interior of the palace may not have been entirely to Mackenzie's taste, a room with pink and yellow walls, combined with 'vivid green curtains'; 'an enormous Gothic mirror—a sort of miniature Westminster Abbey'; and 'no fewer than fifteen reproductions of one particular coloured vase' with cut crystal or gilt furniture. All this pales into insignificance beside Sadiq Muhammad Khan's famous musical silver bed although Mackenzie does not dwell on that unique piece of furniture—perhaps he was shocked. There are images galore of this bed, made to order by Christofle in Paris in 1882. It is an object of appalling wonder, delivered to a nawab with a penchant for European women, later shared by his grandson Sadiq Muhammad Khan V, and proving troublesome to them both. The bed was a giant musical box made of rosewood, clad with silver and with a bronze automaton figure of a life-sized nude woman at each corner. Each one had natural hair of a different shade and each held a fan of ostrich feathers or horse tail to fan the resting nawab while winking at him. It apparently played an air from Gounod's *Faust* and sounds altogether the stuff of hellish nightmares.

There was also a fountain, made in London by W.T. Allen & Co. of Upper Thames Street. It is reputed to have been a gift from Queen Victoria, which may or may not be the case. There is another rumour, still running rife on the Internet, to the amusement of Salahuddin's family, that one of the marble mausoleums at Derawar contains the remains of one of the queen empress's daughters, married off at some point to the nawab. Confusion may have arisen over the Victoria who was Sadiq Muhammad Khan V's favourite English wife and for whom he built Mubarak Manzil, outside the walls of Sadiqgarh, where his grandson still lives when in Bahawalpur. The fountain was also at Sadiqgarh, in front of the palace, and was moved into Bahawalpur city by Sadiq Muhammad Khan V. It still survives, minus the scantily clad nymphs with which it was originally ornamented. They sound a most unlikely gift from Queen Victoria.

As for Sadiq Muhammad Khan IV, there is also a plethora of photographs, each portrait as much an image of glorious costume as of the man. Some of his spectacular coats, encrusted with gold embroidery and lined with layers of tissue silk, still survive, metre upon metre of exquisite fabrics, weighed down with pure gold embroidery. Mackenzie described the nawab as 'about thirty-six years old, six feet tall and well proportioned, he has dark and prominent features, long black curly hair, beard cut close and very long drooping moustaches curling into a ring. He is extremely sensitive, has a strong will and a constitution of iron and is intensely suspicious and jealous, the natural result of his position.' He generally wears two or three watches from a collection of some seventeen hundred, and the *Century* article carried a photograph of the nawab in the diamond crown with its fringe of large pear-shaped pearls. It sounds as if Mackenzie was shown the best of the jewels including the historic 'fifteen uncut rubies' measuring more than one-and-a-half inches in diameter, with the names of the Mughal emperors engraved upon them. Mackenzie commented, 'It is only natural that the young prince, once in possession of his great wealth should desire to spend it.' His 'present income is about fifteen lakhs of rupees a year. He is an absolute monarch' and 'if it suits his pleasure', holds a weekly durbar at which anyone of any station in life can present his petition. He has a bodyguard of 400 mounted Baluchis, 'a wild, dirty and most picturesque set and the most reckless riders I have ever seen'. There were 2000 domestic servants, 300 shikaris, 150 English and Arab horses and two river steamers always ready on the Sutlej. 'Like most Indian princes, he has killed his tiger', and also, like his peers, had an English tutor and spoke good English.

No sooner had Mackenzie witnessed a royal durbar than news came of wild boars surrounded in the desert and off they went in the shikar wagon, drawn by eight mules, at breakneck speed, while the nawab handed round generous quantities of cigars and cigarettes to the eight occupants 'pressed like pickles in a bottle'. The pig-sticking successfully accomplished, the boars liberated from the vast canvas arena hurriedly put up around the cornfield they were grazing and the nawab 'pluckily' jumping off his frightened horse to run his spear through a charging tusker, the party returned to the palace by about eight o'clock at night. After dinner, Mackenzie retired in 'the awful emptiness of the palace' wondering to himself if this was the proper 'environment for a prince who had received an English education and spent the best part of his life in European society'. He had not been alone for long when he was invited to join the nawab, his prime minster and private secretary, for the nautch that continued into the small hours as the assembled company, barring the nawab, indulged in 'gentle sleep'. At last they retired to the roof of the palace, to rest more than to sleep for the narghile was called for and the storytellers came to recite until the nawab should rest.

When Mackenzie woke, he found himself in broad daylight quite alone on the roof, and discovered that the nawab had been given news of more pigs and rushed off to the hunt. Returning at about midday, he watched wrestling all afternoon, went for a drive in the evening and another nautch all night. Mackenzie wrote, 'That is a fair example of the restless life led by an Indian Prince. Of course, no human frame can long endure such a strain but somehow it does when buoyed up by "stimulants".' Perhaps the death of the English wife to whom he was most attached, pushed Sadiq Muhammad Khan to find solace in those stimulants. There are remarkably informal photographs of her in the garden with her husband, a slight young woman with fair hair, in her white dress she looks nothing more than a child, and, for all his curling whiskers, neither does he. In Salahuddin Abbasi's house behind Sadiqgarh, her full-length portrait hangs above a bed in a room believed to be haunted by her, or possibly by another English wife.

Only the names of those women who divorced or were divorced by Sadiq Muhammad Khan IV or V and were so dissatisfied by their treatment by the nawab, or more usually by their pay-off, complained to the British powers, remain in existing India Office Records. In general, the correspondence between residents, and governors, private secretaries and occasionally the viceroy, on the subject of wives, was redolent of exasperation and the feeling that most of the women who set out to capture a wealthy prince were no better than they ought to be. As that same prince's English nanny might well have said. Of the Indian wives, until the last nawab, there are also few records except when a particularly mutually advantageous marriage took place. In such cases the family, if not the given name of the bride, was recorded, or, in the case of a begum acting for her minor son when he inherited the throne. Abbasi daughters were rarely allowed to marry out to other families and remained in their father's, brothers' or uncles' zenana all their lives.

Like so many others, Sadiq Muhammad Khan's young English wife's name has disappeared from memory. She may be buried somewhere at Derawar but where has been forgotten beside the date and the cause. It is known that her husband was so heartbroken that he begged for help from the Sufi mystic and Saraiki poet Khwaja Ghulam Farid (1845–1901) who had grown up in Bahawalpur and to whom he was extremely close. Khwaja Ghulam Farid was said to be deeply antipathetic to British rule but his ability to do his best for the state of Bahawalpur, even at long distance, is legendary and illustrated by a story remembered by Salahuddin Abbasi. He tells of a British offer to pay off the young ruler's debts in exchange for the district of Rahim Yar Khan, a quarter of the state. When the nawab, possibly under the influence of one of several British wives, signed the agreement, one of his durbaris rode hotfoot 150 miles to Khwaja Ghulam Farid and explained what had happened. To his surprise, he was swiftly dismissed by the mystic, who said only, 'Understand one thing. Sadiq Muhammad Khan has written the state away but Ghulam Farid has not.' When the messenger returned to the palace, there was a tremendous hue and cry; the documents had gone missing and were never found again. The mystic duly arrived himself at Sadiqgarh to castigate the young prince for his irresponsibility. The British reaction to this turn of events has disappointingly disappeared.

When the nawab's wife died, he begged the saint to bring her back so that he could see her once more. Khwaja Ghulam Farid eventually agreed on the promise that Sadiq Muhammad Khan would neither speak to nor attempt to touch his dead bride. The story is told that, when she appeared before her husband, he gazed upon her until he could bear it no longer and, putting out his hand, touched hers. The vision vanished and he found himself holding only the hand of Ghulam Farid. The nawab may have welcomed the death in the 1890s of another Englishwoman, the self-styled Sarah, begum of Bahawalpur, as much as the British authorities. They were forced to expend reams of paper and presumably many hours attempting to get to the bottom of the true relationship between Sadiq Muhammad Khan and the woman, formerly known as Mrs Skinner, which they considered 'a very disgraceful business in every way'.

She had previously been, or might still be, married to a Mr Skinner of Meerut, a member of the well-known Anglo-Indian family descended from James Skinner of Skinner's Horse cavalry regiment. Her marital status depended, in the first instance, on the validity of a divorce from him on the grounds of her adultery with one or possibly two of his 'Muhammedan man-servants'. Inevitably, the endgame, if a valid divorce was accepted, focused on the terms of any marriage or other arrangement with the nawab as regards dowry, or other payments and promises that may or may not have been made, kept or broken. It is a grubby tale whereby, whether or not she had ever been Mrs Skinner, Sarah had been more or less procured by one Adamji who was aware of the nawab's tastes and was probably working directly for him in this capacity.

In a summing up of the case, John G.M. Rennie, sessions judge in Multan in March 1897, does not beat about the bush, nor does he go far to conceal the contempt of a man educated at Winchester and King's College Cambridge for the case in front of him:

> In the first place, it is not to be supposed that the lady went to Bahawalpur for love of the Nawab, even of the lowest description. She went there for what she could pick up and it is not reflecting too severely upon her to suppose that she made up her mind to get all she could out of the Nawab.

Attempting some mitigation for her actions, he describes the nawab as having 'reduced himself to a state of semi-imbecility by his dissolute habits and he is certainly not the sort of man to show any self-restraint in gratifying the caprice of the moment'. He judges that the nawab, having set his heart on something, in this case a woman, would do anything required to get her including having 'penned all the trash' in love letters produced as evidence by Sarah Skinner who said that she thought the nawab would have given her 'half of his kingdom for the pleasure of possessing her'. Sarah, in addition, he judged as having lied about her 'self-sacrifice in relinquishing Christianity for 'Muhammedanism' since many of the Skinner family were already Muslim and 'their general appearance is precisely that of the ordinary Delhi Muhammedan'. Nevertheless, there were letters procured from Sarah and given in evidence by Sadiq Muhammad Khan that agreed, on receipt of a 'present' from him of jewels and Rs 12,000, 'we are by this paper taking a divorce from each other, so you have no more hold on me, nor I on you'. She was 'miles from a station in the middle of a Native State without a single influential friend' and 'in a state of actual bodily danger'.[3]

The last word on the case came, at length, from the governor of the Punjab in June 1897, via Louis Dane, chief secretary to the governor of the Punjab. It was judged overall that while everyone had behaved atrociously, Sarah Skinner had no further claim on the nawab beyond her Rs 12,000, and there was 'no reason for bringing the agency of Government to bear upon the settlement of a case which he deeply regrets having to investigate'. A copy of this final judgment was forwarded to the *motamid* or chamberlain of the Bahawalpur Durbar with the governor's disapproving regret that 'such a discreditable case should have come before him'.

Looking back not so very far from the twenty-first century, it is hard to equate that beautiful nawab, one of Leopold Grey's modern young Indian nobles, the jewelled dandy, captured in one photograph after another, with Ottoman tales of zenana jealousies, poisonings, incarceration in ancient fortresses and mysterious deaths. On reflection, however, perhaps the playboy looks combined with royal prerogative, unfettered unless the paramount power should become involved, fits perfectly into that scene. The transcription of such archaic activities into dry civil service language only adds to their arcane unreality, the *One Thousand and One Nights* as a government report. Simultaneously with the Sarah Skinner case, further acres of typescript from Louis Dane show ever closer British involvement in unsatisfactory Bahawalpur affairs. Sadiq Muhammad Khan's excessive drinking and drug taking, reducing him to unconsciousness for two or three days at a time, had been brought to government attention by the wazir of Bahawalpur.

In addition, under the influence of his favourite wife, the nawab was attempting to bypass his eldest living son, Muhammad Mubarik Khan, then aged thirteen or fourteen, as heir to the throne. A curious introduction to the complications of the succession was added by Leopold Grey in his memoir as something of a morality tale on the proper bringing up of young princes. Muhammad Mubarik Khan had not been the firstborn son of the nawab. Shortly after receiving his powers in 1879, his wife had produced an heir 'and great were the rejoicings'. With pursed lips, Grey continued, 'As always, the boy was spoiled; young nobles in India have no chance for flattery and submissiveness surround them from their earliest years.' When he was four or five, the young heir, roaming with his attendant, found a basket of fireworks ready for a festival and wanted to set them off. The attendant demurred but 'the child, never restrained, grew more determined from opposition. Who was the attendant that he should oppose a prince's will!' So, as he protested feebly, the boy set off the fireworks and blew them both up. That wife never had another son, and Grey said, 'the succession passed to my second ward, the son of a hated rival'.[4]

Poor Muhammad Mubarik Khan. He had been sent away to long incarceration in Derawar with no access to suitable education, then freed, at the insistence of the British, to a house at Ahmedpur with his mother and grandmother.[5] In another confused tale, teased out in official documents, the nawab had found his latest favourite wife, Gama Khatun Begum, when she was herself imprisoned in Bahawalpur jail. Legend has it that the young woman, who came from a cattle-stealing desert tribe, refused to look at the prince when he visited the jail but instead sat with the Koran open in front of her. The nawab was so impressed by her piety that he determined to marry her then and there. If it is fair to judge by his other adventures with women, matrimonial or not, it seems likely that Sadiq Muhammad was at least as impressed by the begum's person as her religious sensibility but she became extraordinarily powerful. She adopted the three-year-old son, Haji Khan, of another wife as her own, and, abetted by her brother, 'a notorious bad character', was pushing to have the boy named heir to the throne. The waters were further muddied by the nawab's state of health and competency at the time. There were almost simultaneous requests, in February and again in March 1897, from the wazir of Bahawalpur, for a British doctor to treat the nawab for his various addictions.

Long-established rumours in the Abbasi family suggest he was also being poisoned by Bibi Gama Khatun, and the wazir may have hoped the British would discover the problem and be able to remove the ruler from his wife's purview. It sounds perfectly feasible, given her reported character and machinations, but the doctors only mentioned their belief that his 'feeble condition both of mind and body' was due to heavy opium and alcohol consumption chased down with large doses of chlorals and bromides. While he had been in Lahore during the cold season, he had begun to hallucinate that he had three or four tongues, or had balls in his mouth and threads in his throat. On 11 March, Surgeon-Major Coates gave his opinion to Louis Dane that the nawab was on the verge of insanity and would shortly have to be placed under restraint unless 'there is a complete change in his way of living and his surroundings'.

Some small improvements and the withdrawal of all drugs, except opium, by the team of British doctors engaged in the case, encouraged the surgeon-major a week or so later to advocate the benefits of foreign travel. By early April, the nawab was able to write himself 'to express his obligations' for the exertions on his behalf by the governor and the doctors assigned to his treatment. He had continued to petition against his heir, the British insisting on adhering to the rule of primogeniture.[6] They also pressed for the sahibzada to be sent to Aitchison College, not least to remove him from potential danger in Bahawalpur, although it had been reported that his mother supervised the preparation and tasting of his food. Louis Dane admitted to concerns about the abilities of Mubarik Khan after his detention in Derawar during his formative years. Rumours spread by the rival faction to his succession had suggested real mental impairment, and Dane recommended he be given the additional care and input of a British tutor. Mr Arthur Evill[7] was dispatched from Dharamsala and stayed with the young nawab until he reached his majority.

In spite of the early complications of his life, the prince proved an excellent pupil who passed the entrance exams for the Punjab University. The lieutenant governor of the Punjab, Sir Mackworth Young, was generous in his praise for 'the first ruler of a Princely State of the Punjab who has passed the intermediate exam'; and continued, 'it is a matter of delight that this fine example happened during my tenure'.[8] After his accession, he was described by the vicereine, Mary Minto, in 1906 as 'extremely promising'.[9] A promise sadly unrealized when he passed all too closely in his father's wake into history, leaving another tiny child struggling to survive to sit on his throne.

According to the *Sadiqnamah*, Sadiq Muhammad Khan IV was known to the Muslims of India as 'Subh-i-Sadiq', the Glorious Dawn. The glory was wearing a bit threadbare by the end of his reign. The histories recount that he became very ill on 7 February 1899 and died on 14 February. It is easy to speculate that his death was the result of poisoning by disappointed parties to the inheritance dispute, although he probably remained more useful to them alive than dead. He may have died by the hand of one of his durbar or council officials, who, like his wazir, despaired of his ability to rule properly. Alternatively, his great-great-grandson wonders, could his death have even been engineered by the British through local agency? A melodramatic departure from the continuing policy of non-interference. It seems probable, given his state of health two years earlier, that he would have died of the cumulative effects of drink and drug abuse with or without a dose of poison to hurry mortality along. In spite of the gloss of the *Sadiqnamah* on this Sadiq Muhammad Khan's reign, Leopold Grey, called out of retirement to return to Bahawalpur after the Nawab's death, wrote of finding the state 'destitute of competent officials; the former chief had effectively cleared off all men of any capacity in the state'. He followed up, rather complacently, 'Had I been left in Bahawalpur to guide the chief for a few years, I should not have spent four years there, twenty years later, in repairing his mischief.'

6

ANOTHER CENTURY

The bright young man, who travelled from Aitchison College to Bahawalpur for the dastar-bandi ceremony on 10 March 1899, took his grandfather's name to rule as Muhammad Bahawal Khan V. After the ceremony, he returned to school, a continuing safe haven, leaving his state in the hands of the state council overseen by Colonel Grey. In May 1901, the nawab left Aitchison to tour Bahawalpur and begin to learn the business of administration from the colonel. In July that year he was married. His heir, named immediately Sadiq Muhammad Khan, was born on 29 September 1904. There is an awful Solomon Grundy element to the life of Muhammad Bahawal Khan V: born, imprisoned, educated, enthroned, married, sick, sicker, dead, all at horrible speed. In January 1903, he attended the Delhi Durbar and was photographed by Bourne & Shepherd in all his finery, wearing the diamond crown.

In April, Colonel Grey retired for good, and the state was placed under the supervision of the political agent of the Phulkian states, comprising the Sikh-ruled states of Jind, Nabha and Patiala. The colonel had been busy reorganizing Bahawalpur over the past couple of years. Revenue had risen; improved irrigation had encouraged higher levels of colonization; the demarcation of local borders had been clarified; and an Imperial Service Camel Corps instituted, instead of the traditional irregular cavalry and infantry. A census took place, plans were mooted for a memorial Victoria Hospital and the question was raised for the first time of a weir across the Sutlej and a canal system into the state, a project that would come to haunt the reign of the nawab's heir. In November 1903, Bahawal Khan was invested with his full powers at Bahawalpur by the viceroy, Lord Curzon. It was the first time a viceroy had so enhanced the stature of Bahawalpur and gave Curzon the opportunity for a masterclass on the role and place of princes under the Empire.

> When the British Crown, through the Viceroy, and the Indian Princes in the person of one of their number, are brought together on an occasion of so much importance as an installation ceremony, it is not unnatural that we should reflect for a moment on the nature of the ties that are responsible for this association . . .
>
> It represents a series of relationships that have grown up between the Crown and the Indian Princes under widely differing historical conditions, but which in process of time have gradually conformed to a single type. The sovereignty of the Crown is everywhere unchallenged. It has itself laid down the limitations of its own prerogative. Conversely the duties and the services of the States are implicitly recognised and as a rule faithfully discharged. It is this happy blend of authority with free-will, of sentiment with self-interest, of duties with rights, that distinguishes the Indian Empire under the British Crown from any other dominion of which we read in history. The links that hold it together are not iron fetters that have been forged for the weak by the strong . . . but they are silken strands that have been woven into a strong

cable by the mutual instincts of pride and duty, of self-sacrifice and esteem . . .

In my view, as this process has gone on, the Princes have gained in prestige instead of losing it. Their rank is not diminished, but their privileges have become more secure. They have to do more for the protection that they enjoy, but they also derive more from it; for they are no longer detached appendages of Empire but its participators and instruments. They have ceased to be the architectural adornments of the Imperial edifice and have become the pillars that help to sustain the main roof . . .

Your Highness I am now about to invest you with the powers of administration in your State . . .

There are five duties that I enjoin upon you as you take up the task. Be loyal to your Sovereign, who is the ultimate source and guarantee of your powers. Regard the Government of India and the local Government under which you are immediately placed as your protectors and sponsors . . . Be just and considerate to the nobles of your state; you owe a duty to them just as much as they to you. And lastly, never let a day pass without thinking of your people and praying to Almighty God that you, who have so much, may do something for them, who have so little. If these are the principles by which you regulate your conduct, your subjects and your friends will look back upon this day not as a tamasha that is forgotten as soon as it is over, but as the dawn of a bright and prosperous era for the State of Bahawalpur.[1]

The *Sadiqnamah* rushes to praise this short-lived nawab, the father of the ruler to whom it is dedicated. Its author, Brigadier Shah, struggles to find enough superlatives to recount Bahawal Khan's youthful successes in every field including public works, his encouragement of cricket and football, the founding of the Bahawal Club, his good stable and his efforts to popularize drama, poetry and music in Bahawalpur. He sounds a model of the British public-school system and of Mr Evill's influence. Salahuddin Abbasi believes he was a brilliant young man whose downfall was in his success and the resulting sidelining of vested interests in the court. In 1907 he set off with a large retinue, including his three-year-old son, on the still difficult journey to perform the Hajj at Mecca. On his return, after rejoining his father's ship at Aden, he was poisoned and died. His body was brought back to Derawar; his life is still remembered in local mourning songs.

There are two contrasting photographs among Salahuddin's remaining collection. The first, of Sadiq Muhammad Khan IV on his accession, aged four and a half, is the Victorian image of the richly dressed but wistful childish chieftain, alone but for his fiercely whiskered body servant. In the second, his grandson, Sadiq Muhammad Khan, aged three, is entirely alone, but, this time it is a modern little boy, dressed up for the occasion and with his jewelled fez firmly on his head, who stares resolutely out of the picture. The child may well have been the image of the wilful man, determined to get his own way regardless of the highest levels of British interference in his state. His character appears to less advantage in India Office Records, but he was a man who continued to modernize and improve his state and helped to mitigate some of the worst aspects of Partition in a flashpoint border area. For good or ill, he supported British military endeavours with his own army and engaged in countless charitable ventures both in Bahawalpur and abroad. Sadiq Muhammad Khan V negotiated an obstacle-strewn path through a life and long reign that encompassed two world wars; the apogee as well as the end of British imperialism in India; the fulfilment of Indian nationalism; and the ripping apart of the subcontinent in the realization of the dream of a separate Muslim state. Finally, he followed Muhammad Ali Jinnah into his dream of Pakistan. He made huge efforts to support his new country with his own fortune and the resources of his state until the loss of Bahawalpur encouraged his retirement to more congenial surroundings in Sussex with his Dutch last wife, Olivia.

The photographs and histories of the last generation of rulers of princely states are familiar to most with an interest in the history of the subcontinent. Bahawalpur was forgotten. The state, with all its treasures, was subsumed into Pakistan and became a mere footnote to the Punjab. A huge tract of land, one of the most important princely states, more or less erased from the map, and its leaders vanished from the window of historical view. Surviving photographs of Sadiq Muhammad Khan V, especially in London at the coronation of George VI, are evidence of his standing among his peers, but lack of familiarity with a territory hidden behind the barriers of Islamic Pakistan has 'disappeared' the history of the man and the place comprehensively, compared with those contemporaries of his father and himself who were the last generation of Indian ruling princes. It seems particularly surprising given the remarkable and well-documented level of British interest in Sadiq Muhammad Khan during his minority and reign to protect their financial investment in his state.

Among his older peers were men like Ganga Singh, maharaja of Bikaner, commander of the Bikaner Camel Corps in foreign wars and Indian representative at the Paris Peace Conference, and Ranjitsinjhi, jam saheb of Nawanagar, remarkable cricketer and representative at the League of Nations. Of the next generation, the jam saheb's nephew, Digvijaysinhji, served in the British Army and in the Imperial War Cabinet, and the images of glamorous Yeshwant Rao Holkar of Indore, with his beautiful wife, remain familiar from photographs by Man Ray. Man Singh of Jaipur, who married Gayatri Devi of Cooch Behar was an international polo player, and, after

Independence, Rajpramukh of Rajasthan and Indian ambassador to Spain. There were others, including two generations of fascinating Cooch Behars, Barodas, Scindias of Gwalior and a whole panoply of rulers of states large and small.

Many of the later princes were educated in England, others at Indian schools run on British lines; the 'Chief's Colleges' like Aitchison, Mayo and Rajkumar College in Raipur. Their wives became equally visible in portraits by Beaton and Lenare and in international society pages. They were powerful women, among them Vijaya Raje Scindia of Gwalior and Gayatri Devi of Jaipur, who entered the political arena and took on Indira Gandhi, the princes' nemesis who abolished their privy purses. That the zenana walls, even in Muslim states, had been breached, is illustrated with photographs of the begum of Rampur, who travelled in Europe in the 1930s, and, latterly, the princesses of Hyderabad. The ruling begums of Bhopal, the best known of whom, Shah Jehan, who ruled from 1901–26 and was a constant visibly invisible presence in her burka at every state occasion, could be said to have led the way for their sisters. She transformed her state, travelled all over Europe and fought for the rights of the eldest born to inherit regardless of gender. She abdicated in 1926 to continue to fight for women's rights, discarding purdah in 1928 for the last two years of her life.

In conservative Bahawalpur, the traditions of the zenana survived until the next generation, saving only the occasional public presence of European wives, both named and unknown. All those women, their names rarely recorded or remembered; only known as the mother, grandmother, cousin, aunt, a princess from Baluchistan, a woman from Afghanistan. Their daughters less than that, numberless, anonymous, unseen females except when they suddenly come to notice, sometimes with a name, fighting usually for the right of their son to a throne or to their own right to a jagir, a land grant, given or promised as dowry at marriage or sometimes inherited. In 1921 the begum sahiba applied for an increase in her allowance of Rs 2814 per month with the grant of a jagir as per the precedent of the nawab's mother, her mother-in-law.[2] Almost invariably a woman's identity remains cloaked in the anonymity of her honorific, the begum sahiba, the dowager begum sahiba. The genealogy of the female line is nigh on impossible to trace, individuals only occasionally identifiable in a new link between families in a family tree, or a throwaway 'they were brothers-in-law', 'he was the father-in-law' in the telling of a tale, but women's names are few and far between and quickly forgotten. Sir Nicholas Barrington who served twice in Pakistan, as head of chancery in the 1960s and as high commissioner during 1987–89, made a study of leading Pakistani families that tapped into the memories of their older female relations. Sadly, there are now few left, of those, fewer still able to remember more than 'he was married to the sister of . . .'

It is certain that Sadiq Muhammad Khan's mother watched over the precarious life of her stalwart child and may have requested British assistance in securing his safety. Salahuddin tells of two food tasters and three known episodes of attempted poisoning. Suspicion falls on the same Haji Khan, Sadiq Muhammad Khan's uncle, son of the cattle stealer, attempted usurper of his father's throne and almost certainly responsible for his poisoning at Aden. Haji Khan's daughter later became one of Sadiq Muhammad Khan's wives. There was clear and present danger, and, soon after the child ruler had caught the attention of the assembled throng and the world press at the 1911 Durbar, he was sent to England with a handful of loyal servants. His mother and his older sister, to whom he was extremely close, remained in Bahawalpur where a council of regency administered the state under close supervision from the British. The involvement of the paramount power would dog the nawab's reign and hold him in thrall almost until Independence. Bahawalpur was a feudal territory with an autocratic ruler, his wings pinioned by an occupying power, The Nawab's subjects might address him, 'O Pearl-wearing Nawab, may your kingdom be one of health', but the British authorities, with a financial stake in the state, could take him to task like a naughty child. They may, all the same, have been responsible for keeping him alive, and, in the hands of—for too short a time—his father and the able administrator Colonel Grey, Bahawalpur state had been reorganized within the terms of the time. It is thanks also to Grey that the figures exist from his census and give a relatively clear statistical picture of the state, much condensed below, when Sadiq Muhammad Khan acceded.

What was Bahawalpur state in 1907? A vast area of land, some 17,000 square miles; part of it a huge tract of sparsely inhabited desert; some areas of forest or jungle containing valuable timber; the main population clustered in rich agricultural land criss-crossed by rivers and a growing spread of canals considerably increasing cultivable areas. Crops were, most importantly, wheat, followed by rice, gram, barley and maize for animal fodder, and indigo—valuable but expensive to cultivate and crop. Other crops were foodgrains, cotton, tobacco, poppy for opium, and a standard range of vegetables. Colonel Minchin had established a successful stud in 1867 and Major Grey a system of loans for farmers, the most noticeable effect being to get Muslim farmers out of the hands of those Hindus who combined farming with moneylending as a lucrative sideline. *Bahawalpur Gazetteer* suggests that the major cause of debt among farming Muslims was the requirement on them to offer hospitality and maintain quantities of livestock on otherwise more profitably cultivable land as a matter of izzat. The Hindus were happily free of this compulsion.

In 1901 the population density was forty-eight to the square mile after considerable increases through migration in the previous twenty years. Settlers came from as far afield as Bombay, following construction of new canal systems and because of the famines of 1895–96 and 1899 in other regions, especially Rajputana. Houses, except those belonging to well-to-do Hindu merchants in the towns, were rarely pukka, built of stone or baked brick, but rather *kacho* or *kutcha*, made of friable and impermanent mud brick. The total population for 1901 is given as 7,20,877. In that year, there were ten towns and 960 villages, ancient cities and forts, new palaces and pavilions, industry and antique crafts, zamindars and peasants. The population was predominantly Muslim, and Muslims were said to be longer lived than the Hindus in the region, but how that relates to their greater poverty is hard to tell.

The Hindu population was significant, especially in urban areas. The Sikhs were largely rural, as were the small proportion of Christians. According to the 1901 census they amounted to precisely six Indians and seventy-nine Eurasians and Europeans. Most of the Muslims were Sunni and all were served by shrines and holy places including Uch Sharif, the City of Saints, which may have been founded by or predated Alexander the Great. The pirs or saints of Bahawalpur state did not hold the hereditary temporal power and estates more common among those of such blessed descent in the Punjab. More notoriously, in Sindh, Hindu and Muslim places of worship were given state grants and some remission of land revenue on regulated holdings and became extremely rich.

Foreigners had remarked on the quality of Bahawalpur silk for generations. Muhammad Bahawal Khan II is reputed to have engaged a weaver from Benares to teach local weavers how to make lengths of a cotton and silk mix, a skill in which Bahawal Khan also became so proficient himself as to be able to weave the Koran into a piece of the cloth. In Bahawalpur jail, as in the jails of neighbouring states in Rajputana, carpets and rugs were manufactured for sale, the designs influenced by the taste of European buyers. Clothes manufactured in the state were exported to other regions with silk, carpets, shoes, wheat, fruit, particularly apples, mangoes and oranges for which Bahawalpur was known, and opium. Writing of the Punjab in 1857, Leopold Grey remarked, '. . . everyone grew his own little patch of poppy for home consumption', and bemoaned that the present 'great increase of drinking in the Punjab is perhaps due to our closing this household cultivation' which, due, to a British clampdown on opium growing and use, in spite of the continuing and lucrative trade to China, had been stopped.

The introduction of railways into Bahawalpur state had benefited exports and exporters while adversely affecting the poor as the prices of local goods grew to match export prices. Their lives were also less likely to be improved by greater access to the wider world and even less by easier ingress from Christian missionaries. The rivers had always been travelled and a number of new canals were navigable, while the 839 miles of unmetalled roads were traversed by the usual bullock carts, donkeys, camels and ponies, on the business of daily local commerce and movement. There was one metalled road, built in 1869 for the visit of Sir Donald McLeod, the old cunctator, running 24 miles between McLeodganj and Bahawalpur, by now a town about 3 miles in circumference. Sadiqgarh, at Dera Nawab Sahib, was established as the permanent residence of the nawab, while other smaller, adjacent houses would continue to be built for wives and family members. Out in the desert beyond Derawar, a string of old forts were already falling into disuse and decay as the days of desert invasions faded into memory.

The accuracy, or rather inaccuracy, of dates relating to Sadiq Muhammad Khan's early life combine with little information on the years between his accession and his appearance at the 1911 Durbar. He was probably still with his mother and sister in the zenana. The next gap, when he was spirited away to safety in the English countryside, has been filled to some extent but the details remain sketchy. It would be surprising for an already ruling chief, albeit a child without power, to be removed from India without the involvement, climbing up the administrative scale, first, of the political agent most nearly responsible for Bahawalpur, in this case for the Phulkian states, followed by the lieutenant governor of the Punjab and, finally, signed off almost certainly by the viceroy, after the usual correspondence through his private secretary. No such correspondence has survived in India Office Records, or among the papers of Lord Hardinge, viceroy from 1910 to 1916, who presided over the Coronation Durbar of 1911. He passed through Bahawalpur on his first viceregal tour in early 1911, but his journal offers the merest glimpse of Sadiq Muhammad Khan amid typical British complaints about the weather.

> From Karachi to Dehra Dun we had to pass through the Sind Desert and Bahawalpur, here we were met by the Maharaja, a boy of six, with his ministers on the platform. The journey through the Sind desert had been hot, but I have never felt such heat as when I got out of the train. It really knocked me down.

Perhaps the sensation caused by the little nawab at the durbar encouraged more interest in the child in high places. Bahawalpur was an important state in which the British were already deeply invested, and the death of a young ruler both reflected badly on officials concerned and caused instability. It may be that his mother had applied for British support, or his loyal ministers, but, sometime in 1912–13, Sadiq Muhammad Khan was taken from Bahawalpur and sent to live in the small village of Porlock in Somerset. Why Porlock? There do not seem at first glance to have been families with obvious connections to India living in the area—no great house, for instance, where a former governor of an Indian state might have lived and taken the young nawab into his family.

On investigation, the only obvious connection between Bahawalpur and Porlock arose in a list of the political agents for the Phulkian states agency. Charles Herbert Atkins, who served in the role between 1910 and 1913, thereafter returning to England to live at The Bungalow, Porlock. Charles Atkins had been born in 1870 and, more to the point, had married in 1900 and produced three sons and two daughters. The older children may have been of similar age to the nawab. Charles Atkins was a 'Balliol man' who later moved away from Porlock and took holy orders. He might very well have been seen as a suitable person to oversee Sadiq Muhammad Khan during his stay in England. Shreds of remaining mystery hang about 'The Bungalow', named, one supposes, for Indian etymology. The Atkins tenure of the house falls neatly between censuses, and later occupants had no apparent Indian connections.

Several houses were built in Porlock in the Edwardian era, but who built or owned what and where they came from has been impossible to ascertain from parish or county records. 'The Bungalow' itself has disappeared into new nomenclature. Purely from the look of an Indian bungalow with its surrounding veranda, not unlike British dwellings in Simla and Mussoorie but translated to Edwardian Somerset, a house, now called Doverhay Place, is the strongest contender to be that lost house. Nobody now remembers Doverhay Place under another name but it was built at the turn of the nineteenth and twentieth centuries by a Captain or Major Perkins who never seems to have lived there himself but let the house to various tenants. Perkins seems likely to have seen colonial service and this was certainly the case with some of his tenants.

Salahuddin Abbasi knows little more of his grandfather's stay in England. He remembers only a story of the English tutor who slapped the boy for some misdemeanour in front of one of his Indian servants and was badly beaten for such an assault on his youthful Highness. Sadiq Muhammad Khan's Indian tutor, Maulvi Ghulam Hussain, later became the bane of British civil servants for his strong, and in their eyes, deleterious, influence over the young man. It is difficult to tease out the true character of an ageing man, loyal, possibly to a fault, to his prince and his state, from the remaining weight of India Office correspondence on the subject. The British and, it appears, a considerable proportion of the population of Bahawalpur, viewed the maulvi as an evil genius, the young nawab's Svengali. Like the servant in Porlock, his complete duty was always due to Sadiq Muhammad Khan for whom he had been responsible since childhood. He may have encouraged the nawab's self-indulgence, or, like that earlier servant, blown to kingdom come on the whim of his young master, been unable to say no. His actions suggest he cared less for a puritanical British view of the dignity and behaviour of a prince and may have considered activities that pushed against British-imposed strictures, fiscal or moral, to be entirely fitting to the nawab's royal status. Later, as the maulvi's power grew, he enriched himself and his family, at financial cost to Bahawalpur state and moral cost to the nawab.

The maulvi's family remained highly influential in the state. His son Shams ud-din, who inherited his role as closest adviser to the nawab, against British wishes, was the shared grandfather of Salahuddin Abbasi and his wife, Moniba. The *Sadiqnamah* determined that Sadiq Muhammad Khan remained in England during World War I and became 'interested in mechanical and military matters'.

That came later, because he returned to India in late 1914–15 and, like his father, into the security of Aitchison College. In 1920, he returned to Bahawalpur with a tutor, to learn the administration of his state, and served a cadetship with the Central India Horse at Quetta. He was appointed as an ADC to the Prince of Wales during that young man's ill-judged tour of India at the height of the Khilafat and Non-Cooperation movements, and, in March 1924, on attaining his majority, was installed as nawab of Bahawalpur by the viceroy, Lord Reading.

The Council of Regency that ruled Bahawalpur from 1907 to 1924, with Maulvi Sir Rahim Baksh as president, was to all intents and purposes wholly under the authority of the British. After Sadiq Muhammad left Aitchison College and factions in Bahawalpur began to jockey for influence and the ruler's favour, their task became a good deal more difficult. At a time when the Khilafat movement was stirring in the Punjab, there was no question of a valuable and 'loyal' state like Bahawalpur being allowed a free hand in its governance. At the end of 1914 a movement began to unite the Muslims of Punjab, and, as the situation grew increasingly tense, cooperation was sought from loyal and influential Muslims, like Sir Rahim Baksh and others similarly honoured for service to the British. The bottom fell out of Muslim hopes to unite Islam in a jihad against the British with the divisive revolt by the Sharif of Mecca against the Turkish in 1916 but other problems followed in India. There were risings in 1916 among the Muslim peasantry, specifically against the Hindu moneylenders who held them in thrall, rather than against the British, but any cooperative movement was seen as dangerous at a time of growing unrest and nationalism in India and revolution abroad. Sir Michael O'Dwyer, governor of Punjab from 1912 to 1919, was an autocratic bureaucrat whose watchwords were 'security and duty'.[3] He was one of the prominent supporters of the Defence of India Act in

1915, limiting civil and political liberties, and of the additional limits imposed by the incendiary Rowlatt Act of 1919. Protests against the Rowlatt Act led to widespread unrest across India and, in particular, Punjab. Coercive recruitment policies for the army, particularly in the later stages of World War I, had added to unrest in Punjab and an alarming awakening of political consciousness[4] from which the princely states and, of additional concern, unknown numbers of their rulers, were far from immune. Any political awakening in Bahawalpur was stamped on by a law passed on 14 May 1924:

> In the state premises, for any public meeting it will be incumbent upon the people to take a written permission for the same, 48 hours before the meeting, from the District Magistrate in view of the administrative affairs and on condition that the holders of the meeting will have nothing to do with political movements and campaigns, relating to the British Government and the state of Bahawalpur, which may lead to disturbance in law and order, or which may harm the feelings of any community and religion. The meeting holders will be answerable to legal proceedings, even after these conditions, if they break out a law-and-order situation.[5]

Nevertheless, when income tax laws were imposed, they were first opposed by Hindus led by Mukhi Darya Baksh. This instigated the formation of Muslim groups for the advance and defence of the Muslim population through better religious teaching and practice through the Moid-ul-Islam. In 1925, the inauguration of the Jamiat-ul-Muslimeen, or Group of Muslims, was followed by others under the banner of religion that shielded them from state bans on political parties.

In 1922 the British had commenced the Sutlej Valley Project. In the view of Sir Penderel Moon this negated their 'special obligation' to a minor nawab, 'to see that the interests of his State were fully safeguarded'.[6] The Triple Canals Project, completed during World War I in the Punjab, was followed by more ambitious plans for canalization after the war, of which the Sutlej Valley Project and the Sukkur Barrage were the largest to date. The expectation for the Sutlej Valley Project was its provision of irrigation for 8,00,000 hectares of land, nearly 8000 square miles, in Bahawalpur, the Punjab and Bikaner, by constructing four barrages across the Sutlej River and eleven inundation canals. Three barrages were complete by 1927 and the last by 1930, converting scrub or poor land into arable, capable of producing two crops per year: cotton or rice in the summer and pulses or wheat in the winter.[7] The authorities in Bahawalpur, who had opposed the project from the start on the grounds that the water available in the rivers had been overestimated, were proved correct when the water at two of the barrages in particular was found to be insufficient to feed the canals. 'Miles of canals dug through the deserts of Bahawalpur were later abandoned, and rest houses, built for the accommodation of canal officers, but never occupied, crumbled away forlornly in a barren wilderness.'[8]

Worse than this, the project had hinged on the expected profits of hugely increased yields and land prices, once colony land was populated with migrant farmers. Instead, the inadequacy of the water supply on top of the dramatic fall in agricultural prices in the 1930s, made the land practically unsaleable. British records reported even Bahawalpuris would rather buy more expensive land in the Punjab than the new canal land.[9] To meet its share of the capital cost of a project which had cost nearly two-and-a-half times its original estimate, the state had been forced to take out a loan from the Government of India. By 1936 no repayment had been made, the interest on the debt was in arrears and it had swollen to Rs 14 crores (14,00,00,000). An agreement with the Government of India, for its liquidation in annual payments for the next fifty years until 1986, became the sword over the head of the ruler of Bahawalpur. It was the means of restraint on his lifestyle and spending and the excuse for refusing him the full financial powers he was due as a ruling prince. As things turned out, the sharp rise in agricultural prices after World War II allowed the debt to be paid off much faster than had seemed possible in 1936 and saved the day for Bahawalpur and the nawab. The hoped-for migration to the canal colonies, when and where it did happen, was not unproblematic. New arrivals from the Punjab were, as is the migrant habit, more energetic and enterprising than long-term inhabitants of the state. This created rivalries between the *riasati*, the Saraiki term for those belonging to the state, and the incomers, and led to discrimination between the two that was in no way related to other communal divisions.

Moon wrote sympathetically of Sadiq Muhammad Khan:

> The tight rein on which the Government of India had held him, allowing him no access to state revenues, allotting sums for his personal use, that fell far short of his requirements, and questioning every expenditure, meant that the real responsibility for the State never full rested on the Nawab's shoulders. The army, in which he showed a lifelong interest, was the only important State department where he had a comparatively free hand.'

As a result, Moon considered, his 'interest in the State's administration was not as keen as it might otherwise have been'.[10] The level of Sadiq Muhammad Khan's profligacy and unusually public promiscuity, exhaustively investigated in India Office papers, let alone the frowned-on influence of Maulvi Ghulam Hussain, illustrate the frustrations of a ruler unable to fully rule and kicking over the traces. The paternalistic holders of power, ranged against the nawab, must have seen his behaviour as that of a spoilt child whose actions they were there to mitigate, overtly for the good of his state and, by this time, more covertly for the good of continuing British rule in India.

Moon continued his more empathetic portrayal:

> These were the defects for which the Paramount Power, through its failure to safeguard the Nawab's interests during his minority, was partly responsible. A more determined or more ill-natured man might have made more than he did of his grievance. But the people were not adversely affected. The State was on the whole quite well administered. The Nawab was by no means unpopular; and if the army accounts were never audited, and if there were leakages from various minor departments, the mass of the people were no wiser and felt no worse. Nor did the people at large think ill of a ruler for wishing to spend more of the State revenues on himself than a civil servant would approve. In a State with which I was later associated, I found that an enlightened ruler, highly eulogized by Lord Curzon himself, held no greater place in popular memory and esteem than his successor who had to be deposed from drunkenness and riotous living, having squandered the State's resources on merrymaking, fireworks and colourful debauches. Circuses have more appeal than uplift.[11]

7

THE LAST NAWAB

The portrait of Sadiq Muhammad Khan V constructed from extensive India Office reports, letters, anecdotes and occasional living memory, is often contradictory. It is also uniquely detailed. British financial interest in Bahawalpur, due to the Sutlej Valley Project and its attached debt on the state, meant extraordinary conditions on the nawab's rule, and intrusive scrutiny of all aspects of his life. As Penderel Moon noted, the paramount power overstepped its proper remit in imposing the scheme, and, more damagingly, its cost on a minor prince, for whose care it was ultimately responsible. The Government of India continued to safeguard its own related interests by placing conditions on the nawab and his state that never allowed him the full power and dignity of a ruler, or, one may conjecture, to be the man he might have otherwise become.

The British worried about the effects of the nawab's lifestyle on Bahawalpur and on their financial interest in the state until the war, from which, serendipitously, Bahawalpur did well. The state that chose to follow Muhammad Ali Jinnah into Pakistan was a rich prize and offered an open-door treasury in support of the new country. Until then, under the compulsion of a debt for which the paramount power was largely responsible, the nawab's actions were watched and reported up through the layers of bureaucracy, until the viceroy or his representative reined him in, or rapped him over the knuckles. Why on earth Sadiq Muhammad Khan should have tolerated, with remarkable good grace, the conditions imposed upon him, heaven knows. If he had little choice but to comply, it is still astonishing that he should have continued to put on the show for the British officials and viceroys he entertained, and, throughout, maintained his loyalty to the British Crown and his love of England. Perhaps his experience of life as a small boy in Porlock had left unexpectedly warm memories, or perhaps he simply followed the tradition of loyalty to the British Crown adhered to by his forefathers.

Mr Bolster, Sadiq Muhammad's tutor, reported to the Government of India, that he thought British boundaries that put limits on the young ruler were sensible insurance, given his pupil's youthful proclivities. Government officers, like Penderel Moon, with more experience in princely states, had doubts. The dignity of the ruler was important, not only to himself but to those around him. As Sadiq Muhammad, recently married, reached his eighteenth birthday during the unrest of the Khilafat movement, there were plenty among those closest to him in Bahawalpur ready, for their own ends, to encourage their inexperienced nawab to disregard British strictures. He was a solitary figure, always watched, pushed and pulled between stronger men from two opposing and interfering camps, and without the power to fully rule his state even after his installation as nawab. It is hardly surprising he did not become the model prince and yet, as Moon noted, he was far from unpopular and, in Bahawalpur today, is remembered with near adulation.

Lieutenant Colonel Henry St John, of the political service, described Sadiq Muhammad in 1922 shortly before his eighteenth birthday, as a 'simple-minded unassuming youth of weak character.

Under an apparently frank and engaging manner there is I feel a slight vein of obstinacy and deceit. Otherwise his disposition is kindly and generous.' But he was:

> Distinctly indolent and self-indulgent and these faults, if not checked may prove his undoing. Physically he does not appear over strong but he was looking healthy and fit when I saw him and showed no signs of excess. On the whole I see no reason for undue pessimism regarding the future of Bahawalpur and its ruler.

Not all bad, but not all good. Mr Bolster's observations were more critical, hinting at problems to come. He reported that the nawab's only real interests were troops, stamp collection and the cinema and that he was a difficult subject to deal with: sensual, impulsive and inclined to extravagance, intensely bigoted in religious matters and wedded to the traditions and customs of his forefathers.

He also complained that the Council of Regency allowed the minor nawab free rein to do what he liked 'without let or hindrance'. He was particularly outraged by the durbar's instant ordering of a motor tractor, requested on a whim by the nawab for his garden at Dera Nawab Sahib and for which 'there was no provision in the budget'. Mr Bolster confirmed Sadiq Muhammad's hatred of alcohol but deplored his inclination to indulge too freely in the pleasures of the zenana. He reported the introduction of 'outside women', and was thoroughly annoyed that his charge's marriage had been arranged without reference to his tutor. Bolster believed the greatest hazards to the nawab were his sensuality and extravagance. He was right, albeit those traits that most damaged the young ruler's reputation and made his relationship with the British endlessly difficult were almost a self-fulfilling prophecy in a traditional state referred to and treated by them as 'backward'.

Two brief generations earlier, Leopold Grey had written complacently of Sadiq Muhammad Khan IV, 'As may be supposed, the Bahawalpur Nawab did not interest himself in the canals on which all cultivation depends, or in the revenue administration.' In the twentieth century, the last generation of princes, the grandfathers of some of the notable entrepreneurs, politicians and businessmen and women in contemporary India, were deeply invested in the futures of their states and of the country as a whole. Lord Minto, viceroy from 1905 to 1910, suggested the institution of a Council of Princes 'as a possible counterpoise to The Indian National Congress' and supported a renewed policy of non-interference in the princely states in the interests of promoting greater partnership. The introduction to the *Manual of Instructions to Officers of the Political Department* instructed officers, to 'leave well alone', unless 'misrule reaches a pitch which violates the elementary laws of civilisation'. To this, officialdom might have added less high-minded stipulations, such as, when government revenue was threatened, or the buttoned-up morals of officialdom offended by wayward behaviour. After the Chamber of Princes was established in 1921, the compulsion to attend was used by the British authorities as another reason to curtail the nawab of Bahawalpur's personal choices, especially as to travel arrangements outside his state or his country that might result in costs to the state treasury.

On the plus side, Mr Bolster reported Sadiq Muhammad had a good grounding in English, French, Persian, accounts and practical administrative studies. He did not like games and had given up polo and tennis, although he occasionally played badminton. He was on a two-month course of training with the Central India Horse in Quetta and, after his eighteenth birthday on 30 September it was planned that he should be put in charge of jails, the army, education and judicial departments. He would be familiarized with the workings of the irrigation, revenue and public works departments and gain a 'practical knowledge' of the Sutlej Valley Project. With its debt constantly hung over his head, it is small wonder Sadiq Muhammad, forced, unlike his grandfather, to be interested in canals, detested the project. He was supported in his dislike by those who also hated the British and were seen by them as a threat to the traditions of Bahawalpur and to their own roles in the state.

Mr Bolster considered it unfortunate that Sadiq Muhammad had been surrounded by a crowd of Bahawalpuri retainers during his schooling at Aitchison College. Their 'influence has nullified the efforts of the college staff', he reported, conceding that the young man's six months' deputation with the Prince of Wales during his tour of India had 'a most beneficial effect'. On the strength of this royal service, he was to be granted the KCVO on his birthday and a commission as an honorary lieutenant in the British Army. Bolster suggested the nawab should best be shielded from bad influences at home, after his own departure, by the appointment of a companion, a senior British captain or major, whose duties might include writing the ruler's English letters since his 'composition and spelling are deplorable'.

British concern about dangerous influences on the young nawab during his minority focused initially on the vested interests of unnamed members of the Council of Regency, 'bigoted Mohammedans' in strong 'though covert sympathy with the Khilafat Movement'. By the time Sadiq Muhammad was installed on his throne, all British opprobrium focused on the person and name of 'the maulvi', Maulvi Ghulam Hussain. Records suggest the maulvi did indeed hold the young ruler in thrall; he had, after all, been the most constant figure in his life. That the British were also biased against a powerful and reactionary counterweight to their own power is also certain. It is difficult to discover from the records of only one side of the story how much the maulvi's reported attempts to rule Bahawalpur from behind a puppet throne were for his and his family's personal aggrandizement and enrichment, and how much they were motivated by his detestation of the British and determination to defy the paramount power. His absolute belief in 'Bahawalpur for Bahawalpuris' was undoubtedly his primary motive for conspiring against Government of India officers loaned to the state administration.

A nasty taste of tales of old oriental courts crept into the British sense of the state of affairs in Bahawalpur. The evil genius courtier and his acolytes encouraging a weak ruler towards debauchery and excess. A whiff of the opium pipe and the cup of poisoned sherbet weakening his hold on reality, to allow the villain effectively to rule in his place. Neither this vision nor issues of the fomentation of serious disaffection in an important and indebted state were likely to endear the maulvi or any of his family and supporters to the Government of India, especially in the years of unrest immediately after the Khilafat movement had reared its head in the Punjab, with corresponding Hindu nationalist activity. Reports of an increasingly barbaric use of power and influence by the maulvi's party engendered some sympathy for the British view, more for the nawab himself and for his people, reportedly tyrannized by rapacious and uncontrolled officers of state at all levels.[1]

By October 1925, eighteen months after Sadiq Muhammad's installation, Sir William Malcolm Hailey, governor of the Punjab, was reporting to the political secretary in Simla on the resignation of the Bahawalpur revenue and public works minister, Walter Kennaway, and other provincial service officials. Kennaway reported, 'the State has been more or less allowed to run loose'. Other officials, including Colonel Ayscough, the divisional engineer, and Miss Brown, one of the medical ladies employed to care especially for the ladies of the zenana, had been 'contemptuously dismissed'. A Parsi prostitute from Karachi was being paid Rs 100 more per month than Ayscough, 'not entirely to the latter's satisfaction'.

Hailey wrote, the 'evil genius of the State', the maulvi, held the nawab completely in his power and the chief minister, Nawab Maula Bakhsh was his 'complaisant tool'. The maulvi would tolerate no one who was unwilling to be subservient to him, and his avowed ambition was to rid the state of all, and especially British, lent officers.[2] Kennaway cited the refusal of the nawab to see him, although previously relations had been 'exceptionally friendly', and of official business being carried out without reference to him. The draft 'Colonisation Act' for the allotment of land on Sutlej Valley canals was being held by the maulvi and had not been signed, and there were additional concerns about the use of forced labour on the canal projects. This was more than ever likely to discourage potential colonizers from the Punjab, who were in any case dubious about life in Bahawalpur under an oppressive regime.

Lieutenant Colonel Henry St John, agent to the governor general of the Punjab, acknowledged Kennaway's difficulties but was inclined to play them down on grounds of the revenue minister's 'somewhat jaundiced point of view' due to his inexperience in Indian states and his 'somewhat sensitive nature'. Summing up a series of scandalized communications from Bahawalpur officials, British and Indian, St John took a calmer line on the situation. He did not entirely accept the nawab's assurance that the labour on the canals was famine relief work rather than traditional '*cher*' or enforced cleaning of canals by the local peasantry, and considered a proclamation in the nawab's name against impressed labour, already abolished in the state, to be mere window dressing. At the same time, he believed the nawab wished to remain in good standing with the Government of India. At a meeting, Sadiq Muhammad had assured St John that the influence of the maulvi had been much exaggerated. St John took a positive longer-term view of winning the confidence of the nawab in counterbalance to the maulvi, although he admitted that the young ruler was attempting to assert his authority and allowing his Bahawalpur officials to intrigue against government officers. He finished a report: 'I do not wish to convey the impression that all is well in Bahawalpur. On the contrary, it is causing and will continue to cause anxiety for some time to come.' The nawab must be 'weaned from the reactionary elements on which he is at present dependent'.[3]

Early in 1926, St John was able to report a 'more favourable atmosphere' in Bahawalpur, although nothing was moving regarding colonization or potential buyers of land. At the same time, rumours of a Eurasian woman brought recently from Karachi and exerting considerable influence over the nawab were disquieting although, he wrote, sensual indulgence was 'a common failing of Mahomedan Rulers' and the nawab had been warned about 'excesses of this nature'. Events took a more dramatic turn when Sikander Hayat Khan, later KBE and governor of the Punjab, was forced to resign or was effectively sacked as chief minister of Bahawalpur, after only a few months' service in 1928, on grounds of his 'extreme and continuous insolence' to the nawab.[4] Sikander Khan was thirty-six with no previous government service or experience of district administration but he was a man from a 'very famous Punjab family of Zamindars', with 'considerable and successful experience of business'.[5] Sikander Khan was commended presciently by Sir William Malcolm Hailey as 'the kind of man of whom one would think of in time as a Minister in the Punjab Government'[6] and who should be 'a guarantee to the Punjab public of stability and businesslike administration in Bahawalpur'.

Sikander Khan barely survived half of his initial appointment for a year as chief minister. He did not have a hope against the maulvi, by now described by the British as 'avaricious and ambitious and will stick at nothing to increase his wealth and power' as well as an ignorant and narrow-minded man whose 'violent pro-riasati and pro Mussalman prejudices give a bad name to Bahawalpur throughout the Punjab'.[7] The maulvi may have been as prejudiced, intolerant and selfish as he was painted, but the British were not exactly disinterested onlookers. They feared that the 'capitalist classes', regardless of the lure of good, cheap land, would never be attracted to the colony in large numbers, under such circumstances, which would put the payment of the debt on the Sutlej Valley Project at risk. Sikander Khan's dismissal was squarely laid at the maulvi's door. The government set about collating enough evidence on 'the sinister figure of the Maulvi secure in his hypnotic power over a weak, ignorant and self-willed' young nawab to insist on his banishment from Bahawalpur. Meanwhile, more poison was dripped into the nawab's ears with rumours of a British conspiracy to annex a large portion of his state in payment of the debt.

Sikander Khan mentioned an odd episode in Bombay to illustrate the jealousy of the maulvi family and their efforts to keep their prince away from alternative influence. During the conference of princes and ministers convened by the chancellor of the Chamber of Princes, Khan had been strolling with friends near the Gateway of India when the nawab had happened to drive past and invited them all to the cinema. Shams ud-din had been furious and had thereafter made sure that he or 'some other henchmen of his' were in constant attendance on the nawab. The maulvi, Sikander Khan said, had 'inculcated a belief in evil spirits in the Nawab and his own power to control them', and a 'reign of terror and oppression' existed in Bahawalpur. In retrospect, it is not hard to understand the epithet 'backward' appended to the state when the British themselves began to speak in terms that smack of ancient history and superstition.

Sadiq Muhammad continued to protest that the maulvi and his sons, Shams ud-din and Zia ud-din, had the best interests of his state at heart but the government had heard from other sources that he was 'very afraid' of them and their power to take over his state. Meanwhile, there were more claims of official business being diverted or held up, and further efforts to isolate the nawab from any influence but their own. Government departments were being run badly, inefficiently and corruptly. In particular, Zia ud-din, in charge of the police in all but name, had 'not even passed the Matriculation Examination', and had no training whatsoever. The nominal superintendent of police, Mr Atkinson, appointed at the theoretical determination of the nawab, turned out to have once been a 'subordinate police officer' and now to be the owner of a taxidermy business in Dehra Dun where he chose to spend most of his time. How on earth the maulvi or his sons had found him remained a cause for conjecture. The police force was being run on 'barbarous grounds' and 'rack and pinion' used to 'wring out confessions from the accused whether they be guilty or innocent'.

Sikander Khan was dismissed by Sadiq Khan on 7 September 1928, causing more unease in the population of Bahawalpur and in the Government of India. By 15 November, the viceroy was closely involved with events, and greater pressure was being brought to bear on the nawab. He was forced to sack the taxidermist, who countered accusations against himself with accusations, of misappropriation and spying for the British, against Sikander Hayat Khan. Both accusations against Khan may have held a grain of truth but neither did much for Mr Atkinson, who was forcibly and permanently retired to his animal skins in Dehra Dun.[8]

Sadiq Muhammad Khan wrote a vindication of the maulvi to the viceroy—he 'entered the service of the State as my own tutor and after long years of faithful and loyal service became Home Minister in 1923'. The post had actually been invented for the maulvi. The nawab wrote of twenty-one years of service with no leave, and his grant to his former tutor of one year's furlough and release from his office, the duties of which he would now undertake himself. He wished to save his old and faithful servant from humiliation and to clear up any misunderstanding. This letter was seen as nothing more than procrastination. In a follow-up, the agent to the Government of the Punjab wrote to Charles Watson, the political secretary to the Government of India (GOI) for the viceroy's eyes, 'the state of affairs in Bahawalpur is a scandal'. On 13 December 1928 the requirement of the GOI that the maulvi leave the state was described to the nawab as 'final and irrevocable', and three days later a letter was received from him stating, 'Government orders regarding Home Minister have been carried out.' That represented a break with the past to the extent, thereafter, that the nawab's actions for good and ill were viewed as initiated more by himself than by others,[9] but it was not the end of the story.

Sadiq Muhammad continued to question GOI officials over the reasons the maulvi had been sent away, with no charges against him under the law, and did not take no for an answer even when it was couched as 'imperative that the good repute of the Bahawalpur administration should be rehabilitated' from its bad reputation embodied in the person of the former home minister. In a letter to Charles Watson, Sadiq Muhammad reiterated his wish for the return of the maulvi who was 'wandering about as an exile' away from his home and children. Moreover, he wrote, his own prestige was suffering in the estimation of his people as they believed their nawab's position was not secure, when 'my tutor is suffering the fate of a common exile'. He complained that enemies of the British Raj had lately received 'conciliatory treatment', 'while I as a faithful and loyal friend, am left to brood over my grievances'. Watson and the viceroy, Lord Irwin, were firm. It was too early to consider the return of the maulvi until such time as the 'irrigation scheme' had become such a success that it could not be affected by his return and no other answer was possible at the moment.[10]

Neither the maulvi family nor Sadiq Muhammad paid more than lip service to imperial directives. They merely looked for ways just short of overt defiance to circumvent the GOI. To save the maulvi's face and his own dignity, the nawab had granted him leave of absence for three months, instead of the full year required by government, prior to an announcement of the old man's retirement. When the maulvi's return to Bahawalpur, at the end of December 1929, came to government notice, the nawab announced a statutory requirement for Bahawalpur officials to return to the state for one day before leave could be extended. It hardly made a difference when Shams ud-din had maintained his family's influence as private secretary to the nawab. He had also stepped into his father's shoes as home minister in all but name.

The maulvi was never far away. He had spent the summer in Solon, almost next door to the nawab staying in Simla, and had spent the winter in Delhi, where Sadiq Muhammad also remained, outside all princely precedence. In a letter to Charles Watson, James Fitzpatrick, by then the Bahawalpur revenue minister, considered there were 'compensatory advantages' to the nawab's absence from the domestic hothouse in Dera Nawab Sahib. At the same time, the maulvis had managed to engineer the continuance of their real hold on power in Bahawalpur, about which the new chief minister appointed in early 1929, Khan Bahadur Nabi Bakhsh Mohammed Hussain, now complained. Fitzpatrick considered it would be an improvement to transfer Shams ud-din to the post of foreign secretary, where the 'dominating and injurious influence still exerted on the Nawab by the Maulvis' would be diluted by greater distance. He also advised the better course of removing the whole family from Bahawalpur.[11]

As the maulvi's sons continued to campaign for their father's rehabilitation and attempted to 'thwart and malign' anyone who tried to work honestly and independently as chief minister, government opinion hardened. In mid-January, Watson wrote to the nawab demanding that the retirement of the maulvi should be gazetted and his severance from Bahawalpur state affairs clarified. Shams ud-din should not be allowed to become foreign secretary but Zia ud-din was to be allowed to remain in post as assistant superintendent of police 'where he could do little harm'. Watson believed this small concession might sugar the pill for the nawab but the bargaining continued. Sadiq Muhammad made a counter-bid for Shams ud-din to become financial secretary, and followed up with a further request for him to become education minister with a seat in the cabinet. He was finally gazetted in the 'purely clerical post' of financial secretary on 7 February 1930, just as questions of the remuneration of the maulvi on his retirement arose, regarding a large grant of canal colony land that was part of the security for the Sutlej loan.

It took another six months for the GOI to achieve a formal order. The '5th June 1930 Extraordinary *Sadiq ul Akhbar*, Bahawalpur' announced the final break with the maulvi and of Shams ud-din's 'connection with the personality of His Highness or with the affairs of the State with a view to stop [sic] this false propaganda against the administration of the State'. Whoever had engineered this breakthrough, the GOI were astonished by the sudden capitulation. Fitzpatrick reported, 'I think His Highness has shown unexpected force of character in sticking to his promise', leading to 'universal joy' in the state. The maulvi got his financial reward for his service, barring the gift of land that he might sell off for his own monetary gain or grant to relatives or allies for services rendered.

It is difficult to believe that the maulvi family, outside official view, did not remain to some extent close to the nawab throughout the intervening years until October 1937 when the GOI received an extraordinary request from Nabi Bakhsh, the Bahawalpur chief minister, on behalf of Sadiq Muhammad, requesting permission for the maulvi's return to his state. The request was an encomium to the maulvi that stated, 'Maulvi Ghulam Hussain Sahib was a very reasonable man inspired by praiseworthy ideals and was second to none in his loyalty to the British connection but unfortunately taking advantage of his goodness and simplicity some clever rogues posing as his friends gave him wrong advice and created crisis after crisis for which he was in no way to blame.'[12] This spectacular statement, in the light of the maulvi's probable history, regardless of factional biases, was purportedly given at the behest of 'various zamindars' who wanted the maulvi rehabilitated or at least allowed home. The premise of its authors was based on the reported release of several political prisoners and the restoration of their property in British India.

British doubts as to the wisdom of rescinding the nawab's own gazetted statement of seven years earlier softened under the clear light of present political expediency. They were hardly likely to forget the vast correspondence on the maulvi, that must still have been close to the top of the Bahawalpur files, but there was a current problem of interference with the superintending engineers of the canal development project over which a compromise might be reached to suit all parties. The nawab was obsessed with the idea, inherited from the maulvi, that all state jobs should be given to riasatis, rather than outsiders, although no such competent engineers existed. The home minister and the director of public instruction were seen to be at the forefront of the employment agitation and their removal became the pay-off for the return of the maulvi. Once again, to British surprise, Sadiq Muhammad acceded to this condition, dealing with the matter without further demand or interference.[13]

If the influence of the maulvi and his family became less strong as Sadiq Muhammad gained in stature and experience as nawab of Bahawalpur, or they simply remained outside the notice and interests of the GOI, it was the old and faithful servant who finally facilitated an end to the Sutlej Valley debt, as related in the following chapter. Whatever his faults, magnified or not by the servants of a nervous British Raj mistrustful of his agenda, the maulvi family's continuing importance to the Abbasi of Bahawalpur was marked by the marriage of Shams ud-din's eldest daughter, Shamsa Begum, to Sahibzada Muhammad Abbas, the eldest son and heir of the last nawab. The maulvi bloodline continues twofold in that of the Abbasis, in the persons of Bahawal and Aneeza, Salahuddin and Moniba Abbasi's children, the paternal and maternal great-grandchildren of Maulvi Ghulam Hussain.

8

THE EXERCISE OF POWER

There is an unusually episodic feel to the recorded life of Sadiq Muhammad V. Childhood, boyhood, youth and old age, but more than those eternal ages of man in a life that was lived on the hinge of dramatic change. He was the brave child at the 1911 Durbar; the unlikely boy exile at Porlock, away from family and familiarity; the adolescent at Aitchison College, returning to Bahawalpur to be torn between tradition and the modernity imposed by an exploitative occupying power; the young man and ruler who was forever under surveillance, whose powers were curtailed by an occupying power for its own purposes and whose lifestyle was picked over and frowned upon. He remained nominally loyal to that power, entertained its officials in style and then there were choices to be made, new loyalties to be decided and generously given, so that another outside power could take what it wanted before reneging on the promises made in exchange for that allegiance and generosity. After that, permanent loss of state, status and power, followed by retirement and semi-exile to a foreign country until death.

There was more to Sadiq Muhammad's life as a Muslim prince than the maulvi and the various scandals that appear most immediately in India Office Records—he was an occasional go-between with Arab countries, particularly during World War II, and had a successful visit to Iraq and Iran in 1941. The British ambassador in Iraq at the time had noted the nawab's help in the war effort as he 'strove to dispel the idea that India is struggling under the heavy yoke of British imperialism'. He had also spoken at important shrines in Iraq of the complete religious freedom enjoyed by all Muslims in India and expounded to leading politicians in Baghdad his conviction that Islam must hold on to British friendship. Less satisfactory were the gifts of fifty silver and thirty gold cigarette cases ordered from 'the leading Sabasan goldsmith in Amara' suspected to be gifts for betrothal or marriage ceremonies, after negotiations with the relatives of Shaikh Salah Bahayan, on grounds of common descent from the Abbasid caliphs of Baghdad. The government noted more approvingly that such marriages 'might constitute an important link between people of Irak [sic] and of Mohammedan India'.[1]

In 1943 there were questions from the commander-in-chief of the Indian Army, Sir Claude Auchinleck, as to His Highness's actual usefulness when he proposed a second visit to Iraq, Iran and Saudi Arabia. It was considered that he was not the man to impress Ibn Saud, king of Saudi Arabia, unlike the later maharaja of Bikaner who, although he was a Hindu, 'had the dignity required' to overcome obstacles when 'the Bedou and the Effendi do not easily mingle'.[2] Neither should Sadiq Muhammad go for the purpose of advising Ibn Saud not to be so friendly with the USA, although he could possibly go again to Iraq, Iran and Syria 'where he will do no harm and might do some good'. In the end, excuses were made on grounds of problems with food and transport in Arabia, and, at a time when the question of food supplies in Bahawalpur was critical during the Bengal famine. The nawab wrote that he had already been sending monetary aid to the 'gentry' of Iraq, Syria and Saudi Arabia which was unlikely to endear him any more to the Government of India.

Sadiq Muhammad undoubtedly propagated his relationship with Arabian rulers in support of his own ancestry, in particular with the kings of Iraq and Egypt, the former the Hashemite descendants of the sharifs of Mecca, and the latter of the Ottoman Turks. In 1938, he had proposed a marriage between his eldest son and King Farouk's sister, which resulted in letters whirling round the political department of the Punjab questioning how far 'events have progressed in this delicate matter'. The answer appeared to be not very far since no such marriage took place and there is no further record on the subject. In 1944, by coincidence or design, his second son, Sahibzada Rashid Abbasi, was appointed ADC to Major General F.W. Burch of the Indian Army Liaison Mission in Cairo. A proposal for him with the half-Scottish granddaughter of a Pathan member of the political department in India proved problematic on grounds of the paucity of dowry offered and the backward reputation of Bahawalpur regarding the situation of women attached to the court. In the end, the prince, who joined the Pakistan Foreign Service and was ambassador to Tunisia, married an Englishwoman, Katharine Scott, at Caxton Hall in London. She is described in various online sources as 'the daughter of a railway carter'.[3]

Sadiq Muhammad was intensely and orthodoxly religious, engaging in regular debate with holy men and teachers as well as building mosques and educational establishments, but his orthodoxy did not extend to communalism. When a Hindu movement, propagated through Hindu newspapers and local activists, against cow killing in 1935 was countered by a Muslim ban on Hindu barbers and sweepers, violence threatened. The nawab issued a firman that all those with grievances should come forward to meet him within three days or the ringleaders would be arrested. He insisted that there was no danger of serious trouble and predicted correctly that the police could cope with the situation without bringing in military force. Finally, at Partition, he did his utmost to retain the whole population of his state regardless of religious affiliation.

He failed in his attempt in 1931 to emulate the Aga Khan with a donation to Aligarh University, the great seat of Islamic learning. The donation was to be associated with the name of the viceroy, Lord Irwin, but his lordship denied the request on grounds of the 'somewhat embarrassed condition of Your Highness' finances'.[4] It transpired the money had already been promised to Aligarh, in instalments over four years, but eighteen months after the original agreement, the university had received nothing. Sadiq Muhammad had first been on the pilgrimage to Mecca as a three-year-old on the ill-fated occasion when his father died. He went at least twice more, in 1931 and in 1935, when he took a party of about 400 at his expense and reportedly engaged in the ritual washing, 'ghusl', of the Kaaba with Ibn Saud and the former amir of Afghanistan, Amanullah Khan. The costs of that expedition must have caused the British heartache. They had successfully turned down his request to make the pilgrimage in 1933, muttering in the margins about money, as they insisted on his attendance at the Council of Princes and informed him that time did not allow for suitable arrangements for his reception at Jeddah. On that occasion, the council had also been used to extend a travel ban to the maharaja of Patiala who was keen to go to England for less devout but equally expensive purposes.

British misgivings about the nawab's sybaritic lifestyle were borne out, but the 'indolence' described by St John is an unfair judgement. His true abilities were never fully tested, but he was energetic in pursuit of his interests, however little they appealed to Mr Bolster's Christian manly instincts. He supported a peaceful path towards independence. A proclamation issued by His Highness deplored the 'welter of chaos' around the Round Table Conferences in 1930–32 and appealed to his fellow Muslims to cooperate with Hindus. He attempted to keep a foot in every camp and to do the right thing according to his loyalty or fealty to the British and to his co-religionists. The photographs of convivial shooting weekends and gatherings of notable politicians and diplomats, with one after another viceroy, lanky Linlithgow and Lord Wavell's moustache immediately recognizable, at Dera Nawab Sahib, imply wider discussions than the numbers of duck in the gamebag.

The nawab's interest in the army, machinery and motors might have been more acceptable to the British, had it not been seen as an excuse for the greater extravagance demonstrated by questions over the Vickers Carden tractors he was determined to buy in 1937. He was a passionate stamp collector, a passion inherited by his grandson, Salahuddin. Sadiq Muhammad's collection at his death was third in the world only to George V, whose philately was much mocked, and the papal collection. The postal system was set up in Bahawalpur during the Mudakhalat but taken over by the British Imperial Post in 1870 on grounds of efficiency and run by that body until 15 August 1947.[5] Stamps printed by any feudatory states in India which had their own postal services were only valid within the state but, as a philatelist, Sadiq Muhammad Khan continued to press for the return of the Bahawalpur postal service, and in July 1933 he issued a stamp commemorating the centenary of the alliance between Britain and Bahawalpur. He did not altogether achieve his dream until the brief period after Independence, before the state was absorbed wholly into Pakistan, but in an agreement with the British, Bahawalpur stamps for official mail within the state became valid from 1 January 1945.

Stamps had been made earlier in the reign in part fulfilment of the nawab's postal ambitions and to commemorate important events. They included one, of considerable multicoloured splendour and extreme rarity, to celebrate the silver jubilee of George V. Bahawalpur stamps continue to change hands; those of lesser value are easily available from Internet sites while others, from the short period from 1947 to 1954 when the capital was renamed Baghdad ul-Jadid after Independence, are of enormous value. They were reputed to be the best-designed stamps on the subcontinent. There were orders, which must have rested more in hope than expectation, that all stamps used within the state were to be returned to the ruler. A recorded 5 per cent return sounds a better tally than might have been anticipated.

Stamp collecting and postal services are harmless enough in the eyes of the world. Unfortunately for Sadiq Muhammad, he also loved and collected women. So far as foreign women were concerned, he was a bad picker, the only exception, his last wife, Olivia, who was Dutch and is remembered fondly by Salahuddin. She outlived her husband by only a few months. The rest, in the main, were quite as much on the make as Sarah Skinner had been two generations earlier and did not hesitate to petition the British authorities to support their rights. In this respect, the GOI was even-handed in its disapproval of all parties concerned, and officials displayed the same lofty snobbery as they had in the past to Mrs Skinner. There is record after record, more frowning detailing of extravagances, women and the perceptions, facts and exaggerations of bad behaviour on the part of the nawab. It is the prurient detail of the tabloid translated to the dry prose of bureaucracy; the debt owed by Bahawalpur always an excuse to hold its ruler in particular disfavour.

Depending on the validity of the record, purported children of some of the more questionable 'wives' occasionally appear in records. Sadiq Muhammad's official tally gives an equal score of ten each of named sons and daughters. Not an extraordinary total for a prince of the period with multiple wives, Bhupinder Singh, the maharaja of Patiala had fifty-two children. At the same time, much as the original 'great-great-grandfather' of the Daudputras created conditions of internecine warfare for years to come, so Sadiq Muhammad Khan Abbasi created inter-family problems for his heirs. The political struggle to salvage the heritage and treasure of Bahawalpur for the people of the state and for posterity has also been exacerbated by family strife. In an atmosphere of mistrust, misappropriation and corruption, there has been endless scope for family members to use influence that gelled with the inclinations of the government of the day, to grab or steal more than their proper share of their father's or grandfather's estate. In the process, the greater part has been lost to a higher power in Pakistan, the army.

In 1921, the nawab was married, in the ceremony complained of by Bolster, to Jamila Begum Sahiba, an Abbasi cousin. In and out of the list of British complaints about other women, one or two in particular emerge as thorns in the side of both Sadiq Muhammad and the authorities. Salahuddin Abbasi has never heard of Linda Sayce nor any children she may have produced between her marriage in 1927, which she herself dated to 1930, and her death in 1933. Whatever form the marriage took, it seems to have been accepted as fact by officials like Sir Richard Crofton, British prime minister of Bahawalpur in 1945, on grounds of believable evidence such as a threatening letter from Linda's brother, H.L. Sayce, to the nawab.[6] Lieutenant Sayce demanded Rs 1 lakh from his former brother-in-law on pain of 'resorting to the Crown' or to litigation. In this instance, when the details of the case were brought to his attention, the Crown, in the person of Francis Wylie, political adviser to the Crown representative, was disposed to stand firmly in the nawab's court.

Crofton reported Sayce's history, his sister's marriage and that her four sons were being educated with their half-brothers in Bahawalpur. Sayce had been born in 1910 and, after his sister's marriage to the nawab, had been educated mainly at his expense. He had attended Dartington Hall in Devon, St George's College in Mussoorie and the College of Estate Management in Lincolns Inn Fields in London, during which time he had been given a good deal of financial help. He had been supported, in the first place, while training to be a civil engineer but had changed his mind. He had 'shirked his studies' and got into bad habits, and Sadiq Muhammad had previously expressed his wish for the young man to finish his education and find employment in India.[7] Now, the nawab said, he was delighted that his brother-in-law had gained a commission with the RNVR (Royal Naval Volunteer Reserve) but had been advised to no longer correspond with or support a man who had been so disappointing in failing to find a proper profession despite the large sums spent on his education and maintenance. Further records show Sadiq Muhammad had taken considerable trouble to settle a feckless young man whose extravagance might almost have matched his own and who clearly and mistakenly believed he had tapped into an inexhaustible source of funds. His name does not appear in RNVR records for 1945.

Before her death, Linda, then calling herself Mrs Y.I. Abbasi, had written in March 1933 to the viceroy, Lord Willingdon, declaring herself deceived into marriage with the nawab in 1930, when she was seventeen. She had married, she wrote, for love not money, on the understanding that she would not have to live in purdah and that her husband was estranged from his two previous wives. This did not prove to be the case and, in fact, there were three other wives in the picture. The nawab, who, she informed the viceroy, called her Babs, had not paid her dowry although he had given her a 'toilet table' with all 'enamel equipments'.[8] She was now being accused of infidelities with 'jockeys and such like' during a stay in Poona for medical treatment. Investigations in Bahawalpur discovered that, notwithstanding possible earlier infidelities, Linda had lately taken up with a German, and the nawab had divorced her, allowing her to keep her jewellery and three months' iddat[9] payment but paying no dowry. She was now, to all intents and purposes, attempting blackmail and the viceroy declined to intervene.[10]

Her family, however, believed they had ongoing claims on the nawab. In 1935 Linda's sister, Gladys Bishop, petitioned for British help in getting a copy of Linda's death certificate from the Bahawalpur durbar. She requested that her nieces Theresa and Mary, presently in a convent school in Simla, and her nephews, Princes Mubarak and Daud, be suitably cared for. As evidence she provided photographs of herself, Linda, another sister, Irene, and two children with the nawab and a Dr Pereira.[11] No further action is noted on the 'injudicious' letter marked to be forwarded to the agent to the Government of the Punjab and it seems likely that none was taken. The discrepancies in dates reported by Linda and her family and the variable numbers, sexes and speed of arrival of her children with the nawab, must have rung alarm bells. Lieutenant Sayce gained the most from his sister's marriage but he forgot the story of the goose and the golden eggs.

The Sayce family was not the only one to attempt to enrich itself at the nawab's cost. Edwin Hall, the self-described injured husband of a Sylvia Gwendoline O'Brien, known as Joy, tried to blackmail Sadiq Muhammad as part of a plot cooked up by Joy's grandmother. She was described by the Punjab resident as of a 'highly predatory nature'. Edwin himself was, not unexpectedly, said to be a dubious character, a drunk who had been thrown out of the police force and was quite reconciled to having his wife pimped out for greater gain. It materialized that Joy was actually the stepdaughter of the nawab; her mother had been procured from Bangalore by his emissary on a search there for a wife from the Anglo-Indian community. Joy, then a child, had been educated by her stepfather at a Simla convent and, from there, aged fifteen, had married Edwin Hall without notice to her sponsor. When she requested financial help after the marriage, the nawab refused to have her at Bahawalpur and attempted to send her to England, a plan stymied by her grandmother. There was some question as to whether he had seduced Joy himself but the resident was certain there was no case to answer. He wrote drily to Delhi: 'His Highness has somewhat unusual taste so far as social and marital relations are concerned.'[12]

Such sordid little tales did nothing for Sadiq Muhammad Khan's reputation. His every move was judged by the British and he could do nothing without interference or British sanction, which was seldom given untrammelled with further strictures. The Sutlej loan was a dark cloud over the Bahawalpur durbar and the ruler. It never went away, and efforts by the durbar to take a private loan from another state, initially Gwalior, were thwarted by British refusal to underwrite the debt, on grounds that the Government of India did not guarantee interstate loans. Gwalior was well aware of the nawab's reputation and would accept nothing less, but a loan was eventually agreed with Bhavnagar, a state that regularly made similar transactions. It was sanctioned under conditions where the earnings of the Khanpur–Chachran railway and any customs subsidy were taken as security, and it became an excuse for further curbs and questions on the nawab's spending.

Requests from the Bahawalpur government for restrictions on their ruler's powers to appoint ministers and submit the state budget were refused on grounds that 'the acceptance of this would be likely to give rise to considerable embarrassment', and His Highness's 'persistent and ineradicable extravagance' made it too early to consider any change.[13] The requirement for the state budget to be approved by the resident to the Punjab states continued on grounds of safeguarding the Sutlej Valley repayments. It was always too early for any change, and complaints against Sadiq Muhammad from those with any axe to grind added to the weight of his British chains over the years. Official attitudes towards him varied from paternalistic sympathy to patronizing postscripts and barely veiled sneers.

Attempts by a Bahawalpur courtier in 1925 to curry favour with his ruler by acquiring medals for him from the third Afghan War, to which he was not entitled, reverberated down the years. As a result the World War II medals and foreign decorations awarded to his sons were wholly unfairly scrutinized and questioned. In 1925 Lieutenant Colonel Gourlie of the 21st India Horse complained of his treatment when Sadiq Khan failed to entertain him at Dera Nawab Sahib because he was on shikar in the desert. It is possible, at the time, that the maulvi may have encouraged him to be inhospitable to a British officer.[14] At the same time, his love of his army, well known throughout his life, was then and later often unfairly viewed as merely a hobby, war games played out by a privileged man. Questions of finance put a stop to his selection as a delegate to the League of Nations in Geneva in 1930, although Punjab government officials had recommended approval of a selection that would be 'regarded by him as a signal mark of Government favour after the hard knocks we have had to give him for his own good'.[15]

The ban on entry into Bahawalpur in 1935 of a dangerously seditious pir, Jamaat Ali Shah, intent on 'rousing popular resentment' against the British was not remarkable. The fact that the pir had been invited in the first place was laid at the door of the maulvi, but Sadiq Muhammad's loyalties were again opened to questions on grounds of his religious views. And so it went on through the years, scandal after scandal, however small or domestic, all black marks against the nawab's name. It was reported that the son of the prime minister of

Bahawalpur was in London, claiming to be a prince, and running up enormous debts in good princely style.[16] There was an 'incident' in 1940 at Clifton in Karachi when the nawab's servant, Allah Diwaya, a man well known to Salahuddin in his youth, had beaten up a plain-clothes detective who was engaged in surveillance on the nawab as he strolled, theoretically incognito, on the beach with his latest European paramour. That story varies with its teller but greater opprobrium was reserved for the fact that he had bought a house outside Karachi without reference to the government.[17] Salahuddin tells another tale of Allah Diwaya, the loyal body servant, scaring off a British political agent in Bahawalpur by shooting at him as he sat in his own compound, on successive evenings, until the man requested a transfer from the state.

In 1945, Sadiq Muhammad proposed to establish a trust for the benefit of members of his family, especially for his younger children, modelled on the Moazzam Jah Trust in Hyderabad and funded, first of all, with the proceeds from the sale of Bahawalpur House in Lahore. The correspondence, questioning ownership both of Bahawalpur House, which was already in the hands of the government as prepayment of the Sutlej loan, and of other properties to be used for capital or land for jagirs, finally arrived on the desk of the very last British political secretary in India, Sir Lancelot Cecil Lepel Griffin.[18] It was fitting that a man with an eighteenth-century-sounding name should deal with issues regarding Bahawalpur that were traceable back through India Office Records to the earliest involvement and non-interference of the British in the state.

It took Muhammad Ali Jinnah, the Father of the Nation, to unknot the noose of the Sutlej Valley Project from Sadiq Muhammad Khan's neck. Shortly before Independence, the nawab's mother, who had been highly influential behind the scenes in Bahawalpur during her son's minority, sent her trusted ally, the old maulvi

Ghulam Hussain, on a mission to the nizam of Hyderabad to raise another loan, on collateral of most of her jewellery. This final act in the endless playing out of the Sutlej Valley Project demonstrates, perhaps more than any, the weight of the British-imposed debt on the nawab. Negotiations with the fabulously wealthy and legendarily miserly nizam did not go well; he had no intention of irritating the British, and the maulvi was returning from Hyderabad to Bombay empty-handed when he ran into Jinnah by chance stretching his legs on a station platform. The two knew each other well, and, seeing the old man was upset, Jinnah invited him to join him in his compartment where the whole story was told. A meeting followed in Jinnah's law chambers in Bombay and a solution so simple was discovered that in retrospect it is close to tragic. Jinnah found that the British share of payment for the land for the Khanpur–Chachran railway had never been fully paid to Bahawalpur. It was probable that the figure, including interest, was higher by that time than the residual Sutlej Valley debt: Salahuddin recalls Rs 12 crore against an outstanding eight. After so many years the burden simply fell away, just at the time when Bahawalpur's newly acquired wealth would have allowed for full repayment of the loan. It had been held over the nawab's head by the paramount power for the duration of his reign and had been anticipated not to be fully paid until 1986.

Part 2

A New Country

9

DIVISION AND STATE

The fears of a devout, educated Muslim and his co-religionists in the subcontinent in the 1940s, for the future of India, are exemplified by Mahmood Khan Durrani GC of the 1st Bahawalpur Infantry in his memoir of the war. On the occasion at Flagstaff House in Delhi during the Cabinet Mission of 1946 when he was informed by Field Marshal Lord Auchinleck of his award of the George Cross for 'acts of the greatest heroism or of the most conspicuous courage in circumstances of extreme danger', he tackled the Secretary of State for India, Lord Pethick-Lawrence, on the subject of Pakistan. When he received an inconclusive reply to his question on the division of India, he answered:

> From the people I have been talking about, I mean the Muslims of India, their circumstances are pathetic. Briefly, I may explain, the Muslims of India have had an extremely bitter experience of a common political, economic and social life with the non-Muslims, who have made their day-to-day life hot for them. The non-Muslims have a great superiority over the Muslims in a share in the administration of the country. They have a complete

> economic hold over the agricultural produce and the trade and commerce of the country. Educationally they are much more advanced than the Muslims. In politics, they have manoeuvred themselves into a position of monopoly. Therefore, they claim to be the sole representatives of the people of India. Besides this they are staunch in their social, cultural and religious prejudice against the Muslims, Therefore, it has become, by now, a passion with all of them to eliminate the Muslims from India which they claim to be only their Motherland. Thus, the Hindus and Sikhs show utmost fanaticism and aggressiveness in their daily dealings with Muslims, whom they spare no pains to keep subjugated and submerged.
>
> My past experiences in India and Malaya, where the Indian non-Muslims had more freedom to pursue such policies, leave me in no doubt about it. It is in pursuit of this policy that the Hindus are bringing every possible influence to bear upon the British Government to recognize them as their only legitimate successors and leave the minorities in the lurch. Every Muslim, even one in the street, is conscious of the Hindu menaces, which is his daily experience. Everywhere he is faced with forces that are there to deprive him of what he possesses, to dislodge him from a position of profit, to segregate him, to stifle his voice and to threaten to encircle and annihilate him. Therefore, in view of his past history and tradition, having nothing in common with that of the Hindus, the menace he faces every day and the prospects of humiliation, death and destruction in a United India, the Indian Muslim cannot have hope or confidence in anything but Pakistan.

Mahmood Khan Durrani was about to graduate from university when a relation serving with the Bahawalpur state forces persuaded him to come to Dera Nawab Sahib to be interviewed by the nawab for enlistment in his bodyguard troops. Durrani had the necessary qualifications, education and breeding; he was descended from the Afghan Durrani royal family; had a certificate for entrance to the Indian Military Academy; and, most importantly, he was 6 feet 4 inches tall. The nawab was determined to have tall soldiers in the bodyguard. In 1941, Durrani's unit was posted to Malaya. Detailed to hold and build up the defences of the aerodromes in north Malaya, Durrani wrote of his respect and liking for his commanding officer (CO), Lt Col. Fletcher, who was recalled to India to command another unit. This British officer was the exception to the rule. Indian officers were universally treated extremely badly by their British counterparts and superiors, and there was general discontent among the Indian troops. Durrani records that punishments inflicted on them were more than those accorded to all the other forces in Malaya, and the nawab himself flew in to deal with trouble among the Bahawalpur troops due to difficulties between the officers. Durrani 'wondered if this treatment was a natural return for all the enthusiasm with which we offered to defend the British Empire'.

The Japanese invaded Malaya on 8 December 1941 and Indian prisoners of war (POWs) were encouraged or forced by the Japanese to volunteer for the newly formed Indian National Army (INA), led first by Captain Mohan Singh, a Sikh officer of the 14th Punjab, to cooperate with Japan in furtherance of Indian independence and to free Asia 'from the crushing yoke of the Anglo-Americans'.[1] The officer in charge of the Bahawalpur troops, Lt Col. Gilani, became second in command to Mohan Singh but Durrani, whatever his low opinion of the British, saw collaboration with the Japanese as the death knell for India and, more than that, for Indian Muslims. The Japanese claimed kinship and common culture with Hindus, who were also a dominant race. The Sikh prisoners, he believed, hurried to volunteer on the promise of a separate kingdom when the hated

British had been driven out of India. Durrani's actions throughout the remainder of the war, beginning with the organization of a Muslim boycott of the INA, and followed by his fearless efforts to work from the inside to thwart the INA and Japanese plans to infiltrate agents into India, were based on his belief in the danger threatening the honour, lives, culture and religion of Indian and Far Eastern Muslims.

By the end of 1942, Mohan Singh had realized that the INA was being used by the Japanese in a wholly unequal partnership. He was removed from command and imprisoned. In May 1943, suspicion fell on Durrani after a spell in the INA hospital with dysentery and starvation. It is hard to tell if it was a miracle he had got away with his sabotage of the INA for as long as he did or if the atmosphere of total chaos he describes in Singapore and Malaya between the Japanese and Indians, who were both prisoners and, nominally, allies, provided excellent cover for individual initiative. Severely tortured by the Japanese, Durrani was sentenced to death by Netaji Subhas Chandra Bose himself, after he arrived in Malaya in June 1943 to revive the INA. Durrani's sentence, giving him the 'privilege' of being shot by an Indian firing squad, was later commuted in favour of more torture to extract any further information he might have about activities against the INA. He somehow survived until the liberation of Singapore.

As the British became both liberators and his new captors, Durrani saw Indians divided once again into groups based on religion and mutual distrust. He was sent for by Lt Col. Gilani, then imprisoned by the British, who asked Durrani to make a statement on his behalf denying the level of his INA involvement. He was cashiered after the war but escaped further retribution, and his later career suggested a clever man with the gift of the gab, unscrupulously able to turn events always to his own advantage and get himself out of trouble. Gilani was able to boast to Durrani of his friendship with an Australian officer in Pearl's Hill Jail who had allowed him freedom of movement, food and alcohol. It comes as no surprise that he cropped up again a little later in Bahawalpur, turning another disaster towards his own ends.

Durrani quoted his remembered conversation with Pethick-Lawrence in his unhappy memoir of the war. In *The Sixth Column* any self-recognition of his own remarkable valour is overshadowed by the events he had witnessed and the appalling torture by the Japanese, when his actions were discovered, that left him a legacy of sickness and pain. He had not, in addition, been wholly immune to the controversial treatment of INA troops on their repatriation to India when some were tried for treason and he was suspect to all sides. The book was published long after Partition and after Bahawalpur state had ceased to exist. Whether the conversation took place as related with Pethick-Lawrence or whether it was remembered with hindsight of later events, he described the hatred, uncertainty, divisions and fear that bred the violence of the tearing apart of the subcontinent.

Any books mentioning the events of Partition in Bahawalpur, usually only as an adjunct to those in the Punjab, freely quote Sir Edward Penderel Moon. This chapter will be no exception. It is hard to improve on an eyewitness account, especially one written with the 'clarity, detachment and mastery of complex detail', noted in his entry in the *Oxford Dictionary of National Biography*. In addition, Yaqoob Khan Bangash, in *A Princely Affair: The Accession and Integration of the Princely States of Pakistan, 1947-1955*, has explored exhaustively the events of this short but transforming period in the princely states. He has accessed records in Pakistan not easily opened to a foreigner, and his research and scholarship are also drawn on and quoted with regard to Bahawalpur during the period. Ayres

Wilcox's 1963 *Consolidation of a Nation,* with its clear overview of the situation between Bahawalpur and the new Pakistan Muslim League (PML) government, is also drawn on at some length below.

Penderel Moon arrived in Bahawalpur as revenue minister in April 1947 under Prime Minister Mushtaq Ahmed Gurmani, later governor of West Pakistan and remembered by Salahuddin Abbasi as a 'lovely little roly-poly man'. He took over from Sir Richard Crofton who had been in the post since 1942, the first of the two British prime ministers of Bahawalpur. Moon commented on a 'vague hostility' to the arrival of another British official, which he put down in part to the desire to see at last the end of the British and secondly to a tradition of 'anti-western, obscurantist and reactionary Islam' in Bahawalpur. In the former complaint, the population must have been disappointed to get a second British prime minister after Independence. In the latter, such opinions may have been part of the earlier clash of the British with tradition embodied in Maulvi Ghulam Hussain. They were not overtly shared by the anglophile nawab. However, in the years since Bahawalpur was absorbed into the Punjab, marginalized, forgotten and impoverished in the enrichment of the upper Punjab, reactionary Islam has gained ground in Bahawalpur once more. The huge support, moral and financial, given by the nawab of Bahawalpur to the Quaid-i-Azam and the new Islamic state of Pakistan at its birth has been in no wise remembered and only reciprocated in broken promises to the state.

As the most important Muslim-majority state with a Muslim ruler, leaving aside the different story and geographical location of Hyderabad, and with geographical borders with Sindh and Punjab, Bahawalpur's accession to Pakistan must have appeared certain. Moon wrote, the people of the state 'knew nothing of any other possibility'. The Muslim population was 'well content' with the prospect and most of the minority communities accepted it without serious concern. It was only as panic grew, and Muslims from Rajputana began to move into Bahawalpur, in the weeks leading up to the transfer of power, that their migration was mirrored by that of the Hindu population. They were, in particular, the proprietors of urban businesses, that the nawab hoped and tried to retain in Bahawalpur.

Sadiq Muhammad Khan was close enough to Jinnah, who had advised the family legally and in relation to the Sutlej Valley Project loan, to have had him as a regular guest at his house, Al Qamar, in Karachi. Eventually, he presented the Quaid with 15 acres of land and ordered that a house should be built for him on it. Jinnah also took a laissez-faire attitude to the princes, so that their expectations of at least semi-independence within Pakistan, and, in Bahawalpur's case, absolute belief in promises of provincial status in due course, would have more allure than any offer from a Congress government in India. One of his grandfather's servants, deputed to look after Jinnah's building work in Karachi reported no such easy-going attitude in other areas of the Quaid's life. The servant, who was an unusually big man, six and a half feet tall, told Salahuddin that Jinnah was so imperious, he used to tremble in front of him.

In a riposte to the resolution of 14 June 1947 of the All-India Congress Committee (AICC) that suggested that the lapse of paramountcy did not lead to the independence of states as they could not exist separate from the rest of India, Jinnah had made a statement on 17 June: 'The Indian states will be independent sovereign states on the termination of paramountcy and they will be free to adopt any course they like. We do not wish to interfere with internal affairs of any state', and '. . . we shall be glad to discuss with them and come to settlement which will be in the interest of both.'[2]

Things were not so simple. Moon wrote of his astonishment when Gurmani, himself an Indian unionist, informed him that the nawab was 'being advised in certain quarters to accede to India'. Dr Umbreen Javaid, former lecturer at Islamia University in Bahawalpur and professor in the department of political science at the University of Punjab, has written of meetings between the nawab and Jawaharlal Nehru in London and, with his sister Vijaya Lakshmi Pandit, at Sadiqgarh, when he was offered incentives to join India. Gurmani was additionally concerned with the situation regarding the division of the Sutlej Valley between two national authorities. He believed that if Bahawalpur was in Pakistan, and India controlled the headwaters of the river, they might reduce the supply to Bahawalpur, returning farmland to the desert. In fact, this was exactly what happened in the 1950s leading to the start of the Indus River diversion project. Meanwhile, it was all horse-trading. Rumour and counter-rumour ran from Delhi to London, through the states of Rajputana and into Bahawalpur, as rulers bargained accession for the best deal and greatest level of independence within the new parameters.

The states contiguous to Pakistan—Bikaner, Jaisalmer and, in particular, Jodhpur—flirted with offers to them made by Muslim League leaders. Likewise, it was believed, the nawab of Bahawalpur might extract greater concessions if he acceded to India. Wayne Ayres Wilcox described Bahawalpur as 'lying along the Sutlej River, with its irrigated face toward the Punjab and its arid back to the great Indian desert'.[3] When Sadiq Muhammad Khan flew to London for negotiations with the British government, the British floated the idea, rumoured to have been proposed originally by Prime Minister Gurmani, of a regional unit of neighbouring states, a Rajputana States Confederation, as a buffer zone between the two countries. Sadiq Muhammad Khan was offered the first presidency. In answer, he said, 'I believe we are all gentlemen here. My front door faces Pakistan, my servants' entrance faces India. I believe a gentleman usually enters his house through his front door'. His grandson adds, 'We have been regretting it ever since.'

On 15th August 1947 the nawab declared himself amir and Jalalat-ul-Mulk ala Hazrat, His Majesty the king of the independent state of Bahawalpur. His action was considered inflammatory by the Muslim League. It resulted in a progression of events described below by Wayne Ayres Wilcox, in *The Consolidation of a Nation,* and also quoting Moon. The nawab's satisfactory simile to describe his intentions to the British may have suggested more clarity of intent than was genuinely the case.

Lieutenant Colonel A.S.B. Shah, the secretary of the ministry for states, later testified to the Pakistan government's reaction:

> I had recommended that the Government should not recognize the new title assumed by the ruler. The new titles appeared to me to be incongruous because the Nawab had not possessed them before Partition and in the Political Department we were very jealous of the Rulers assuming titles to which they were not justified.
>
> Equally serious was the lack of a Standstill Agreement between the state and the central government. Two missions visited the state in 1947—the first, under Major Short, from July until September; the second, led by General Iftikhar of the Pakistan Army and Mr. Ikramullah, secretary of the Ministry of Foreign Affairs, arrived in connection with very serious communal riots, but the presence of a ranking political officer belied its dual nature.[4]

Gurmani had discussed a Standstill Agreement with representatives of both governments on 'matters of common concern', to which the Government of Pakistan had agreed. The Government of India would only accept the Standstill Agreement in the standard form prepared for all states in case any exceptions created difficulties with other states. On 14 August 1947, Gurmani signed the agreement between the Government of India and Bahawalpur on matters relating to 'currency and coinage, extradition, irrigation, motor vehicles, relief from double income tax, and other arrangements relating to existing privileges and immunities enjoyed by the rulers'. Such a document, regarding a state that would almost certainly be attached in some form to Pakistan, was not likely to hold much relevance. Gurmani informed Ikramullah, the secretary of the ministry of external affairs and commonwealth relations, observing, 'It will take some time to get agreement and arrangements in regard to the matters of common concern between the Pakistan Government and Bahawalpur State.'[5]

At this point, Gurmani and the nawab themselves went into a standstill mode of delay and hesitation, with the intention of retaining as much independence as possible. Ten days after Partition, the nawab made a statement of his intentions, which was somewhat contradictory: 'The States have once again become fully independent and sovereign territories. These important and far-reaching changes enable us to shape our own destinies.'[6]

The nawab foresaw Bahawalpur's future as an Islamic state, but at the same time alluded to the need for the protection of minority rights, called for religious freedom and justice, and asked for cordial relations with all his neighbours. He added:

> In view of the geographical position of my State and its cultural and economic affinities with the Pakistan Dominion, my representatives should participate in the labours and deliberations of the Pakistan Constituent Assembly . . . which will enable the two states to arrive at a satisfactory constitutional arrangement with regard to certain important matters of common concern.[7]

The speech clarified nothing except that Bahawalpur would negotiate with Pakistan as a separate legal entity.

No accession was forthcoming by the end of September, and Liaquat Ali Khan told Colonel Shah that there was a 'hitch' in Bahawalpur's accession and asked the secretary to try to secure an instrument through the good offices of Mr Amjad Ali, a friend of Gurmani. In October, after several delays, the reluctant chief minister came to Karachi with a signed agreement, which was accepted by the governor general on 5 October 1947.

Eleven years later, the whole affair was raked up in a libel suit filed by Gurmani against the editor of the *Times of Karachi*, who published a letter which was alleged to have been sent by Gurmani to Sardar Patel. It offered the accession of Bahawalpur to India if Sadiq Muhammad Khan was appointed rajpramukh of Bahawalpur, Bikaner and Jaisalmer. The nawab testified at the trial that Gurmani did not approach him concerning accession to India, that he was in London during the critical months, and that he had been advised to assume the royal title because he had not acceded to either dominion on 14 August 1947. Some observers expected the nawab to implicate his chief minister because of the personal enmity between them, but there was no way in which the nawab could extricate himself from the same charge since he was obviously free at any time to sign a binding instrument of accession.

The circumstances by which such a letter would get back to Gurmani's political foes eleven years later were so implausible and unsavoury that the court was indignant. The letter was ruled a forgery, and the then prime minister, Firoz Khan Noon, was exposed and censured for his involvement. Noon later told Gurmani that he did not think that Gurmani would contest the issue and raise other disputes. Certainly, the trial revealed some of the outlines of the delay and manoeuvring associated with the accession of the state. It was pointed out by some that in the period between his alleged treason and the trial, Gurmani was the minister for states and could have destroyed all of the official records that might have been incriminating. Others, some in high places, believed that such a letter did exist but that its original was unavailable and the forgery was concocted only to expose the facts. Still another viewpoint was that the whole affair was an inner-Punjab vendetta, artificially inflated to national proportion. There may have been a degree of truth in parts of each charge. Unquestionably there was a delay over the accession of Bahawalpur without much good excuse.

The role of Nawab Sadiq Muhammad Khan has never been fully explored. It is altogether possible that his was the most decisive voice in Bahawalpur's accession process. His minister for revenue and works, Penderel Moon, has written that the spirit of the state administration was one of independence, for:

> If we went cap in hand to Pakistan, we should put ourselves at their mercy and enable them to assert the Paramountcy of the old British Indian Government. The Nawab and Gurmani were anxious to avoid this and considered it both possible and desirable that Bahawalpur should maintain a quasi-independent existence.

The trial, at which Sadiq Muhammad Khan gave evidence, saw the Lahore High Court convened in Noor Mahal Palace because the ruler of a state was exempt from appearing in court, but, had in this case, volunteered. His grandson is unaware of enmity between Gurmani and his grandfather, although it is possible that the nawab did not wholly trust the machinations of the consummate civil servant and held his former prime minister responsible for losses to Bahawalpur at the time of Partition. This would have included the nawab's inability, despite his own efforts, to retain the valued Hindu population in his state. He was, however, quite clear in his statement that Gurmani had no authority to go against his wishes at the time of Independence and that he had personally already declared himself to Jinnah.

The nawab of Junagadh, ruler of a state with borders contiguous with Indian territory on three sides, the fourth being to the Arabian Sea, and a predominantly Hindu population, was officially the first state to accede to Pakistan on 15 September 1947. By late October, the effects of an Indian blockade on Junagadh had resulted in the flight of the nawab and his family to Karachi and compelled the diwan, Sir Shah Nawaz Bhutto, Zulfikar Ali Bhutto's father, to request the Government of India to take over the administration. On 10 November, the accession to Pakistan was rescinded, and a plebiscite carried out under the auspices of the Indian Army in February 1948 confirmed popular approval for accession to India. Thus, Bahawalpur was the first state fully and permanently to accede to Pakistan followed by Khairpur two days later. Kalat, geographically important for its border with Persia, was the last to accede, holding out for independence until March 1948.

There can be no doubt of the importance of Bahawalpur to Pakistan, geographically, and, most vitally and immediately, for its wealth. It was the only region in the new country with a budget surplus and a successful economy, quite apart from the well-appointed Bahawalpur army and the personal wealth of the nawab. With each Supplementary Instrument of Accession after Independence, Bahawalpur was compelled to give up more state resources. Initially, the nawab supplied the empty exchequer of the new country of his own free will. The Pakistani rupee was shored up with gold deposits previously held in England, and six months of government salaries were paid by the Bahawalpur exchequer. The Bahawalpur Infantry battalions, at full strength about 11,000-strong, were merged into the

Pakistan Army, first as the Bahawalpur Regiment in 1952 and then merged with the Baluch Regiment in 1956.

State finances and the army were central to Penderel Moon and Prime Minister Gurmani's actions in Bahawalpur to restore order as quickly as possible, while the Punjab was in a state of continuing and increasing anarchy. Moon considered the military 'potentially by far the most dangerous source of anarchy', yet nothing could be done without them as escorts for trains, frontier and river patrols and protection for labour parties. Salahuddin Abbasi believes that Moon, at some stage, fell out with his grandfather. It is possible to speculate that the revenue minister's mistrust of the nawab's army, the one area of state with which he had been allowed full rein and of which he was excessively proud, may have had something to do with it, but that came later. The immediate and pressing needs were to stop violence, create better security, reduce fear and deal with the refugees flooding into India. Fear of financial breakdown and the 'symbolic significance' of the empty treasury under these extraordinary circumstances were a serious concern.

Bahawalpur, as previously discussed, had recovered from earlier financial hardship thanks to World War II. Repayment of the debt to the Government of India had nevertheless used up all surpluses, leaving the state virtually debt-free but low on immediate resources for emergencies that might include feeding thousands of destitute refugees for months. On the nawab's behalf, neither Moon nor Gurmani anticipated or wished for any assistance from the financially precarious Pakistan government that might use any such request as an excuse to 'assert the Paramountcy of the old British-Indian Government'. At this stage, Bahawalpur had only acceded in respect of the state's foreign affairs and defence.

It was essential for the state to remain financially solvent. For that purpose, the civil supplies and cooperative departments were pressed into service to collect, or buy at falling prices, all the grain stocks abandoned or sold by Hindus leaving the state. They were then able to feed thousands of refugees at low cost at the same time as settling new refugees as quickly as possible, quickly enough in fact that they could reap standing crops and resow for winter crops. By October 1947, the most immediate and dangerous issue, beyond feeding and settling a new population as quickly and economically as possible, was to help Hindu migrants, by then desperate to leave, to evacuate the state safely in the opposite direction, towards India.

Gurmani also contributed generously to the efforts to rehabilitate Muslim refugees coming from India. He sent two cheques of Rs 2,50,000 each (totalling Rs 5 lakh) as a donation from the amir of Bahawalpur to the Quaid-i-Azam Refugees Relief Fund. Gurmani was the chairman of the fund. Gurmani also helped settle 70,000 refugees from East Punjab, Bikaner and the Punjab states on lands within the state and provided them with accommodation, agricultural implements and necessary food, houses and shops in towns, and *mandis* in the state. Jinnah particularly appreciated Gurmani's services and noted that he 'worked day and night for our Muslim brethren in distress'.[8]

In June 1947, Penderel Moon found that minor disturbances in Bahawalpur had largely died down. The Hindu population had been reassured by assurances from Gurmani of his protection although, as revenue minister, Moon had felt unable to offer the same to Sikh colonists who had come to see him, and he felt they would leave in the absence of such guarantees. Through July, the state had remained calm even as the situation deteriorated elsewhere. At the beginning of August, refugees began to arrive; the first were informed by Gurmani that they had not arrived in Pakistan and had better go on to Punjab. The nawab, meanwhile, was summering as usual in England, albeit in close touch with events at home and in Delhi.

The first violent incident of Partition to impact seriously on Bahawalpur happened on 9 August 1947 when a special train, due to pass through Bahawalpur and filled with clerical staff for the new Pakistan government, was derailed by a bomb placed on the track by Sikhs. Moon writes that although a few passengers were injured and only two or three killed, as nothing compared with later atrocities, the event made an impression on Bahawalpur Muslims. For Moon himself, full realization came when he set out for a break at Simla on 15 August, his astonishing timing suggesting how extraordinarily secure Bahawalpur had felt. At Simla, he found Hindu migrants from Punjab whom he had known for years, and, for the next few days, the news got worse. On his return to Bahawalpur, he and Gurmani began to understand the new reality when they set out for Bahawalnagar where trouble had been reported.

On the way, they came across a small group of Hindu villagers who had converted to Islam, 'as it were at the point of the sword'. The pathetic spectacle of these villagers with their green rag on a stick by way of a Pakistan flag, a talisman to be invoked for the sake of their lives, was underlined by a run-in with looters, who were apprehended with the assistance of the police in the next town. Nonetheless, the ministers allowed themselves to journey on in a 'mood of complacent self-congratulation' that problems in Bahawalpur were so minor. It was only when they reached the colony town of Hasilpur that they discovered a massacre of men, women and children 'arms and legs akimbo in all sorts of attitudes and postures, some of them so life-like that one could hardly believe they were really dead'. The situation was compounded by a meeting with Brigadier Marden,[9] in command of the Bahawalpur troops. He now questioned the reliability of his men under present circumstances and reported the presence in the area of armed gangs of Pathan seasonal migrant labour, from the North-West Frontier, who had already mopped up the survivors of the Hasilpur massacre who had requested their help.

That was the beginning. Moon, Gurmani and other state officials worked non-stop, and with considerable success, to solve immediate problems in the state and mitigate against worse atrocities and the total breakdown of order. As he recorded details of the tragedy that continued to unfold, Moon conveyed a feeling of disbelief at the events he witnessed. He and Brigadier Marden were proved correct in their concerns over the possible behaviour of the Bahawalpur troops. When they were used to escort a large group of Sikhs, over 2000 strong, from Rahim Yar Khan across the desert to Jaisalmer and India, the troops first robbed their charges of all their possessions including the camels and beasts of burden supplied for the transport of women and children across the desert. Within a few miles of the border, under the pretext of a night raid on the column by a group of Hurs[10] ahead of them, the women were separated from the men, the young women distributed among the soldiers and the children and older women told to run for the border in the dark. An unknown number were shot by soldiers firing from both directions. The tragedy came to light, with the escape of many of the young women who had been carried back to Rahim Yar Khan and were given sanctuary by local inhabitants. The matter was reported to the deputy commissioner, and the commanding officer was arrested, only to be allowed to escape to Punjab a week later.

When a request was made for his extradition, Gurmani reported its absolute refusal. There were rumours of intercession on the officer's behalf by a high-ranking British officer, who had probably served with him during the war. Moon commented:

> It would have been quite natural and in keeping with current sentiment for the Punjab Government to refuse extradition.

> Despite noble professions, there was no real desire to punish those who robbed, raped and murdered the minority communities. Rather there was a disposition to punish those who tried to protect them. There were many incidents in those days, both in India and Pakistan far exceeding the story of this ill-starred expedition in horror, atrocity and the extent of the bloodshed; but I know of none that surpass it in calculated perfidy.

On 13 September, disturbances, mob looting and killing broke out in Bahawalpur city on the signal of an explosion outside the main mosque. A great number of Hindus, who had come for safety from surrounding villages and had been housed in a large Hindu school, were killed. During this time, Moon remarked:

> A complete breakdown, or rather reversal, of the ordinary moral values. To kill a Sikh had become almost a duty; to kill a Hindu was hardly a crime. To rob them was innocent pleasure, carrying no moral stigma; to refrain was a mark not of virtue but of lack of enterprise. A new scale of values had been introduced and the old one had been almost universally discarded.

With hindsight, Moon described the 'somewhat panicky decision' to evacuate the entire Hindu population of fourteen or fifteen thousand to India, initially moving them to the new jail for their safety, as right but made on the wrong premise. The casualties were some two or three hundred. He had not at that stage realized that loot was more important than lives, although at some point one would inevitably get in the way of the other. Looting was the lesser evil. Indeed, it turned out to be impossible to stop theft, in which the Bahawalpur troops were fully complicit on the orders, Moon was assured, of their commanding officer. He was that same Gilani,

Mahmood Khan Durrani's enemy, of the INA. He had been kicked out of the Bahawalpur army, but was a younger brother of the high court judge presently acting as assistant district magistrate, and Gurmani had thought his influence with the troops, at the same time as his desire to gain the good opinion of the prime minister to win reinstatement, might be useful. Brigadier Marden had been shot in the knee while endeavouring to restore order.

Ultimately, Moon points out, Bahawalpur was evacuated under circumstances 'equivalent in effect to agreements of the type often reached during wars in earlier times, whereby a city was delivered over to be sacked by the soldiery, but the lives of its inhabitants were spared'. By and large, the Hindus were saved from further slaughter, but their property became 'legitimate spoil'. The crammed trains taking refugees from Bahawalpur, unlike so many others, safely delivered their human cargo to India, under guard from the unreliable troops on whose heads had been laid a solemn responsibility to follow instructions. The dispatch took six nerve-racking days. Muslim officials complained at the belongings Hindus were allowed to carry away. 'There was a sort of idea that their property belonged really to Pakistan and so should not be taken out of it.' At the same time, displays between old friends of 'sentimental affection for the Hindus subsisted along with the desire to benefit from their plight'.

By late November, nearly all the remaining Hindus in Bahawalpur state, who had lived in the Rahim Yah Khan area, had left their villages and were staying in the towns for security. The more prosperous slipped away to migrate via Karachi to Bombay, or managed to bribe their way to a secure passage for Hindumalkot, the first station in India, in Bikaner state and only 5 or 6 miles from McLeodganj Road, the last in Bahawalpur. Some 60,000 Hindus remained and could not safely be transported by train out of the state unless special trains were provided. The nawab was still determined to keep his 'loyal Hindu subjects' and, Moon records, was already trying to persuade those who had left to return. Finally, Bahawalpuri refugees who had reached Delhi, invoked the assistance of the Government of India, and, in December, a British colonel arrived with the offer of the necessary trains. The nawab, at the time in Karachi, continued to say no and turned down the offer despite his personal train being more or less ambushed by desperate Hindu suppliants as he returned to Ahmedpur. They were sent packing by his staff. In Delhi, Mahatma Gandhi, trying to stop the flow of refugees in both directions, was petitioned again by Bahawalpuri Hindus but supported the nawab's assurance that those Hindus who remained could 'live in Bahawalpur in peace and safety and no-one would interfere with their religion'.

Under greater pressure, Gandhi, with the agreement of the nawab, sent Dr Sushila Nayyar, formerly his personal physician, with Leslie Cross of the Friends Ambulance Association, to Bahawalpur at the end of January 1948. These emissaries were convinced of the Nawab's ability to guarantee the safety of his Hindu subjects, but Moon intervened—in another instance of a direct clash with the views of the ruler, he pointed out that the nawab would go to England in April for the summer. Moon doubted the ruler's ability to safeguard the lives of his Hindu subjects in Rahim Yar Khan from those distant shores. Thereafter, Dr Nayyar and Mr Cross visited groups of Hindus, asking for a show of hands of those willing to remain in the state and finding not one in favour. The emissaries realized that most of the wealthier families by now having left by any means, those who remained were displaced from homes and places of work, and were not only fearful for their safety but had also lost the livelihoods that had for so long been so valuable to the state and valued by its ruler. When the emissaries stopped at Lahore, on their return journey to Delhi, they learnt that Mahatma Gandhi had been assassinated.

The Hindus of Rahim Yar Khan were evacuated at last, in sixteen special trains, over a number of weeks. Moon considered that the departure of the Hindus from the capital of the state was the signal that it would lose all its Hindu inhabitants and become a 'purely Muslim territory'. Like the nawab, he had thought it possible that Bahawalpur, like Sindh at that stage, might retain much of its Hindu population. At the same time, the evacuation had been carried out with massively less loss of life among Hindus and Sikhs than in the Punjab, or among Muslims in some of the princely states of East Punjab such as Patiala and Kapurthala. Throughout Punjab, Moon wrote, the 'forces of law and order proved unreliable', and the police and army in Bahawalpur behaved better than those in some other areas. The worst problem for officials was the lack of any alternative to local forces of law and order. The Government of India in other regions could draft in Gurkhas or Madrasi troops who were more or less untouched by local communal feeling. Even if Bahawalpur had applied to the Pakistan government, it was in no position to offer help, and the Pakistan Army was 'largely infected with the general contagion'. V.P. Menon described Bahawalpur as a 'paradise compared to East Punjab'. Moon assessed the overall number of deaths in the state not to have exceeded 3000. So, he wrote, 'the Nawab's good intentions towards his loyal Hindu subjects, were honourably carried into effect'.

10

PAKISTAN

Seventy years later, the tearing apart of the subcontinent in the violence of Partition appears not only as the pain-filled birth process of a new country but also the shrugging off of millennia of Indian history. That long narrative should have remained as much a part of Pakistan and the memory of its people as of India and hers. However, in India, Independence was merely the end of one more invading empire that would itself disappear, one more episode in a far longer story. In Pakistan, history ended with Partition, Pakistan Zindabad. Meanwhile, the servants of that last empire continued for the time being to busy themselves in the separate affairs of two countries. When the new finance minister arrived in his new office in Karachi, the capital of his new country, on 15 August 1947, he found nothing there except one table. The treasury was almost as bare.

Although Pakistan was owed 18.75 per cent of the current cash balances in Delhi, Rs 750 million, to be paid in two instalments, the country was in immediate debt to the tune of almost Rs 400 million and had hardly enough cash to pay the army for four months. governor general Jinnah's loan of Rs 200 million from the nizam of Hyderabad is recorded. His close relationship with the wealthy nawab of Bahawalpur yielded a further Rs 7 crore (70,000,000), funds that were more in the nature of a gift, both to the Quaid and to the new Muslim nation. All the salaries of government departments for one month were also met by Bahawalpur. Given Penderel Moon's concerns about the Bahawalpur state finances, it seems likely that much of the funding was supplied from the nawab's personal wealth, or from the confluence that had been of such concern to the British authorities in the past, where state and royal treasuries merged. For a brief period of independence, Bahawalpur was the gift that kept on giving, until it disappeared. If Jinnah was more favourably inclined towards the princes than the new regime in India, any idea of their nominally independent states surviving within Pakistan for long, in the new world after August 1947, now seems incredible. Especially so after Jinnah died in September 1948.

The states and frontier regions ministry (SAFRON) was set up in July 1948 under Jinnah himself while several experienced old-style India hands, Pakistani and British, initially became governors or commissioners in the Pakistan princely states. Yaqoob Khan Bangash described the integration of the princely states into Pakistan, pointing out that the appointment of prime ministers of states had always been a contentious issue between rulers and the political department. The British, we know, had latterly been particularly keen to have a hand on, if not a hand in, appointments in Bahawalpur, to safeguard their financial interest in the state. The Pakistan government equally wished to exercise a level of control over any state. In the case of Bahawalpur, where the army was of considerable strength, there was an additional imperative to bring such a regular force under government control. Bahawalpur also had other commodities of value to the centre. By the time the state merged fully into Pakistan, its wealth was being well spent. There was free education and healthcare, grants for university seats in Lahore and scholarships abroad, all funded by the state treasury or the nawab himself. Literacy rates were the highest in Pakistan, reputedly higher than Pakistan today, and the state bureaucracy was highly educated and well-trained. Just as Sadiq Muhammad Khan had once spotted a potential loyal servant in Kapurthala, he had an eye for talent beyond Bahawalpur and was in a position to pay highly for services. After 1954 the revenue and canal departments of West Pakistan were among those run by former Bahawalpur bureaucrats.

In October 1948, the nawab of Bahawalpur signed the Supplementary Instrument of Accession for Bahawalpur. By the end of the year there were changes in the administration in Bahawalpur as Penderel Moon moved on to take up his final post in India, in Himachal Pradesh, and Prime Minster Gurmani prepared to join the Pakistan government as a minister without portfolio. In 1949, Gurmani signed the Karachi Agreement, establishing a ceasefire after the first Indo-Pakistan war and the Line of Control between the areas of Indian and Pakistan-administered Kashmir. Lt Col. A.S.B. Shah, permanent secretary at SAFRON, was aware of the nawab's desire to have his own choice of an Englishman as his new prime minister in Bahawalpur. This would reinstitute the pre-Partition status quo of British PM and Indian revenue minister, but the Pakistan government was now in a position to insist on the appointment of their own nominee. Colonel John, later Sir John Dring, who had been chief secretary to the Government of the North-West Frontier Province (NWFP), was given the post.

The government continued to flex its muscles when Lt Col. Shah informed the nawab that control and command of the Bahawalpur army must be handed over to a government-appointed commanding officer, taking over from Brigadier Marden. Marden, by now advanced to General Marden, was appointed controller-in-general of properties by the nawab. A demand by Shah for a sanction from the

Nawab Sadiq Muhammad Khan IV

Nawab Muhammad Bahawal Khan V

Derawar Fort

Sadiqgarh Palace

The mosque at Derawar

Derawar interior, 2017

The tomb at Derawar mistakenly identified as that of one of Queen Victoria's daughters'

Sadiqgarh Palace in 2017

Muhammad Abbas Abbasi as a young boy

Nawab Sadiq Muhammad Khan IV

Nawab Muhammad Bahawal Khan V with attendants

Bahawalpur Motor Transport

1882 watercolour of the Christofle bed with female automata made for Sadiq Muhammad Khan IV

Muhammad Abbas Abbasi

Amir Muhammad Abbas Khan with Bahawalpur troops

1877 Delhi Durbar, with Viceroy Lord Lytton on the throne and Sadiq Muhammad Khan IV, aged nine, in the front row of the princes

A durbar held by Muhammad Sadiq Khan V at Gulzar Mahal; Abbas Khan sits to his right

Sadiq Muhammad Khan IV and his best-loved English wife

Sadiq Muhammad Khan V with President Ayub Khan at Bahawalpur

Sadiq Muhammad Khan IV with shikaris

Maulvi Ghulam Hussain

Sadiq Muhammad Khan V and his family before the coronation of Queen Elizabeth II in 1953

Daulat Khaana, birthplace of Sadiq Muhammad Khan V, in Bahawalpur City

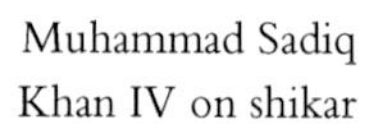

Muhammad Sadiq Khan IV on shikar

Muhammad Sadiq Khan IV wearing the diamond crown

Muhammad Abbas Abbasi with Khawaja Nazimuddin, prime minister of Pakistan (1951–53) (in the front seat of the jeep)

Sadiq Muhammad Khan V and Muhammad Abbas Abbasi with Khawaja Nazimuddin and others

Muhammad Sadiq Khan V with Muhammad Ali and Fatima Jinnah

A durbar at Gulzar Mahal

Sadiq Muhammad Khan V and Muhammad Abbas Abbasi with an unknown guest

Bahawalpur House, Delhi

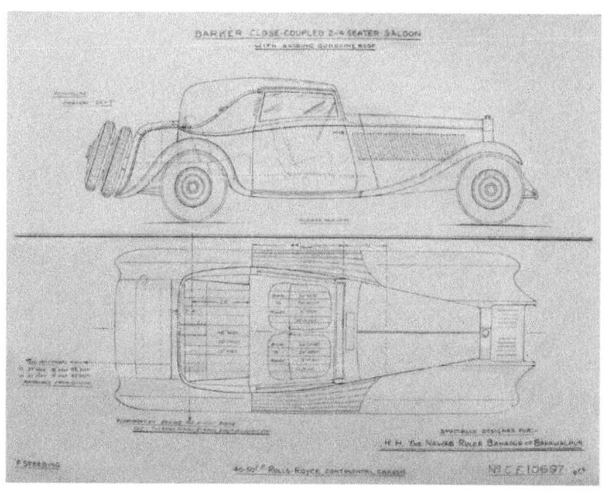

The plan for a Rolls Royce customized by Barker for Muhammad Sadiq Khan V

Amir Salahuddin Abbasi and Coco

The stand for the Bahawalpur banner at the 1877 Delhi Durbar

The Bahawalpur coat of arms

nawab of army expenses of Rs 1 crore (10 million) per annum on top of an immediate Rs 1 crore for expenses in upgrading and retraining was an extra sting in the tail. The nawab countered with a request to maintain half the Bahawalpur forces as his personal bodyguard under his direct command. Shah argued against this on grounds of the inevitable inferiority in respect of training, efficiency and resources of such a force compared with the Pakistan Army. Bangash is correct in regarding these measures as 'a clear attempt by the Government of Pakistan to resurrect the doctrine of paramountcy in an even more powerful form through the complete takeover of the states' forces' and 'the beginning of a process of ultimate integration of the whole state with Pakistan'. Shah knew exactly what he was doing, and the time between Independence and the complete integration and loss of statehood for the population and ruling family of Bahawalpur was little more than a gap between lines in the story of Pakistan over the past seventy years.[1]

Colonel Dring had a difficult time as prime minister of Bahawalpur and political agent of the Pakistan government. Bangash notes 'numerous misunderstandings' and quotes Shah remarking, in a telegram to Prime Minister Liaquat Ali Khan,

> I still fail to understand why he was so anxious to rush me through everything in one afternoon, and why, when he saw that I was going to tackle my task in my own way, he took it upon himself to present me with a fait accompli, and why he sent the ruler away on tour and himself proceeded to Karachi.

Shah was inclined to ascribe Dring's unsatisfactory behaviour towards Pakistan to latent British imperialism: 'Unfortunately he has still not reconciled himself completely to the fact that the British rule has gone and that we meant to do our work in our own way.'

Lt Col. Arthur John Dring's family had been in India since 1830. They were one of those families who were the backbone of administration in the subcontinent; his grandfather had been chief paymaster of the army. John and his wife, Deborah, appear in Charles Allen's *Plain Tales of the Raj* and he is said to be the model for Ralph Whelan in the television series *Indian Summers,* which adds a touch of greater exoticism to John Dring than was probably the reality.[2] All the same, his short memorial essay among the India Office Records points to a particularly active and interesting career in India. He was commissioner in Peshawar during the height of Red Shirt activity, and was appointed assistant commissioner in Charsadda immediately after the evacuation of his predecessor following three assassination attempts against him. He had spent two years as assistant private secretary to the viceroy, Lord Willingdon, a post where he had met everyone from Gandhi and Jinnah to the members of the Cripps Mission, and he had a particular fondness for the tribes of the NWFP. As chief secretary of NWFP, he had been extremely unimpressed by Nehru's ill-judged visit to Waziristan, the Khyber and Malakand, in 1946, to push the Congress cause at a time of high communal tension.

Dring had been in Peshawar during the misery of Partition, of which he said, 'Basically Pakistan exported riches and imported poverty.' A few months later, he was offered the post of prime minister of Bahawalpur, with instructions to convert the princely state into a democratic unit with its own ministers and assembly. Initially he found the nawab 'decidedly awkward', and resenting the loss of all his powers, but 'he gradually mellowed and accepted the change as inevitable', although 'he exuded loyalty to the old regime and voiced his antipathy to the political leaders and their parties'. Dring also noted, His Highness 'even had his own postal stamps, including air mail, printed by De La Rue', and his impressions were confirmed 'that the Princes in general were a very spoiled class'.

Early doubts aside about his position as the only white civil officer in Bahawalpur, he found a state with somewhat antiquated institutions but considerable wealth from 'the rich land irrigated by the Panjnad barrage on the Jhelum and from minor head-works under the Sutlej Colonisation Scheme'. The state public works department was particularly efficient and enterprising. It had managed to start a supplementary canal from Panjnad, to irrigate land in the south of the state, enabling Rahim Yar Khan to be established as an industrial centre. Cotton and sugar mills were set up, and Unilever built a large factory for vegetable products. Dring noted, the 'Pakistan Government lost no time in demanding a formidable annual contribution to the Central Treasury'. Shah was probably right to an extent about Dring's loyalties. Given his name still attached to the Dring Stadium in Bahawalpur, Salahuddin Abbasi believes Sir John's heart was more closely attached to the nawab and his state, if not to the older British paternalistic status quo that was both in his blood and his experience, than to the Pakistan government.[3]

Shah was determined 'to get the people of Bahawalpur behind the Government of Pakistan without any further delay' and to sideline the nawab to a purely constitutional role. The 1949 Government of Bahawalpur Act was the codification of a series of reforms since November 1948. They were first announced as the new state constitution by the nawab at celebrations for his silver jubilee at Gulzar Mahal in Baghdad-ul-Jadid, on 8 March 1949, in the presence of Prime Minister Liaquat Ali Khan and his wife who were visiting the state. They are summed up as follows:

> The State Majlis i.e. the legislature was constituted in June 1949. It had sixteen elected and nine nominated members. The Majlis

> had full power of legislation in regard to Transferred subjects i.e. agriculture, forests, etc. It could also legislate for the reserved Subjects i.e. revenue, irrigation, police etc., but such legislature was subject to veto and certification by the Prime Minister of Bahawalpur. The Majlis held two sessions during 1949–50 and passed the following bills: a) Shariat Application Bill, 1950, b) Prevention of Corruption Bill, 1950, c) Transferred Subjects Legislation Validating Bill, 1950, d) Income tax (Amendment) Bill, 1950. Bahawalpur State was allocated one seat in the Pakistan Constituent Assembly and Maulvi Fazl-e-Husain ex-Chief Judge of the State was nominated as the representative. Col. A.J. Dring was appointed as the Prime Minister of Bahawalpur State in accordance with the provisions of the Government of Bahawalpur Act, 1949. The Prime Minister was appointed by the Nawab in consultation with the Government of Pakistan. All this was stated in the new constitution of the State.

The ruler still had power to dissolve the majlis (state assembly) and appoint the prime minister, but his appointment had to be agreed by the Pakistan government. The prime minister was effectively able to overrule the majlis and enact new laws on grounds of state security or in the better interests of the state. In effect, the majlis was precisely the same toothless collection of councillors as their predecessors, the advisers to the autocratic and absolute rulers of the past, but now the ruler himself was equally gagged. Instead, the Pakistan government, through the instrument of executive powers conferred on their appointed prime minister, was in charge. Everything else was window dressing and that too would shortly be stripped away. Elections (for the majlis) in Bahawalpur in May 1949 had given the Muslim League a landslide victory, fifteen out of the sixteen seats, opening the field to popular demands for 'fully elected assemblies and 'popularly elected ministers', and smoothing the central government's path towards implementation of further reforms in 1951. In addition to reiterating the nawab's role as ruler, the four articles of the agreement limited the money the nawab could withdraw from the state treasury for personal use, required him to provide an inventory of his property to the government, and allowed the royal family to retain their titles in exchange for a government guarantee 'that the method of appointing the heir to the throne shall be in accordance of the laid down rules and traditions of the State'.

On 29 April 1951, Sadiq Muhammad Khan and Sir Khawaja Nazimuddin, governor general of Pakistan, signed a pact, the Second Supplementary Instrument of Accession, placing Bahawalpur on the same footing as other provinces. Bahawalpur's contribution towards the defence budget was replaced by net receipts of central taxes, and the government took over the responsibility and administration of the reserved subjects. Under the Government of Bahawalpur (Interim Constitution) Act of March 1952, Bahawalpur became a federal unit of Pakistan with the status of a province, administered by a forty-nine-member legislative assembly elected for a five-year term on the basis of universal suffrage. The nawab at this stage retained the power to dissolve the assembly and to veto legislation. Also, no case against the nawab could be admitted in court. With the Third Supplementary Instrument of Accession signed by the nawab on 3 March 1952, the power of the nawab, except insofar as his role and rights existed in the traditions and emotions of his subjects, came to an end.[4] He agreed

> that an experienced officer shall be appointed by me in consultation with the governor general of Pakistan, as my adviser to aid and advise me in the exercise of my powers and authority as

> the Constitutional Ruler of my State and in the discharge of my functions in respect of matters with respect to which the federal Legislature has powers to make laws for my State and in respect to which the executive authority vests in the Governor-General of Pakistan, with a view to ensuring that due effect is given within this State to the provisions of the constitution and laws of Pakistan.

It finishes by saying that should the nawab 'differ from the advice extended to me by my ministers of the Kabina or by my said adviser, I shall seek the advice of the Government of Pakistan thereon and shall accept it accordingly'.[5]

John Dring retired as prime minister of Bahawalpur in 1952, replaced for an interim period by Makhdoomzada Hasan Mahmud, and by A.R. Khan from 1953 to 1955 acting as chief minister and adviser to the nawab. In the provincial elections of 1952 in Bahawalpur, the Muslim League won thirty-five out of forty-nine seats; the Islamic parties Hizb-i-Iktalaf and Jamaat-e-Islami eleven and two seats respectively, with the remaining seat going to an independent candidate. Confirmation of Bahawalpur's provincial status within Pakistan in 1952 has been central to Salahuddin Abbasi's political life. When Bahawalpur merged with West Pakistan, at the creation of the One Unit, described below, in 1955, it merged with the status of a province, and an understanding was given to the nawab that if or when One Unit was broken, Bahawalpur would be restored as a separate province in a federal Pakistan.

The promotion and facilitation of Bahawalpur as a welfare state that had begun with Independence had not stopped, and the nawab continued as instigator or figurehead of new projects in education, health, communication and social uplift assisted by grants from the central government. He gave 2000 acres of land and funding for the construction of Sadiq Public School in Bahawalpur. The foundation stone was laid by him on 4 March 1953, and the school opened less than a year later on 18 January 1954. To quote the *Sadiqnamah*, the 'constitutional set-up in the Bahawalpur State had burst into full and fragrant bloom'. Less floridly, new democratic principles and an organized judiciary were working in support of new initiatives, whether schools, the Jamia mosque, designed with a shopping centre and commercial offices on the ground floor, or textile and flour mills, model dairies, fruit farms, soap and ghee factories, and the revival of cottage industries and handicrafts. The effects of Partition, flight and influx of populations if not without problems, had been unusually well organized from the outset and new settlers absorbed successfully into the state. Pakistan could not do without Bahawalpur until the time came when the former state's wealth had been so deeply looted in favour of upper Punjab that motorways built from Lahore to Multan have no need to stretch as far as the backwater that the former province has become.

After the assassination of Liaquat Ali Khan in October 1951, Khawaja Nazimuddin took his place as prime minister, until he was replaced by Muhammad Ali Bogra in April 1953. Bogra was, like Nazimuddin, a Bengali attempting to administer a country with two wings, East Bengal and the composite of the provinces and states of West Pakistan. East and West were divided by 1600 kilometres of Indian, essentially enemy, territory, and were disparate in almost every respect except religion. East Pakistan blamed economic woes on a central government invested and based in faraway West Pakistan, and agitation for greater autonomy for the East grew. The success of the United Front of nationalist and leftist parties against the Muslim League in East Bengal in the legislative election of 1954 resulted in a power struggle in the central government and the announcement of emergency rule in Pakistan by the governor general. This led to the announcement of a One-Unit policy framework by Prime Minister

Bogra in November 1954, in which 'there will be no Bengalis, no Punjabis, no Sindhis, no Pathans, no Balochis, no Bahawalpuris, no Khairpuris', and, 'the disappearance of these groups will strengthen the integrity of Pakistan'. The two wings of the country were intended to have relative autonomy, one from the other, and would each, as a cohesive unit, have the space and capacity to grow without the handicap of the other.

According to a 2011 'In Memoriam' in *Dawn*, 'it became expedient for the political unity of the Dominion for a merger to take place between the two States which the late ruler agreed to'. On 17 December 1954, the nawab signed the Bahawalpur Merger Agreement:

> Whereas in the best interests of the State of Bahawalpur as well as of the Dominion of Pakistan it is desirable to provide for the cession of the territories of the said State to the Dominion of Pakistan and for the merger of the same in the proposed Unit of the said Dominion to be known as West Pakistan,
>
> As from the said day the Government of the Dominion of Pakistan shall exercise all powers, authority and jurisdiction for the governance of the said State and territories in such manner and through such agency as it may think fit.
>
> This agreement abrogates all the Instruments of Accession and agreements between the governor general of Pakistan and His Highness the Ameer of Bahawalpur signed so far.

Bahawalpur state became an administrative division with three districts: Bahawalpur, Bahawalnagar and Rahim Yar Khan. The amir was given a yearly stipend of Rs 32 lakh (32,00,000). He was not an old man but it was nearly half a century since he had, in the first place almost literally, inherited the poisoned chalice of kingship, from his father. It was more than forty years since that determined little boy had caught all eyes at one of the last gigantic jamborees of the British Raj. It was all over.

In his valedictory message to the people of Bahawalpur, the amir said:

> The relations between you and my family which carried on for the last few hundred years are now going to end. I thank you for your love, affection, cooperation and loyalty, which you have provided to me for the last fifty years. I am confident that you will be loyal friends towards Pakistan. Till my death I shall be interested in your betterment and welfare. I pray to Allah that may God always bless you with his blessings. May God always take care of you and be with you and lead you towards the right path.

Sadiq Muhammad Khan continued to spend time in Bahawalpur but his life became that of a wealthy, retired and generally retiring, gentleman in Sussex and London. His eldest son Muhammad Abbas Abbasi entered the political lists against his father's will and at the request of the president, General Ayub Khan, through the complications of the Basic Democrats voting system. This was imposed by Ayub Khan to elect a National Assembly in 1960 and, again, to re-elect him as president in 1965 after his electoral win against Fatima Jinnah amid accusations of vote rigging and murder. Abbas Abbasi was always elected unopposed. His father considered this somehow more respectable than a fight with a local opponent. In wilder regions of Pakistan, tribal leaders fought on against government and each other much as they always had. In 2006, in Baluchistan, Nawab Akbar Bugti died, aged eighty, in the mouth of a mountain cave under government fire, fighting for greater autonomy for Baluchistan. Bahawalpur's recent, vicious, family and state battles have been fought in more contemporary arenas, through the judicial and democratic processes of a theoretically contemporary and civilized country.

The glitter and the glory days of his London life of the 1930s and '40s, with a suite at the Savoy and others for his courtiers and servants, the display and spending of 1937, were over for Sadiq Muhammad Khan. He may have continued to lunch at Quaglino's and to frequent Asprey of Bond Street and Garrard the Crown Jewellers in Regent Street. There, the walls of a boardroom were still hung with the designs for Bahawalpur jewels but Sadiq Muhammad Khan had become an old and sick man; his royal life had been hollowed out and he was relatively impoverished. He was suffering from diabetes and led a largely isolated life outside the circles of British society, the social rounds of the season, the sporting events and the parties and country weekends that had continued after the war. Some old habits died hard. His grandson knows he continued to make a regular order from royal florist, Moyses Stevens, for flowers and his card to be sent to the queen at Buckingham Palace, just as they had always been to the sovereign or his consort on the nawab's arrival in England. He did not shoot and was not a polo player, unlike his son, but he had been a regular visitor to Buckingham Palace in the past. Now, there was an anonymous apartment in Westminster, or his house in Sussex, with his wife, Olivia, Lady O. Sadiq Muhammad Khan, who is rumoured to have bequeathed a considerable amount of jewellery to his stepdaughter, Lady O's daughter, from an earlier marriage.

He fostered the same loyalties among those who worked for him in England as he had with General Marden in Bahawalpur and, as Penderel Moon remarked, those over whom he ruled. Salahuddin Abbasi remembers Alfred Simmons, who appears to have been his adviser and general factotum, and another Mr Simmons, Alfred's brother, who was his grandfather's tailor and came to Bahawalpur in that capacity. There was an English chauffeur and another named Smith, for his wife, and Mr and Mrs Husband, the butler and his wife. Then there were maids, in particular and fondly remembered by Salahuddin, Irish Miss Griffon, who had been his grandmother's lady's maid, and went on to look after him and his house in London, going out to stock up on groceries until she was in her nineties.

Sadiq Muhammad Khan Abbasi died in London on 24 May 1966. His body was returned to Pakistan to be carried into the desert on a gun carriage for burial at Derawar.

The last years of his life in England were remembered by Sheila Covey, the daughter of his former head gardener in Sussex, in an article in the *Graffham Parish News* in 2009:

> The Ameer started coming to England for his annual 'holiday' in the 1930s having bought a beautiful house in the outskirts of Farnham, Surrey. During the 1939-45 war, he was unable to leave his country. He handed over his house to the authorities to become a children's nursery (presumably for evacuees). He also provided a mobile canteen to serve the people in the blitz areas. At the end of the war, his house was handed back and was restored, and he continued his annual holiday in England. In 1948 Selham House came on the market. His Highness sold his house in Farnham and moved to Selham. My father, William Tilbury, was employed by the Ameer as Manager/Head Gardener and moved with him to Selham. He worked for him for 35 years in total, and, looking back, he was 'on call' 24 hours a day.
>
> While at Selham, the Ameer kept a permanent cook, butler and housemaid as well as employing additional local people when in residence. His chauffeur lived in London, where the Ameer spent 2–3 days a week. The English staff ran the household,

however personal servants were brought over from Bahawalpur each year and had their own apartment. The Ameer liked to walk through the servants' quarters and expected them to say 'Good Afternoon, Your Highness'. Unfortunately, the English servants didn't always recognise him. He was a lively character, with a love of exotic birds and animals. At Selham House he had a Macaw, parrots, doves, rare breeds of rabbits, bantams, dogs, cats, cows, and of course, his beautiful horses which he rode around his property and the woodland surrounding Selham House.

Although the house was beautifully furnished, he wanted the animals to have complete freedom—it didn't really worry him if they did any damage. One animal was a grey parrot which spoke fluently. I think it was the butler who taught it to say 'left, right, left, right, whoah', and it also called out 'Mr Tilbury' in the butler's voice. It could speak in a woman's voice too, and imitate a running tap, a telephone and the pips on the radio. He bought the cows so that he could have his own dairy produce, but Her Highness, the Begum, put on too much weight and said she didn't want so much cream, so the cows were sold. In the garden, the Ameer liked bright colours. My father always did formal bedding, and used to take over a thousand cuttings each year. He took all his own seed (except sweet peas). My father had six staff in the gardens. There was also a head kitchen gardener, a Mr Alf Sargent, who lived in Selham. The Ameer enjoyed his cars which were always silver and black and included a Rolls Royce. 'Mrs Highness', as my father called the Begum, always had a little blue Jaguar. The Ameer was also a keen philatelist, owning an extensive collection. He also had a love of toy trains, and had a magnificent layout including miniature trains from many countries.

The Ameer was a very generous man. On one occasion he came across some children playing cricket in the road near The

> Three Moles. As soon as he got back he rang Mr Simmonds, his London solicitor, and asked him to arrange for the correct cricket equipment to be sent to the children. He put on a party every year for many years for local children in the Empire Hall. They had first-class entertainers and caterers and all received lovely presents. The presents were all sent down from London. The parties started in the late 1940s and continued into the 1960s. He was a very polite man, a gentleman. Before he went back to Pakistan he always shook my father's hand and gave him a monogrammed gift. He continued to have his holidays at Selham until 1954. He then discovered his house in Farnham was on the market again, and promptly bought it and moved back, putting Selham House up for sale. Sadly for the Ameer, Selham House did not sell, so he was advised to put both properties on the market. The Farnham House sold quickly, so once again he moved back to Selham. He continued to visit every year until his death in the mid sixties.

In June 1966 Brigadier His Highness Muhammad Abbas Khan Abbasi was formally recognized by the president of the Islamic Republic of Pakistan, General Ayub Khan, as amir of Bahawalpur. He received a privy purse of Rs 16,000, tax-free, to cover all the expenses of the amir and his family including 'personal staff, bodyguard, tours, hospitality, maintenance of his residences, marriages and all family ceremonies', on condition that he 'conscientiously discharge the obligations of a citizen of Pakistan'.[6]

11

CHILDHOOD AND MEMORY

Salahuddin Abbasi's first political memory is the assassination of Prime Minister Liaquat Ali Khan on 16 October 1951. He was five. He recalls a commotion in the middle of the night at home at his parents' house, Al-Abbas, outside the walls of the palace at Dera Nawab Sahib. The house has since been inherited by more distant relations, in the division of Bahawalpur property between the competing heirs to his grandfather's estate, but the memory of his father hurrying to get ready to drive over 600 miles on bad roads to Karachi for the funeral has remained. As he recalls, his mother explained what had happened and the word assassination, heard for the first time, stuck in his mind. Conspiracy rumours still swirl about the murder of the first Pakistan prime minister in Company Bagh, Rawalpindi, just as they do about the assassination of Benazir Bhutto fifty-six years later in the same place. By then, it had been renamed Liaquat National Bagh. In an odd twist of fate, the doctor who attended Bhutto after she was shot was the son of the doctor who had attended her predecessor in 1951 under similar fatal circumstances.

Liaquat Khan was shot by Said Akbar, a former brigadier in the Afghan Army, as he began his address to a vast meeting of the Muslim League. The assassin had lived in Pakistan since 1947 and, depending on sources, was a pensioner of the pre-Partition Government of India, the British Army or the Pakistan government. The prime minister, respected by the public for his close ties to Jinnah, his belief in democracy and his personal honesty, had told his wife that he was about to make the most important speech of his life. Like Jinnah, he was a muhajir, an immigrant whose family had come from India, and, like Jinnah, he had 'compensated for the lack of a local power base in Pakistan by his moral authority based on a reputation for honesty and duty'.[1] As Roger Long notes in his recent *History of Pakistan*, Liaquat's reputation has grown over time. His death began a chaotic period in the political life of Pakistan, when former bureaucrats jockeying for power, notably, roly-poly Mushtaq Ahmed Gurmani, and Malik Ghulam Muhammad, who became governor general after Liaquat's death, 'were increasingly transformed from the state's servants to its masters'. In particular, the divisions between so-called 'Bengali' and 'Punjabi' groups in the central government exacerbated the divisions between the East and West arms of Pakistan and opened the way to the collapse of democratic government in 1958 and the advent and habit of military dictatorship.

That was all to come as Liaquat lay on the ground, shot at close range by Said Akbar, who had been sitting with his eleven-year-old son immediately in front of the dais where the prime minister had just begun to speak. Conspiracy theories continue to swirl. What about the lack of blood on Liaquat's chest if he had been shot from the front? What about the timing of the first two and then a third shot believed to have been fired at him? The immediate shooting of the suspect by a sub-inspector of police under orders from his superintendent provided a satisfactory and conveniently dead scapegoat. The suspicion, based on the prime minister's wounds, was that he had been shot in the back, and, far from being an assassin, Said Akbar, had brought out his own pistol as a protective measure after the shots had been fired. He had then been identified as the assailant and set upon by the crowd before being shot.

Whoever's hand had wielded the weapon, what was the motive for the murder? Which hidden individual, faction or country had promulgated the assassination? Theories about Said Akbar's potential motive ranged from a moment of insanity, religious or Pashtun nationalist fanaticism to anger over Liaquat's Kashmir policy and avoidance of jihad against India. Beyond him, the finger of suspicion wavers over Liaquat's political rivals. Gurmani and Muhammad were not present at the rally; why not? Others pointed at the Americans, determined to stop war breaking out between Pakistan and India as Pandit Nehru engineered Constituent Assembly elections in Indian-held Kashmir. With the Indian Army formed up along the border, there was a fear that public opinion would push the Pakistani government over the brink. Liaquat himself, the Americans believed, was angry enough not to heed their fears of a dangerous change in the balance between India, supported by Russia, Pakistan supported by the US, and the overarching and ever-present danger of a domestic, communist, threat, supported by China. There were also concerns over problems flaring up in Iran and the Middle East. Might the prime minister in any case have been turning towards Moscow at the cost of US relations and his relationship with those at home who saw the US as their best ally? Or was it simply the improbable act of a lone assassin sacrificing himself for the cause, whatever cause, in the presence of his young son?

In his autobiography, General Ayub Khan remembered the assassination and its effects on the leadership of the country.

> When I returned to Pakistan, I met several members of the new cabinet in Karachi—Prime Minister Khawaja Nazimuddin,

> Chaudhari Muhammad Ali, Mushtaq Ahmed Gurmani, and others. Not one of them mentioned Liaquat Ali Khan's name, nor did I hear a word of sympathy or regret from any of them. Governor general Ghulam Muhammad seemed equally unaware of the fact that the country had lost an eminent and capable Prime Minister through the fell act of an assassin. I wondered at how callous, cold-blooded, and selfish people could be. It seemed that every one of them had got himself promoted in one way or another. The termination of the Prime Minister's life had come as the beginning of a new career for them. It was disgusting and revolting. It may be a harsh thing to say, but I got the distinct impression that they were all feeling relieved that the only person who might have kept them under control had disappeared from the scene. The political arena was now available to them for a free-for-all. The assassination of the Prime Minister caused universal anguish. There were all kinds of wild rumours and some cabinet ministers and highly placed individuals were accused of having plotted the murder. I did not for a moment believe that any one of them was directly or indirectly involved in an assassination. I know that Begum Liaquat Ali Khan still thinks the government did not try hard enough to investigate the assassination and bring the culprits to book. I have seen the report of the expert who was called from Scotland Yard: he could find no evidence to show that the assassination was anything but the act of an individual. Had there been any complicity or involvement of any kind, I have no doubt that it would have been discovered. These things do not remain hidden.[2]

Salahuddin's view is that Liaquat, although he took enormous care to appoint ministers who were not seen to have residual familial ties to India, was an Indian agent. There is family history here. Salahuddin's maternal great-uncle, General Muhammad Akbar Khan, not, he points out, the General Akbar who was brigadier in charge in Kashmir during the 1947 Indo-Pakistan War, had been very close to Jinnah. He had advised the Quaid, to no avail, that his trust in Liaquat was misplaced and that his prime minister was working against him. After Jinnah's death, whether because Liaquat wanted him where he could see him or because he was an overwhelmingly powerful personality, Liaquat invited Akbar Khan to become first Pakistani chief of the Pakistan Army after General Sir Douglas Gracey and was refused. The young Akbar Khan had run away to join the British Army during World War I, lying about his age, and had been taken prisoner by the Turks in Mesopotamia. He escaped, was recaptured and escaped again, this time, from all accounts, without his clothes, which had been confiscated to stop any such further attempt. He somehow reached Britain, and from there, home to India.

After the war, he was offered land to cultivate, as a traditional reward for his bravery, but turned it down, determined instead to do whatever it took to gain a commission in the British Army. He succeeded at last, ending up as a major general at the end of World War II. When Liaquat followed up his request for the general's service with an order vested in his power as Governor-General, General Akbar is reported to have told him: 'You can't order me, only King George VI can order me. I am a British officer and you have no authority over me. If you get His Majesty to deliver the order, then I will serve.' Instead, Liaquat passed the mantle successfully to Akbar Khan's younger brother, General Iftikhar Khan. He was killed before he could take up his appointment, probably assassinated, with his wife and other high-ranking army officers. when their flight from Lahore, after an important meeting, crashed near Karachi, leaving the way clear for Ayub Khan to become commander-in-chief in 1951.

The new C-in-C was well known to General Akbar. His son, Khaled, told Salahuddin of an episode when Ayub, a known philanderer throughout his career, had begged the old general for help. He was in danger of court martial for an affair with an Englishwoman. The matter had been dealt with and the commander-in-chief had continued to consult Akbar Khan, flying to Karachi to ask his advice several times before and during the Indo-Pakistan War of 1965. In a final postscript to General Akbar's own war with long-dead Liaquat, when Zia ul-Haq became commander-in-chief under Zulfikar Ali Bhutto, he sent army intelligence agents into the old man's house under the false pretence of paying their respects to an honoured military commander. They removed all his files relating to Liaquat Ali Khan. In other hands and other times, they might have brought the truth of hidden loyalties and that first assassination of a leader of Pakistan out of the shadows. Unexpectedly, General Akbar was also a novelist. Salahuddin remembers his mother correcting his poor English in books written under the pseudonym, 'Rangroot' meaning recruit or rookie.

Whatever the truth of Liaquat Ali Khan's death, it was the beginning of the end of the dream of a parliamentary democracy based on a Western model. Even as the centre ate away Bahawalpur's sovereignty, power was passing from the politicians, first to the bureaucracy and then, as provincial politics added to national instability, into the hands of the military, starting with a two-month taster period of martial law in Lahore during anti-Ahmadi riots in 1953, and supported by a bureaucratic oligarchy. For Salahuddin, politics, the backdrop against which both his and his father's life have been played, had not yet obtruded beyond that one remembered bloody episode. By that time, more terrible events had already dramatically changed the script for India's princes and encarmined the South Asian stage.

The panther, gifted to Salahuddin at his birth by the maharaja of Travancore, or maybe the Francophile Sikh maharaja of Kapurthala, and banished to alternative captivity after eating his mother's cat, was part of a different existence that had faded during his childhood and adolescence. His grandfather was close to Kapurthala and visited often. He had employed one of his favourite servants from the Kapurthala court, a man whose main job, so far as Salahuddin remembers, was to buy and send fresh fish from Karachi by train to the palace in Bahawalpur when his grandfather was in residence. Privilege and respect remained part of Salahuddin's childhood, but changes in Bahawalpur were reflected in reductions in the trappings of royalty, if not yet of greatly reduced financial circumstances. Indian properties like Bahawalpur House in Delhi were gone, and also Al-Hilal in Palampur, with its glass roof, where he had been born and where most of the hill station belonged to his grandfather. There were at least ten other houses built for family and courtiers after travel to England became impossible during the war. There were still English nannies, but the monogrammed perambulators that Salahuddin thinks were part of his father's babyhood were a thing of the past. His grandfather was both a distant figure, to whom proper greeting and respect must be given, and the man who would pick up his young grandsons, Salahuddin and his brother Falahuddin, even as they bent to touch his feet. Salahuddin just about remembers the pomp and ceremony of Sadiq Muhammad Khan's durbar, with all the durbaris in uniform with swords. Some of the sword blades still lie around in the residual rubble of Bahawalpur stores, all made in Britain, mainly by Wilkinson.

Of his nannies and their regime, aside from the difficult question of sago for breakfast and everything else well boiled, he remembers his favourite, Nanny Coleman. She was probably in her early thirties and wore a white skirt and blouse with some sort of half-recalled respectable head covering. Phyllis Coleman's piles of pictorial magazines, a constant part of the luggage carried between Karachi and Bahawalpur, introduced her charges to images of British royalty, particularly at the 1953 Coronation and, most memorably, of the queen in the famous Annigoni portrait. Beyond such English curiosities there was a wealth of toys from the British Toy House in either Victoria Road or Elphinstone Street, the main Karachi shopping streets. In the summer holidays, there were twice-weekly trips to the beach with those maternal aunts closest to Salahuddin in age. Deemed too young to travel abroad with their father, they were looked after by Salahuddin's parents in his absence. At some point, when he joined the aunts at St Patrick's convent school in Karachi, which was also attended by the future general Musharraf, the nannies disappeared. He thinks his maternal grandmother considered herself better able to cope with Falahuddin's severe asthma. Salahuddin never saw Phyllis Coleman again but he believes she may have remained in the melting pot of Karachi where she had a sweetheart of 'dubious birth', Greek or Albanian, who was a mechanic at the General Motors plant. Karachi maintained its richly mixed population for years after Independence, but Nanny Coleman vanished entirely into its labyrinth.

Other odd memories of childhood remain, of scraps of adult conversations overheard; what, for instance, should be done about Lord Linlithgow when he visited as viceroy? He was too tall to fit any of the palace beds and one had to be brought especially from England. There was the memory of his grandfather, Sadiq Muhammad Khan, challenging a British sports car enthusiast to a race and then realizing he did not have a suitable car to drive on roads that were being specially made for the competition. His agents trawled the country for a sports car, eventually buying a Mercedes previously ordered by the nawab of Bhopal for tiger shooting, until he changed his mind or had run out of funds. Sadiq Muhammad Khan won his race in this unlikely shooting vehicle, which had an alarming propensity to catch fire, and which was later rebuilt by the nawab's favourite British coachbuilders, Barkers. After the nawab attended the coronation of George VI in 1937, the car returned to India as part of a large shipment, which was the cause of considerable trouble with the British authorities due to a sensational article in the *Sunday Express*.

Sadiq Muhammad Khan had already struck the rock of obdurate officialdom with regard to his spending in England. In 1935, in spite of his written assurances to the Government of India that he would not incur further debts, he was believed to have entered into agreement with the Army & Navy Stores and the Goldsmiths & Silversmiths Company for new credit. The two businesses were warned off by the government, but too late to avoid the execution of a fresh order to the Goldsmiths & Silversmiths for 'presumed re-setting of stones' at a cost of £7000.[3] In 1937, the *Express* reported, 'All the Indian princes in London have done a great deal of shopping but the Nawab has surpassed them all.' It is quite surprising, even at sterling values of the time, that his reported 50 tons of luggage, including 100 cases and ten crates, were quoted only to have cost £30,000, especially when additions included 'a limousine with gold fittings', gold-plated wireless sets, grand pianos, a large amount of furniture, uniforms for servants and clothes for himself valued at hundreds of pounds. That is not to mention the collapsible boat which for some reason particularly offended the authorities. Salahuddin says that £30,000 was pocket money compared with levels of expenditure in the brief years of Bahawalpur's independence, but for that short part of his life, the nawab of Bahawalpur was, at last, his own master.

The 1937 correspondence between a somewhat mendacious nawab and the British questioning his version of events has its entertaining moments. An outraged letter based on events as reported by the *Sunday Express*, and a report collating the grievances of recent years over spending by His Highness in the light of the Sutlej Valley Project debt, apostrophized him as, 'of a nature that can most suitably be described as devious'. Following this, a letter to the nawab from the resident to the Punjab states inquired whether

'Your Highness is quite correct in saying that the only motor-car brought out with you was an old "Mercedes"?'

> In the *Country Life*, dated 24th July 1937—a most reputable publication, by the way—there appeared a photograph of a new Rolls Royce which you had bought from Messrs Barker and Hooper. Somewhat expensive details were touched on in the letter press about this car, and, as it has cost in London probably well over £3,000 it would not have been possible for the car to be delivered in Bahawalpur for less than Rs 50,000. No doubt Your Highness has overlooked this item.

Salahuddin Abbasi, and his son Bahawal, share Sadiq Muhammad Khan's passion for motor vehicles. Nowadays, Salahuddin uses a beautifully preserved Jaguar or a Mercedes, both with the diplomatic plates still permitted to the family by a grudging Government of Pakistan. Of the old treasury of motor vehicles, one or two ancient American Dodges or Cadillacs remain in the coach houses at Sadiqgarh. The rest have gone, lost, stolen or sold; their proceeds shared under sharia law between numerous family claimants to Sadiq Muhammad Khan's estate. The last nawab may not have bought Rolls by the half-dozen like the profligate young ruler of Bharatpur. Darbhanga had thirty, and the story of another princely car buyer is well known: spoken to dismissively by a Rolls-Royce salesman, he bought the entire stock of cars in the showroom and used them as dustcarts in his state. The story was probably not about Bahawalpur, although it might have been: there is a photograph of lined-up Rolls-Royces that Salahuddin is sure were used for rubbish collection. The maharaja of Patiala had forty-four Rolls-Royces to transport his numerous wives, and Salahuddin well remembers the complications of travel in the covered purdah cars used by his grandmother. Remaining in strict purdah, she barely went outside Bahawalpur and never outside Pakistan.

Today, in deeply conservative Bahawalpur, Moniba Abbasi and her daughter Aneeza are, to their irritation, still required to respect tradition and travel through the confines of the former state with screens over the closed windows of the cars and their heads suitably covered. Bahawalpur has also been veiled from public interest behind the Pakistan border. The state is unnamed in a recent documentary on Rolls-Royce in India and undocumented in any recent publication on Indian royal cars but, of the 840 Rolls-Royces imported into India between 1908 and Independence, Sadiq Muhammad Khan had his fair share. They were lent, as was often the case with princely vehicles, to add grandeur to the image of British officials who could certainly not afford such luxury themselves. There are photographs of viceroys and high officialdom arriving on quasi-royal tours at palaces in Bahawalpur and throughout the princely states. The abhorred extravagance of the illustrious but humbled rulers was able to support the dignity of the paramount power.

Jinnah was also loaned a Bahawalpur Rolls-Royce by Sadiq Muhammad Khan. Whether or not his Rolls-Royces were used as dustcarts, his cars were practical machines as much as royal ornaments. There is a photograph of his London Rolls after hideous modifications to heighten the roof so that he could comfortably wear his top hat to drive to Royal Ascot. Later, there were cheaper cars, half a dozen Fords for the price of a single Rolls. Daimlers were a Bahawalpur favourite as were the huge Americans, those Dodges and Cadillacs. When Salahuddin went to St Patrick's school, he and his young aunts piled into a small Renault for the school run. He wonders now how they all fitted, with children sitting in layers on each other's laps for the twice-daily journey through the near-traffic-free, peaceful streets of Karachi in the 1950s.

12

PUBLIC LIVES

By the time Salahuddin Abbasi moved on from St Patrick's to Aitchison College, Lahore, in 1959, Field Marshal Ayub Khan had become president of Pakistan. In 1960, Muhammad Abbas Khan, Salahuddin's father, became a member of Parliament after the field marshal prevailed upon Sadiq Muhammad Khan for permission to enlist his son. According to Salahuddin, Ayub was in awe of Sadiq Muhammad Khan's standing and experience, but the feeling was not necessarily reciprocated in spite of the former ruler's abiding love of and respect for the army. After Ayub had cleaned his nails in front of him on an occasion when both men were travelling to England, Sadiq Muhammad Khan refused to see the general for six months. On regular visits to England, the field marshal generally stayed or dined at the former nawab's house in Surrey, and, Salahuddin says, was in the habit of hinting at gifts he would like to receive. It sounds like the stories of Queen Mary, although her kleptomania never reached the conspicuity of the glass-roofed Daimler eventually handed over to General Ayub by his host.

Abbas Khan, young, tall and smiling, in photographs with his father at public events, and, in full dress uniform in formal portraits, sadder in later images of dinners and entertainments at Sadiqgarh Palace as an older man, was an icon of former princely style pushed unwillingly on to the public stage to add gloss to the newest regime. He remains, thirty years after his death, a shadowy, private figure. Salahuddin's description of his father does not greatly illuminate the image of a good man living in difficult times who was pushed and pulled by those who then held power. Like other former princes, he was forced to become an ornament to be used or discarded on a whim by the rulers of their countries. Overshadowed by his own father, whose power grew in his lifetime until it was lost altogether, he was, according to his daughter-in-law, Moniba, a 'beautiful human being who had a special relationship with everyone around him' and of whom she has nothing but fond memories.

He was born and lived in difficult times for an honourable man, the favourite and eldest son and the bridge between his siblings and their father in his lifetime; after Sadiq Muhammad Khan's death, they fought their brother tooth and nail for their slice of his inheritance. After Abbas Khan's own early death, due to diabetes like his father, the battle continued with his sons, Salahuddin and Falahuddin, as they tried to salvage the Bahawalpur heritage. Salahuddin, perhaps a more natural fighter than his father, has taken on both his wider family and the government for his own, and his son Bahawal's, rights and inheritance, and for restitution for the people of Bahawalpur. Looting of family property by the government and military has been exacerbated by public family rows over ownership. To the distant viewer, the family quarrel is a microcosm of Pakistan where power has so often been grabbed by the strongest in the face of the indecision and quarrels over detail that divide their more liberal opposition. In the early days after Sadiq Muhammad's death, there was plenty of Bahawalpur loot to be taken: gold and silver howdahs, massive sets of plate and cutlery, even the pillars of durbar tents were encased in silver or gold, their cloth shot through with pure gold thread. That was just the beginning.

Brigadier H.H. Jalalat ul-Mulk, Rukn ud-Daula, Saif ud-Daula, Hafiz ul-Mulk, Mukhlis ud-Daula wa Muin ud-Daula, Nawab Muhammad Abbas Khan Abbasi Bahadur Al-Haj, Nusrat Jung, amir of the God-gifted kingdom of Bahawalpur may have been weighed down by titles he retained until they were finally abolished in 1972. Only the religious title amir remained, recognized by the government and legally and formally inherited by his son, Salahuddin. Abbas Khan was a gentle soul, albeit a sportsman, a good polo player and keen shot, the perfect sporting gentleman whose instincts would have met with the approval of the British tutors of earlier generations. His reputation was confirmed by his honourable military service in World War II. He was also deputy chief commissioner of the Boy Scouts, leading the Pakistani delegation to the 1957 jamboree at Sutton Coldfield.

The nawabs' *shikargarh*, hunting ground, in the Cholistan Desert remained extant into the 1970s, extending to a reserve with a 100-mile perimeter round Derawar Fort. As a boy, Salahuddin shot doves, a taste of free meat for his servants to take home, and went on shooting trips with his father, shooting deer from the driving seat of a jeep while steering with his thighs. Salahuddin never much enjoyed shooting himself and was put off altogether when he watched a deer he had shot have its throat cut to make it halal. The last time he remembers holding a gun with intent to kill was in 1962. All the same, he deeply regrets the loss or theft of the collection of 500 or so antique pistols and sporting guns belonging to his forefathers. They included innumerable pairs of Holland & Holland shotguns from London held in the armoury at Sadiqgarh Palace and stolen after the palace was sealed under Zia ul-Haq pending court cases over inheritance. It is surprising perhaps that Z.A. Bhutto, with his own notable private collection of guns and acquisitive zeal, did not get there first.

Salahuddin's early memories of home and childhood are, in the main, the hazy recollections of those lucky enough to have had happy childhoods, only occasionally punctured or highlighted by a major family or national event. It was their grandfather, Sadiq Muhammad Khan, whom he and his brother feared, respect for the nawab drummed into them from babyhood. Their grandfather metaphorically held a big stick with which he instilled that same respect and fear in all, except the colonial authorities of his youth. Years after his death, Salahuddin and his brother, Falahuddin, found duplicates of their regular report cards sent secretly by Aitchison College directly to their grandfather so that he could monitor their progress. Although Salahuddin says school was sometimes like imprisonment, it sounds as if the two boys passed muster. They may not have travelled to school by elephant from Bahawalpur House like their great-great-grandfather, but they were still princes. They had their own private room with bathroom and two servants in adjacent accommodation. They were close enough to the swimming pool to sneak out for a cooling swim in the hot weather, and there were Saturday afternoon bicycle excursions to the cinema in Lahore. They enjoyed themselves, but it sounds as if they were also hard workers who continued their educations at London University and Cornell, and who had never been required to answer for their academic records to their demanding grandfather.

Abbas Khan was close to his children and an indulgent father. A genuine family man, he was deeply in love with his wife, Shamsa Begum, whom he showered with jewellery, which, according to her son, was against her own inclinations. Unusually for a traditional family, even in the second half of the twentieth century, when women might still remain between *chaadar* and *chardiwari,*[1]

Shamsa Begum travelled everywhere with her husband. Her highly educated, modern and emancipated younger sister, Suraiya Aslam, remembers the scene when she came as a bride to her parents-in-law's traditional village near Attock on the borders of the Punjab and NWFP in the 1960s. Collected by car from the train with her new husband, she was carried from the edge of the village into the compound of the house in a covered *dooly* or litter. Once inside, she was shown her rooms in the joint family house by her mother-in-law, who presented her with a burka to be worn at all times outside the house. She roars with laughter, telling the story at the distance of half a century, but at the time, she says, she was outraged and hurled the garment into the corner of the room, flatly refusing to wear it. Eventually she negotiated a modus operandi with her father-in-law that did not involve the burka. It is an entirely believable story of the character she remains today, a charming and determined behind-the-scenes facilitator of honesty, optimism and the female voice in Pakistan politics.

All the same, times and characters had changed, neither sister had to make space for other wives and, Salahuddin says, thank God nobody tried to make his mother wear a burka. On the contrary, she was absolutely free in Karachi, although in Bahawalpur her car was almost completely covered. Shamsa Begum is in evidence in all the photographs of her husband. The kind and hospitable amir played generous host to rows of dignitaries, often imposed upon him by those forces determined to divert or subjugate the mystique of former princely families for their own end. He had grown up the dutiful son of one strong man, later to be used by others whom he had little power to resist. On the contrary, it appeared imperative to work with and for the leaders of his country if he was to save what he could of the Bahawalpur heritage and ultimately to redeem the promise of provincial status for the former state. Like his son,

Salahuddin, and most of the older generation in Pakistan today, he admired President Ayub Khan, his sponsor into national politics. In their case there is particular personal regard for the only Pakistani leader who, whatever his failings, formulated a plan whereby all claimants to the Bahawalpur inheritance would be satisfied in the best interests of the family and preservation of the state heritage for the future.

The chaotic democracy between 1947 and 1958 in Pakistan has been described by Professor Roger Long as 'procedural' rather than 'social'. The former amounting to little more than the 'holding of regular ballots while the latter implies a participatory element in the exercise of power and the removal of social inequalities'.[2] Regardless of universal franchise, the characteristics of social democracy were absent in a country where the status quo remained as it had always been, with local power held by landowning elites and bureaucrats turned politicians protecting group interests from the centre. Field Marshal Ayub Khan justified his coup in 1958 on grounds of the breakdown of law and order. The khan of Kalat had revolted in a late, and swiftly suppressed, bid for autonomy that stirred the rest of Baluchistan into rebellion; there was a crime wave in Karachi; smuggling and black marketeering increased; prices rose; foreign exchange reserves shrank and everyday commodities became scarce; the economy was failing. Politicians at the centre blew with the wind; corruption, nepotism and jobbery were rampant, and the country was in danger of total collapse.

The army under Commander-in-Chief Ayub Khan took over on 7 October 1958, with Iskander Mirza as president. Martial law was implemented, according to its architect, as 'a reformatory law to rehabilitate the country on sound lines'.[3] Ayub Khan was named administrator until he dismissed President Iskander Mirza three weeks later and took on the double role. Mirza, great-grandson of

Mir Jafar, nawab of Bengal, had been a regular visitor to Bahawalpur for Sadiq Muhammad Khan's shooting parties and was close to the Abbasi family. After his dismissal, he was exiled to England on little more than his military pension and was supported, among others, by Sadiq Muhammad Khan who offered him use of his own property in Whitehall. When President Ayub commented on this philanthropic gesture, Sadiq Muhammad Khan is reported to have told him, 'Whenever you are thrown out, you are also welcome to my hospitality.'

Ayub Khan was seen as the builder of the nation, the promoter of progress, business and modernization, ready to push Pakistan into the world and open the doors of the country to outside influence and investment. In London, the queen's older courtiers remember him well as the commanding figure and smiling face of the young Pakistan. Later leaders seldom stood out one from the next. The historian F.S. Aijazuddin, in an article on the seventieth anniversary of Independence,[4] described Ayub Khan as the 'Potohari Bonaparte', for the extraordinarily 'steep trajectory' and speed of his climb to power. Aijazuddin had no intention of garlanding this hefty Napoleon with a laurel wreath but Ayub Khan did have some of the aura of those convinced they are born to rule. That conviction was most certainly inherent in the make-up of Ayub's nemesis and successor Z.A. Bhutto. Like other leaders, before and since, Bhutto's hero was the first emperor of the French. In the late 1950s and early 1960s, with a shattering world war, and the civilian upheavals that followed it, close in memory, the truth was, for good or ill, that people trusted a proper military leader to do the right thing for his country.

All this was exemplified in the founding of a beautifully planned new capital city, Islamabad, adjacent to army HQ in Rawalpindi and not far from President Ayub's home village. That is the glossed history of a president who, regardless of failures or successes, did provide something close to a settled period in his country's history, during the 'Decade of Development' from 1958–69. The alternative view is one of good intentions, badly implemented. Ayub's leadership ended in an avalanche of protest and violence and opened the door for worse to come. If he personified the more benign face of military dictatorship, he created a precedent in Pakistan where army takeover has often been greeted with an initial sigh of relief in the aftermath of sheer havoc, seldom to the country's longer-term advantage. It is perhaps not surprising, in that first case, that a leader whose epitaph might reasonably have been *après moi le déluge* should be so venerated in memories shadowed by what came after.

Ayub Khan's good intentions are apparent from his collection of speeches and articles published as *Pakistan Perspective*[5] and smartly packaged with other laudatory publications from the information departments of various Pakistan embassies abroad. He became a major player on the international stage; Robert McNamara, president of the World Bank, proclaimed Pakistan 'one of the greatest successes of development in the World'. Ayub Khan's critics point to growth based on foreign aid and increased concentration of new wealth in the hands of the few with no effect on the many who were touched only by the presidential rhetoric. The effects of land reforms in 1959 were seen as ineffective when landowners transferred excessive landholdings no further than to family members. Landowners were courted by Ayub Khan to recreate a relationship of co-dependency through the Basic Democracy System, first used in elections in 1960 to endorse and legitimize the president.[6] The relationship of dependency with a powerful bureaucracy likewise maintained. In his farewell to his ministers, Ayub admitted, 'Quite frankly I have failed' but, 'if nothing else, I have held this country together for ten years. It was like keeping frogs in a basket.'[7]

In Bahawalpur, Sadiq Muhammad Khan took a philanthropic approach to land reform initiatives. In the spirit of Bahawalpur's welfare state, he gave most of his better agricultural land to the newly formed Sadiq Muhammad Khan Hamas Trust—Hamas meaning thrift. Trustees included the commissioner of Bahawalpur and were otherwise short-term local appointees. The beneficiaries were the Sadiq Public School; the Jamia Abbasia University; the Shahi Masjid, a building with an exterior of surpassing beauty; the orphanage founded by the family; and the family tombs at Derawar whose upkeep was funded by the trust. Later, under Z.A. Bhutto, the trust was systematically looted through the rejuvenated Auqaf or religious affairs department. As Bhutto 'oscillated between socialist developmentalist rhetoric and Islamic symbolism',[8] tracts of property from family trusts were transferred to the pirs and religious leaders he courted and, in the guise of land for the cultivators, to his own supporters and cronies. The Jamia Abbasia was renamed Jamia Islamia.

The definition and laws for waqf, or religious property and trusts, were clarified under the Punjab Waqf Properties Ordinance of 1979, ten days after Bhutto's execution. The definition of waqf property is 'property of any kind permanently dedicated by a person professing Islam for any purpose recognised by Islam as religious, pious or charitable, but does not include property under which benefit is for the time being claimed for himself by the person by whom the waqf was created or by any member of his family or descendants'.[9] The ordinance quotes the Mussalman Validating Act of 1913 stating that no one has any right over a waqf nor can it be invalidated until 'after the extinction of the family, children or descendants of the person creating the wakf'. Simply, charity starts at home. Sadiq Muhammad's intentions in setting up his trust were, at that stage of his life, highly unlikely to have been other than religious and charitable. Others may have seen charitable trusts as a loophole to mitigate the effects of land reforms. Regardless of motive, under the Islamic law appropriated by Bhutto for his own ends, nobody else had any right to any part of a trust then nominally waqf until such time as the family chose. The rhetoric of land reform in Pakistan has rarely transformed into better provision for the poor. Rather, it has been another means for the powerful to take what they want: Salahuddin recalls Nawab Qizilbash, a leader of the Shia community who was chief minister of West Pakistan for a few months during 1958, and later ambassador to France. Qizilbash family lands had been granted by the British, for whom they had once provided troops, and encompassed a large area of Lahore. They too were confiscated to be divided among the cultivators and probably, like so much Abbasi property, ended up as part of the vast estate of the Pakistan Army.

In the early 1990s, after Abbas Khan's death in 1988, Salahuddin proposed the institution of a new trust to preserve the three remarkable buildings that had come to epitomize the rule of the Abbasi nawabs and were the most recognizable images of Bahawalpur: Derawar Fort, and the palaces of Noor Mahal and Sadiqgarh. He envisaged Sadiqgarh as the repository of Abbasi family history for posterity, and Noor Mahal of Bahawalpuri and Saraiki culture, a centre for regional language, culture and craft. It was a last-ditch practical solution to end family fallout and battles over property. The treaties between Bahawalpur state and Pakistan had already indicated acceptance of Sadiq Muhammad's distribution of property to his wider family; the rest to be passed in perpetuity to his son and heir and to succeeding generations through the direct line. As the family fought during Abbas Khan's lifetime, the palaces and properties of the nawabs were sealed by the Bhutto government pending a settlement. The imposition of sharia law by Zia ul-Haq in

1982 as part of his Islamization of Pakistan was used by claimants in support of actions against Abbas Khan, judged in their favour when he refused to bribe the court for a favourable judgment.

Meanwhile, the army had expanded massively in Bahawalpur as fears grew of an Indian invasion across Cholistan and the Great Indian Desert. Abbas Khan's attachment to the military he had served encouraged him to strike a verbal agreement with the army for a temporary three-month use of two-thirds of Noor Mahal while a permanent officer's mess was constructed in the cantonment. At that stage the palace remained under some level of family control; Salahuddin was able to use it as his HQ during elections in 1976. The official story of Noor Mahal's continued ownership by the military today is clearly, if mendaciously, stated in an ill-phrased framed notice inside the entrance to the soaring durbar hall, now lit by the plain-glass of the demilune window high overhead: 'In 1956, when Bahawalpur State was merged into Pakistan, the building was taken over by Auqaf department. The palace was leased to Army in 1971 who later acquired it in 1997 for a sum of 119 million.' No such money has ever changed hands. In 2001, after a variety of other uses, the palace was confirmed as the officers' club and mess for the Bahawalpur garrison. At the same time, it was declared a protected monument by the department of archaeology. Most of its original artefacts have long since gone to adorn the houses of a succession of army generals. Part of the army's business model of confiscation and reward.

These events, however, were hidden in future darkness during Ayub Khan's conservative but religiously liberal leadership. If Western social scientists saw the system he created in Pakistan as a model of development,[10] his efforts to keep the frogs in the basket had long since made him fall back on the status quo of power holders and brokers. His daughter married the last wali *ahad*, Aurangzeb, heir to the remarkable Jehan Zeb, wali of Swat. In the late 1980s, one of Aurangzeb's younger brothers, a second lieutenant in the Pakistan Army, died under mysterious circumstances after an extraordinary meeting with Salahuddin at his house when he begged Salahuddin to be a witness to his own anticipated murder by his family. At the time, Salahuddin, who did not know him, thought the story unbelievable; the man was after all an army officer. A few weeks later he was dead. Another brother who became minister of education for NWFP was killed by a roadside bomb in 2007. Marriage alliances aside, President Ayub's power in West Pakistan was vested in the governor, Amir Mohammed Khan, the nawab of Kalabagh, the embodiment of feudal tradition and a man of extreme, almost obsessive, rectitude in public office and loyalty to Ayub Khan, but notorious for his brutality.

Salahuddin describes the Kalabagh family as 'very overbearing people', of the Awan tribe from the northern Punjab, close to Nowshera and the tribal areas. They claim descent from Qutb Shahi of Ghazni and through him from Ali, son-in-law of the Prophet. Salahuddin was told the following story by the well-known international artist and poet, Raja Changez Sultan, about his father who had fallen foul of the ruthless nawab over the murder of a peasant. The Kalabagh clan had been trying to suppress the story when Raja reported to the deputy commissioner what had happened and was summoned by the nawab and asked to change his story. When he refused, Nawab Kalabagh told him that he was on the way to a position of great power and threatened him with the loss of all the Raja land. The nawab had successfully positioned himself, with major donations to the Muslim League in 1940, when the Pakistan Resolution was passed. He had entertained future leaders of the country, such as Ayub Khan and Iskander Mirza, on hunting grounds that once extended to over 100 square miles. In 1959,

Kalabagh became chairman of the Pakistan Industrial Development Corporation, and in 1960 was appointed governor of West Pakistan by President Ayub. When the capital was moved from Karachi to Islamabad, most of the level land lying in the shade of the mountains designated for the new city was owned by the Raja family. The governor ensured that it was systematically taken from them without compensation until, eventually, repeated representations to the government extracted a face-saving Re 1 per revenue unit. Sometimes it does not pay to fight the system, and in Pakistan there have rarely been rewards for standing against it. In Pakistan, second sight is the only insurance against future payback. Nawab Kalabagh was murdered in 1967 by one of his own sons.[11]

If Salahuddin Abbasi is not blind to President Ayub's failings, the field marshal was a relatively safe pair of hands in comparison with anything that came later. Due to his relationship with Abbas Khan and his respect for Sadiq Muhammad Khan, a supporter of the army and the former ruler of a state with institutions that were, at the time of integration, a beacon of progress to the rest of West Pakistan, Ayub Khan did not interfere in Abbasi affairs. At the same time, the Indus Water Treaty, signed by Indian prime minister Jawaharlal Nehru and President Ayub in 1960, not only undid most of the eventual good effects of the contentious Sutlej Valley Project but destroyed other canal systems that had been in use for 100 years. Under the Indus agreement, Punjab's three eastern rivers, the Ravi, Beas and Sutlej, went to India while the western Chenab and Jhelum were under Pakistani control. In some ways remarkable for surviving three Indo-Pakistan wars, the Permanent Indus Commission has hardly presided over fair shares. Since all the rivers flow from their source first through India, India has always held the better hand; Pakistan, not least due to the apathy of its own successive governments, has come off considerably the worse.

As for Bahawalpur, where Alexander Burnes punted upriver with Ranjit Singh's horses, nobody seems to have noticed or cared that the Sutlej was the lifeblood of the Cholistan region. It was the beginning of the marginalization of the lower in favour of the political power base of the upper Punjab. Now the Sutlej Valley canals are filled with sand, the bridges are ruinous and water scarce to non-existent in the dust-dry desert, where animals and people wait for rare rains to fill empty ponds. Underground aquifers have been depleted and are severely contaminated, and later-planned canal projects have never been implemented as successive Pakistan governments have, almost literally, buried their heads in the sand. The 300 kilometres of the Sutlej River belt are habitually barren and dry. Conversely, in years of heavy monsoons, careless water management in India and poor infrastructure in Pakistan have resulted in severe flooding. The Sutlej waters, when they run, are so polluted with industrial waste that they are deemed highly unfit for drinking drinking. Impurities have seeped into the banks, compounding contamination of underground supplies, and deformities have been reported in babies among populations with no other water supply. On the other side of the Cholistan Desert, in Rajasthan, India, the desert is metamorphosing into fertile land; prosperity is illustrated by the brick houses in villages where there was once only mud and straw. Tour operators are hard-pressed to find a sand dune for camel-mounted clients to watch the sunset, and some owe more to bulldozers than nature. The contrast cannot be laid wholly at India's door. The Pakistan government and the military does little if anything for those poor parts of the country with no political influence, only snatching at the remaining shreds of past wealth and leaving deprivation behind.

Altaf Gauhar, formerly information secretary and speech-writer to President Ayub, wrote of the end of the presidency in his biography *Ayub Khan: Pakistan's First Military Ruler*: 'After that

Ayub lay back like Gulliver, all tied and laced up, at the mercy of the Lilliputians.'[12] Gauhar had been the ghostwriter of Ayub's 1967 autobiography *Friends Not Masters*. The biography, written after his subject's death, told a different story. The book acknowledges Ayub's faults but, after its author's experiences and imprisonments during the Bhutto years, nevertheless supports the portrait of a better man and a safer pair of hands than those that followed. In the last few days before martial law was reimposed in Pakistan on 25 March 1969 under General Yahya Khan, Gauhar wrote, 'Ayub would go to sleep and wake up with the question "How did it all go wrong?"'[13]

Professor Ian Talbot sees Ayub's presidency as a 'hinge period'. High rates of growth and yet greater inequality; national integration endangered by Punjabi domination and the 'beginnings of the nexus between the army and Islamic groups', as this president, like those who have followed him as leaders of Pakistan, was forced to moderate his modernizing intentions and fall back on Islamist support to legitimize his regime. This was the formative period for Milbus,[14] the term for 'military capital that is used for the personal benefit of the military fraternity, especially the officer cadre, but is neither recorded nor part of the defence budget', first notoriously coined by Ayesha Siddiqa in her book, *Military Inc.*[15] The mirror image of Ayub's positive international persona was a catalogue of failures and growing discontent at home. His controversial victory in the 1965 election against opposition led by Fatima Jinnah, the Mother of the Nation, was marred by violence and accusations of vote rigging. The notional endorsement of his presidency led, circuitously, given the serpentine machinations of Zulfikar Ali Bhutto in the background, to the 1965 war against India.

The unpopularity of the Tashkent Declaration of peace with a West Pakistani population primed, like Foreign Minister Bhutto, for a resumption of hostilities unless a plebiscite was agreed for

Kashmir, was another straw on the camel's back. Bhutto resigned to lead opposition to Ayub and to found the Pakistan Peoples Party (PPP), placing himself as champion of the poor and neglected, with the slogan '*Roti, Kapra, Makan*'[16] and spinning a web of left-wing alliances at home and abroad. In East Pakistan cessation of hostilities was conversely greeted with huge relief, but the war had added to the East's sense of isolation and marginalization. Sheikh Mujibur Rahman's Awami League accused Ayub of endangering the East with the hostilities, but the grievances of Bengal had far deeper roots. The burgeoning of Punjab as the economic and political power base for Pakistan, at greatest cost to the East, promulgated dissatisfaction over political, economic and ethnic inequality in other regions. The activism of the left embodied by Bhutto and Mujibur, was augmented by disaffection in Sindh and in the so-called Saraiki belt of south Punjab with parts of Sindh and Baluchistan, to bring renewed ethno-linguistic nationalism into the narrative of Pakistan politics.

The resentment that sowed the seed of the Saraiki province movement, based on linguistic identity, was the precursor to, and sometime rival of, the more ethnically inclusive Bahawalpur province movement, which was based purely on the issue of regional status. In the general elections of 1970, candidates for the Bahawalpur movement won 80 per cent of the votes.[17] The Pakistan Muslim League had passed a resolution supporting the movement, and Sheikh Mujibur Rahman was, perhaps unsurprisingly, a supporter of provincial status for Bahawalpur to honour the 1954 Constitution after the One Unit of West Pakistan was dissolved. The movement lost momentum after the shock of the loss of East Pakistan in 1971, which Salahuddin Abbasi remembers as devastating, like losing an arm. Salahuddin continued throughout his political career to lobby for Bahawalpur. The history of the struggle for provincial status is explored in Chapter 17 below. Salahuddin formally relaunched the Bahawalpur province movement as the Bahawalpur Awami Party in the gardens of Sadiqgarh Palace on 14 April 2011, forty years later and in another century and another millennium. Between President Ayub Khan and President Asif Zardari, a lot of the hopes of the people of Pakistan as well as the lifeblood of the former state of Bahawalpur had drained away.

13

THE ABUSE OF GREATNESS

Salahuddin Abbasi's view of Zulfikar Ali Bhutto is epitomized by Stanley Wolpert's opening remarks on his subject in his 1995 biography of Bhutto: 'Zulfi Bhutto roused such diametrically opposed passions and has left such divergent images among his disciples and adversaries that it remains virtually impossible to reconcile them as reflections of any single personality.'[1] Salahuddin was forced to return from university in London, and a congenial if relatively impoverished student life, when his father, faced with Bhutto's depredations of his estate, of Bahawalpur, and of his personal standing, needed the help and support of his young and energetic heir. Salahuddin takes a dim view of Pakistan's leaders in general, especially with regard to their dealings with Bahawalpur, but Bhutto was the worst and the most vicious. He says, 'Bhutto was the one who first cut our throats.' Asked whom he would have trusted, had it ever been possible, to help to make Bahawalpur the place it could or should have become, he returns, whatever the field marshal's failings, to Ayub Khan. Salahuddin expresses some sympathy with Ayub's well-known weakness for beautiful women. Women, he says, were one of his own main interests as a young man about

London in the 1960s. Bhutto was also passionate about women. But Bhutto, Salahuddin remembers, later enjoyed humiliating those he had pursued for his brief gratification.

Bhutto used his personal power and subverted the state to shred and loot the residual trappings of nawabi life that should have survived to ornament the history of Pakistan. He cleared the path towards the greater devastation of Pakistan's heritage at the same time as he laid the explosive charge for the destruction of the reputation of his country after his death. In his lifetime, he was the golden image of Pakistan's future, who charmed world leaders wherever he went. And yet, there is a level of grudging admiration in Salahuddin for a unique character and the leader he could have been, or the man who had taken a fancy to the amir of Bahawalpur's combative young heir on his return from London.

Bhutto's casually overbearing appropriation of the property and dignity of the amir is exemplified by one particular event that has passed into Abbasi family legend, complete with photographic record. Salahuddin tells the story, the duality of his feelings for the then president apparent, as his expressed loathing for Bhutto's high-handed bullying gives way to astonishment at the man's quick-witted skill in dealing with a potentially highly embarrassing situation. In the pomp of his new presidential role in 1973, with a week's warning, Bhutto informed Abbas Khan of his intention to bring all the foreign ambassadors serving in Islamabad, and their wives, by special train to Sadiqgarh for a grand lunch. He inquired whether this could be arranged. Abbas Khan was more infuriated by the implication that it might not be possible, than by such an order thinly velveted as a request. The unwanted guests, including most of the cabinet, were feasted like kings on quail and venison. With considerable difficulty, several bottles of Bhutto's own favourite whisky, the elusive Black Dog,[2] were procured, and, well refreshed, he afterwards addressed a large meeting in Ahmedpur. He began by listing all the things he had eaten at lunch, omitting only, Salahuddin says, 'a hell of a lot' of whisky and pointed out all the luxuries available to 'Nawab Sahib'. Now, he said, the time had come when he, Zulfikar Ali Bhutto, should take all those things and give them to the people. Did his audience agree? His audience proceeded to make their views nakedly apparent; the first man who opened his dhoti and bared himself to the president was followed by others who dropped their salwars. The rest took off their shoes and shook them at the podium. Bhutto was speaking against their prince and ruler. Making his voice heard again above the hubbub, he said, 'Yes, I understand the price of leather is very high now. Give me one day—let me get back to Islamabad and I will make shoes cheaper for you.' But, Salahuddin says, he could not finish his address all the same.

It was a pyrrhic victory for the former ruling family. Bhutto never forgot a conversation[3] or a slight. Despite his wealthy Sindhi background, vast landholdings and power base, he resented that he could never claim the grandeur of royal status. His father, Sir Shahnawaz, had been prime minister of the former princely state of Junagadh in India, a spot on the map compared with Bahawalpur, although of importance to India when its Muslim ruler attempted to accede to Pakistan at Partition. Sir Shahnawaz and Zulfikar, who inherited further estates from his uncle, ruled vast swathes of land, greater than some princely states, from their base in Larkana. They were among the most influential of the Sindh *wadero*s, but Zulfikar was not a prince. Salmaan Taseer wrote of Bhutto, 'he could not bear equals',[4] still less could he bear anyone who might be seen as superior, socially or intellectually. In Salahuddin's opinion, Zulfikar's arrogance was such that he probably believed even his early role model, Jawaharlal Nehru, to have been his intellectual inferior. Now, Salahuddin believes, Bhutto was determined to neutralize the former princes and others antagonistic to his rule.[5] They would, with the rest of his new fiefdom of Pakistan, be made to bend the knee to Zulfikar's personal version of divine right, his long-held conviction that he had been born to lead. They were his to use or abuse on a whim or to pay off a grudge, to appropriate to add lustre to his power, or to be humiliated as living proof of his strength. By the time of that glittering gathering at Sadiqgarh, he had already confiscated the passports of the former ruling families, imposed quotas on any goods brought by them into the country and removed their privy purses and any remaining rights and privileges.

After the abolition of One Unit in 1970 under President Yahya Khan, the people of Bahawalpur were in perfect accord with their amir in their dismay at the breaking of the promise of provincial status. They watched the resources of their former state spent on other parts of Punjab, putting a final full stop to hopes of building on the progress begun during nawabi rule. It was an 'extreme injustice'[6] and the strong feelings engendered were demonstrated in the 1970 elections. Out of a total of 10,30,000 votes, 7,14,000 were cast in favour of the Bahawalpur province movement. The elected members of the National Assembly (MNAs), Mian Nizamuddin Haider and Makhdoom Noor Muhammad Qureshi from Bahawalpur, sat in opposition to Bhutto and his PPP. They protested by refusing to sign the 1973 Constitution. Any real hopes of restoration of provincial status had vanished with Mujibur Rahman and Bangladesh in 1971.[7]

Salahuddin remembers those from Bahawalpur who held to their principles but he remembers better those easily bought off with political preferment. He snorts with disgust at the thought of his father's youngest half-brother, Muhammad Said ur-Rashid Abbasi. He had been entrusted with Abbas Khan's own former political seat but was successfully bribed to acquiesce to the status quo with the offer of a 'mere parliamentary secretaryship'. He later became minister of state for science, technology and tourism. Faced with others who were less faithless, Bhutto turned the screws on Bahawalpur and the amir. He used the Antiquities Act to legitimize his attempted confiscation of Sadiqgarh and threatened Abbas Khan with the imposition of new laws when Sadiqgarh nonetheless fell inside the definition of an ancient building by a handful of years.[8] By the 1968 Act, buildings predated as recently as 1957 were considered ancient.[9] In spite of Bhutto's telephoned threat to the amir, who had declined to appear on demand in Islamabad, he failed to modify the Act to suit his purpose. Since then, laws on antiquities have nominally become more stringent at both federal and provincial level. Implementation, in the face of corruption, avarice, army acquisition and lack of care for the past is an entirely different matter.

Bhutto's land reforms and nationalization programme after he became prime minister in 1973, were, Salmaan Taseer wrote, for all their unpopularity among feudal and industrial society, at least more successful than Ayub Khan's. They brought the greater balance in 'wealth differentials' and ongoing benefits to the poor,[10] that might be expected of any true socialist, although Zulfikar's socialism was worn or discarded like a shawl, according to expediency. That said, there have been plenty of so-called socialists, leaders who behaved like kings and fostered their personality cult. Not so many of them also held estates worthy of a sovereign. On his forty-fifth birthday in January 1973, Bhutto was able to give land deeds to 105 previously landless peasants from his personal landholdings and have 'Sindh's red dust' kissed from his shoes in exchange.[11] An interesting contrast to the Royal Maundy, when Christian kings both gave gifts to the poor and also washed their feet. The foot washing went out of fashion in the eighteenth century but it was not documented that the poor kissed the king's feet in return on receipt of their Maundy pittance.

A little later that January, Bhutto entertained his fellow ruler Shah Reza Pahlavi of Iran. The shah, he noted, 'was "intensely envious" of him', and, 'respected and feared his capabilities'. He wrote of the Shah's fall, 'his grandiose designs and fanciful ambitions . . . contributed in no small measure to his ruin'.[12] That he was providing insight into his own downfall cannot at that stage have been in Zulfikar's mind. The shah was foisted, like the diplomatic corps before him, on to Abbas Khan during his stay for a taste of Pakistani royal hospitality and a demonstration of the power of the country's president over all the ranks of its citizens.

Bhutto broke spirits for his own aggrandizement in a way that Indira Gandhi did not achieve when she removed the princes' privy purses in India. Later, in Zia ul-Haq's regime, and into the twenty-first century, family strife and the use and misuse of sharia swung the wrecking ball harder among the palaces of Bahawalpur and Dera Nawab Sahib. Zia used the courts and the law to divide the spoils of Bahawalpur between heirs recognized under sharia. It could and should have been done better and within the stipulations of Sadiq Khan's will and wish. There should have been no dissent, and there might not have been any had not Bhutto first opened the breach, sealing palaces as he chose—three times in the case of Sadiqgarh. He attended appropriations and nullified the status quo to allow space for the opportunistic and aggrieved wider family of the last ruler to pour in. In time, it was the army who most successfully filled the vacuum left as the family fought among themselves. Bahawalpur had been the biggest, richest and most comprehensively governed of the states acceding to Pakistan. A quarter of a century after Independence, nearly a decade after One Unit, after it had failed to receive the promised provincial status when Yahya Khan rescinded One Unit in 1970, it still had the most to lose. Abbas Khan, was forced, against his nature, instinct and breeding, to conciliate Bhutto where he could to salvage what was left.

When Zulfikar's old friend and drinking partner, the powerful Punjabi feudal landlord, Ghulam Mustafa Khar, who had been successively the first governor, then chief minister of Punjab, and again in 1975, governor, and was popularly known as the Quaid-i-Punjab, began to oppose Bhutto's land reform and nationalization programme and to make difficulties, Bhutto looked for a replacement. He was also faced with challenges of provincial and linguistic regionalism. At the same time in the Punjab, pressure had grown from reactionary Islamic groups. The religious parties, in particular conservative Sunni sects, accused Bhutto of favouring the minority Shias to whom he belonged. He mollified fundamental Islamists to some extent when he gave in to pressure to relegate the contentious Ahmadiya sect to non-Muslim status, but, even in his home base of Sindh, growing factionalism had to be 'neutralised' if Bhutto was to survive. In Punjab, the Bahawalpur province movement had foundered after the breakaway of East Pakistan in 1971, but the Saraiki Suba, demanding the establishment of 'Saraikistan', to include Multan, Dera Ghazi Khan in Bahawalpur and Muzaffargarh, now rose. At the same time, Punjabi MNAs attacked Bhutto for his 'alleged prejudice against Punjab and Punjabis and his marginalisation of their province'.[13] He replaced Governor G.M. Khar with Amir Abbas Khan Abbasi 'primarily to assuage separatist susceptibilities'.[14]

As Bhutto's courtship of the religious opposition to his rule intensified and he looked for new bones to throw to his political rivals, he became both the appeaser of the forces he feared and the tyrant who must be appeased. Perhaps the true dictator would have murdered his visible and potential rivals. Abbas Khan, unwilling 'though he might be', had little choice but to serve in the traditions of his royal duty and appease the appeaser for the survival of what was left of his inheritance. As Salahuddin relates, he had previously been offered the governorship and turned it down more than once.

This time, there was no escape for the man who 'didn't want to be Governor, he didn't want to be anything. He inherited the mantle of the Amir of Bahawalpur, that was bigger than anything any Government could offer him but, in the end, of course . . .'[15] In the end there was no alternative. The amir accepted the hair shirt for the greater good. Bhutto's chief minister was another feudal landlord, Sadiq Hussain Qureshi from Multan. Later, Bhutto sought to reduce regional factionalism and loyalties by moving governors outside their native provinces, and Abbas Khan accepted the offer of 'the Frontier',[16] Khyber Pakhtunkhwa, but never took up the post. By that time, it was too close to the end of all things for Zulfikar Ali Bhutto, and his successor had other ideas.

Had Abbas Khan hoped for some restitution of his birthright as reward for working faithfully with the ruling powers? The alliances of other powerful feudal leaders constantly mutated as they plotted change and snatched advantage. Salahuddin is convinced no such light of hope brightened his father's horizons. Instead, he was taking out insurance for what was left by serving, doing his duty both temporal and spiritual, and maintaining the dignity of his family and the amir for Bahawalpur and for his descendants. Unfortunately for him, no gentlemanly behaviour could insure against the megalomania and greed of a leader of his country, of whom one of Salahuddin's uncles said, 'I think there was no blood in his veins, it was all politics.'[17] The rigorous conservative religiosity of Bhutto's successor, who strove to impose a medieval system of life and law on the country and its institutions, and the growing grasp and acquisitiveness of the army he had commanded, killed hope. The less scrupulous intentions of the amir's own relatives, and their use of influence in whichever system to feed their own avarice, were the final nail in the coffin.

Salahuddin considers his father's major achievement, for the people of Bahawalpur and Cholistan, during Bhutto's heedless programme of land distribution, was to have saved the shikargarh, the vast shooting grounds of the nawabs. This was not done for family, but for the nomadic herders of the desert, the Tirni-Vhar, 'those who grazed their animals', under their traditional and customary rights. The amir was entrusted by Bhutto to arrange the first distributions of land and was able to explain the size of the holding, 12.5 acres, owed by tradition to each family, upon which they paid a minuscule but recorded land tax. This was proof of their identities as true desert dwellers as opposed to migrant land settlers. The governor's role was largely ceremonial. It included the chancellorship of all universities in Punjab and a constant round of entertaining. His wife was a great favourite with the Bhuttos; she and Husna Sheikh, Zulfikar's later partner, were friends, and Zulfikar expected to stay at Government House when he chose and to use it to entertain international guests such as King Sihanouk of Cambodia and the king of Jordan. It is hard not to wonder at the forbearance of Abbas Khan and his wife, who came herself from a highly politicized family, but Salahuddin describes both more as diplomats than as politicians. They kept their own counsel, their religious faith, and their held faith with the people of Bahawalpur. They upheld the honour of their country, and, regardless of the damage done by its leaders, maintained a civilized face on those leaders' behalf.

When martial law was imposed under Zia ul-Haq, the new president unexpectedly behaved with considerable grace towards the retiring governor of Punjab whose fearful staff were packing their bags as fast as they could. Personally lacking the acquisitive tendencies of his predecessor, Zia might have been impressed by another man who had never feathered his own nest. Abbas Khan had taken a token Re 1 a year in payment for his service and used as many as possible of his own staff at Government House in Lahore. Orders came from the new president that the governor's staff including the military secretary should remain in post until the governor was ready to leave for Bahawalpur, with all his staff, in the governor's railway saloon. By that time, Salahuddin had entered the National Assembly, and Abbas Khan's half-brother, Lieutenant General Sahibzada Muhammad Sadiq ur-Rashid Ibrahim Abbasi, had become martial administrator of Baluchistan. In 1978, he too became governor of Punjab. Salahuddin believes that it was because of his uncle's growing closeness to dangerous feudal factions in Sindh that Zia attempted to redress the balance by persuading Abbas Khan, whom he could trust to act for his country, to engage in government as a member of his cabinet. Abbas Khan's reluctance was eventually overcome through the intervention of a close friend, described by Salahuddin as an unofficial uncle, who advised him to become a minister without portfolio. Later, he became minister for religious affairs, with responsibility for Hajj arrangements for Pakistani pilgrims to Saudi Arabia. It was an honourable and fitting position for the amir that lasted until he had a stroke and was forced to retire.

One remaining story of a raid on the Abbasi heritage by Zulfikar Bhutto is decidedly surreal, a rare moment of marvellous farce in the decline of Bahawalpur and the Abbasi heritage. Elements of it may be made more believable by Zulfikar's reputed faith in the horoscope drawn up, after his birth, by an old Brahmin astrologer at the behest of Lakhi Bai, his Muslim convert mother, to whom he was extremely close and who 'never lost her Hindu faith in astrology'.[18] It is hardly credible that the highly educated, proudly progressive leader of a theoretically modern country in the late twentieth century should believe a story of buried treasure in an ancient fortress, whatever his inherited superstitions. Still less so that the same man should go on a wild goose chase at the same time as developing an atomic bomb.

The story of the legendary treasure of Derawar was related to me by Salahuddin. The treasure, it was said, was held for the use of any nawab of Bahawalpur in time of need. Down the generations, only a single treasurer had successively inherited the secret of its location among the palaces and pavilions, the courtyards, gardens and myriad underground spaces of the fort. The nawab of the time was led, with covered eyes, by the treasurer to the hoard and could take whatever he needed, or, more practically, what he could carry, before his eyes were re-covered and he was led from the secret treasury. Salahuddin is not sure which of his ancestors tried to cheat the process, but it was said that the treasurer decreed that the treasure would be lost for three generations or perhaps it was five or seven, whereupon the secret would be revealed once more. There are other versions of the story with earlier provenance as related by the travel writer Salman Rashid[19] in a 2011 article and told to him by Salahuddin's cousin, Omar Abbasi and by the late Obaidullah Baig, scholar, writer and film-maker.

> Alexander, having conquered Sehwan, paused to take stock. Putting together a vast treasure collected over the years of conquest, a hundred camel loads' worth, he entrusted it to his general Nearchus, instructing him to travel six days in a north-easterly direction to the midst of the great sandy desert [Cholistan]. There, so the king ordered, he was to bury it.

According to Obaidullah Baig, Salman Rashid wrote, a journey of six days on the given bearing would have brought the navarch Nearchus to the vicinity of Derawar.

> When the first Abbasi wrested Derawar from the Rajputs back in the 1730s, the keeper of the treasure agreed to lead one man, only one, to the treasure in the subterranean labyrinths. Shortly, the two men re-emerged from the dark catacombs back into the presence of the Nawab. The keys to the vaults were handed over and before

anyone could stop him, the Rajput keeper of the treasure had leapt over the crenellations of the fort to his death. Though the Nawab's man confirmed to his master that there was indeed a treasure beyond imagination, all attempts by the man to locate the vaults in the maze for his Nawab failed. Suspecting treachery and greed on the part of his man, the Nawab had him tortured and executed. And so the treasure remains hidden under Derawar.

Rashid continued,

And then I read *Tareekh-e-Masumi.* Completed by Mir Masum Shah in the early years of the 17th century, this history tells us yet another tale concerning the treasure of Derawar. In 1525, Shah Hasan Arghun, whose father, Shah Beg had earlier established himself in Sindh, wrested Multan from the ruling Langahs. There, a turncoat named Iqbal Langah, offering his services to the Mongol, told him of the 'immense riches and buried treasures . . . the wealth amassed by the Sultans . . . stored in Derawar'. Hearing that the fort lay in a sandy waste, the Arghun ordered collection of provisions to last a full month before the army was sent under Sumbul Khan to the desert. Shah Hasan followed up four days behind. Comprising cavalry, artillery and infantry, the Arghun army laid siege to Derawar and began pounding its walls. In an allusion to the Holy Koran, the historian tells us that Derawar was 'like Zulquarnain's wall [that the king built against the barbarian tribe of Gog and Magog] in its loftiness and strength'. As the siege proceeded, the Rajput defenders steadfastly held out even in the face of sharp artillery barrages and a decreasing food supply inside the fort. Time came when even 'boiled hide' was not available to be eaten for nourishment. Then Shah Hasan ordered mining of the fort walls on two sides. As the mud brick fortification came down,

> the Mongols stormed the breach and took Derawar. Mir Masum Shah tells us that, having collected the hidden treasures, Shah Hasan 'distributed a large portion of the gold among his troops, and took a considerable portion of it for his own coffers'. He does not disclose, however, if some of the treasure was left behind for future use. But what was taken must indeed have been considerable to permit the Arghun to rule over Sindh comfortably for so many years.

Salahuddin says his grandfather, Sadiq Muhammad Khan, had certainly searched for the treasure. Now it was the turn of Zulfikar Ali Bhutto, Quaid-i-Azam and prime minister of Pakistan. He telephoned Abbas Khan with a warning, which must for a change have raised little alarm, of the arrival of a soothsayer at Derawar to divine the hidden treasure. Abbas Khan, who had been heard to say that if the treasure should be meant for him, the amir, it would be shown to him by God without digging for it, was nonetheless touchy about Derawar, the seat of his family's power and past and the site of their tombs. He refused point-blank to allow anyone inside. The army had previously severely damaged the interior searching for arms that had been supplied by the last nawab for his Bahawalpur army, and it was agreed that the soothsayer should remain outside the walls. According to Salahuddin, 'this idiot', the benighted soothsayer, thought for some time before decreeing that a river flowing with milk should be made to run around the base of the walls and the treasure would be seen to float forth on the milk. The local administration was forced to provide quantities of milk that flowed and disappeared straight into the sand. No treasure came forth. For Salahuddin, the treasure is a just a good story. He sees it, in terms of his family, as a metaphor for the perpetual goodwill towards them that survived the worst slings and arrows of history, and the Bhutto era, and continues through the vicissitudes of Pakistan in the twenty-first century.

14

SALAHUDDIN

When Salahuddin Abbasi left Karachi in 1966, shortly after his grandfather's death, to study business administration in London, he did not expect to be thrown so soon into the maelstrom of Pakistani politics. Although he demurs, saying that he would have liked the life of a craftsman, a carpenter, such dreams were for another life or another man who had arrived in the world unencumbered by family history and tradition. He admits, looking back, that his mind was already half on home and Pakistan while he enjoyed his student life. His father had developed the diabetes suffered by his father, Sadiq Muhammad Khan, and Bhutto cohorts would soon be on the doorstep of Sadiqgarh Palace to place wax seals on the doors in the name of the government. The tradition of duty, however impugned by some of his more unsatisfactory ancestors, has steered the life of the last officially recognized amir of Bahawalpur, regardless of his personal dreams. Only in the manner of his service to Bahawalpur and to Pakistan has he had free will, retaining a sense of propriety and a level of independence that is maverick, almost eccentric, among the slippery loyalties and mutable alliances of the country's self-interested power holders.

It is his ability to remain separate, retain his integrity, his honour, and live, in important respects, within the true and orthodox tenets of his faith, which have created a reputation whereby an ordinary policeman will stop his car, with apologies, just to shake his hand. Those qualities are rare these days in any political world; in Pakistan, they are both a handicap and of high worth to the few with eyes to see. To them, Salahuddin, outspoken as he is, adds another value much prized by him in others, good manners. In the Islamic Republic of Pakistan, more heed might be paid to the hadith of Sahih-al-Bukhari translated as 'the best amongst you are those who have the best manners and character'. Salahuddin's determination to find the 'gentleman' in the character of his acquaintances and associates has occasionally led to some judgements that are surprising to the outside observer. They are based in part on ordinary good manners but also on that person's empathy with Salahuddin's lifelong fight for the recognition of Bahawalpur within Pakistan. He describes the former 'First Gentleman' of Pakistan, Benazir Bhutto's husband Asif Ali Zardari, as a gentleman, 'in the beginning'.

After long experience, Salahuddin trusts very few; his brother, Falahuddin, who died of cancer in London in 2016, was his closest friend and ally. The brothers supported their father and, when he died in 1988 aged only sixty-four, it was the two of them against the rest of their rapacious family and, if need be, against the rest of the world. Salahuddin remembers twenty years working with his brother, writing endless letters—he did the typing—to one or other government department, fighting for their heritage and for Bahawalpur. It was all, he says, a waste of time. This is hardly true that constant correspondence and the family and public battles for the Bahawalpur inheritance were only part of Salahuddin's early political career. Salahuddin says, 'I had to go into politics to survive,' to save what he could, but he admits there were other ways he might have achieved those ends. He says, 'Quite honestly, they were good days, politics became dirty in the mid-1990s. It might have been dirty then but to a much lesser extent.' He always believed he could achieve higher living standards for his people by playing the political game, with the goal of provincial status for Bahawalpur always in sight.

His political life began when he left the UK to return to Pakistan in 1970. He had an honours degree but had been called back before he was able to finish his postgraduate course. He had arrived at university in London and loved it. He had no money to speak of; his grandfather had recently died in London leaving his property abroad to his last wife, Lady O, also known by her Muslim name as Jamelia. The Surrey house, Selham, where she had lived with her husband when not holidaying at Torquay, her favourite place on the so-called English Riviera, had been sold and she, like Sadiq Muhammad's four other living widows, became his heir's pensioner and was given an annual allowance for her maintenance and staff. By then she was already dying, staying in the family's apartment in Westminster, after being diagnosed with cancer. Salahuddin says if she had offered him financial help, he would not have taken it. He was not fond of her; she was too aloof and he believed her attitude to his father was negative, an opinion revised in retrospect due to his mother's warmer opinion. Whatever his views, he witnessed her death and was upset that, among the family members who drifted in and out of her room, no one prayed for her. He remembers starting to pray then in a way he had not done before, that unexpected and unlooked-for spark enlightening for the first time the rituals he had learnt as a small child from his mother's maid and creating the foundation for the habit of a lifetime.

Possibly, it was that very personal discovery of his faith that has informed a private religious discipline of orthodox belief but unconventional practice in terms of the fervidly competitive demonstrations of faith, that have become the public face of Islam in Pakistan since Zia ul-Haq. Bhutto's successor, Zia ul-Haq, 'believed he had a divine obligation to establish an Islamic society ruled in accordance with the Qu'ran and shariah'.[1] That Islamic society included the only constant holders of power in Pakistan, the army. No leader of the country since has dared do other than kowtow to the religion of an army that marches under the flag of the Islamic Republic of Pakistan and bears its faith like another weapon. Zulfikar Ali Bhutto, like Jinnah before him, had his whisky and, through fork-tongued rhetoric, publicly forced his religion into complicated alliance with his socialism to achieve his goals. That he was not averse to the popular expressions of superstitious belief enjoyed by his people has been demonstrated by his faith in a most ineffectual soothsayer. That may have been an aberration borne of boyish dreams of buried treasure but, later, he 'turned to Sufism as an alternative source of Islamic legitimacy',[2] patronizing the shrine of the Sindhi saint Lal Shahbaz Qalandar, just as other politicians have sought solace, inspiration or power through the magical or mystical tradition of religion in Pakistan and elsewhere.

It is in that tradition that the power of the hereditary pirs or saints, their descendants among the most notorious feudal landowners and politicians, has become legendary. If heredity was ever synonymous with sanctity, it is no longer the case. Outside the country, the best known was the sixth Pir Pagara, who fought the British with his private army of fanatical 'Hur' followers and was finally hanged by them in 1943. There is another version of the execution in which he wasn't hanged at all but shipped out to sea and dropped overboard to be eaten by sharks. Salahuddin favours the more picturesque but unverifiable shark option. To all intents and purposes, the selling of indulgences, the role of the pir as a *safarshi* or intercessor between man and god is entirely against the precepts of the Koran but carries hard currency with the poor in cash or votes. While Salahuddin well understands the importance of the pir tradition for those who have often to survive on little more than their faith, he abhors the stupidity of the wealthy and well educated in its propagation.

The sixth Pir Pagara's sons were educated in the UK, the eldest returning to succeed his father in his religious role and to become the president of the Pakistan Muslim League (PML) (F). His son, the eighth Pir Pagara, inherited both his father's religious and political roles, and his son, Pirzada Sadaruddin Shah, is an MNA, leader of the same party, and allied with former prime minister Nawaz Sharif's PML(N). He became minister of overseas Pakistanis and human resource development under Nawaz and, after the prime minister met his nadir with the publication of the Panama Papers, was reappointed under his successor, Shahid Khaqan Abbasi. According to Salahuddin, Benazir Bhutto and Nawaz Sharif shared another soothsayer who sat under a tree with a birch rod to beat his disciples as a painful cure for any ill. Superstition as comfort, insurance or wishful thinking is all well and good—who has not avoided walking under a ladder? But Benazir covered her head with that iconic white dupatta, not previously worn by her or the women of her family, before she sought to lead the Islamic Republic of Pakistan and had to prove her good Muslim credentials. More than that, to overcome the handicap of her gender and single status, she married a man she barely knew in an attempt to appease the religious status quo. Salahuddin has neither used nor abused his personal beliefs nor felt the need to make his religious practice a matter for public consumption with the sole exception of making the Hajj pilgrimage. He is amir of Bahawalpur and that will do. Like others of his and older generations, the rest of his religious practice and his own reading of the Koran is for him alone.

Lady O died little more than a year after her husband and there was no hidden trove of funds to support a wealthy lifestyle for Salahuddin in London, in spite of Sadiq Muhammad Khan's long history in England. The costs of the Indo-Pakistan war in 1965, loss of foreign aid in its aftermath, and the related squeeze on foreign currency were very much against students and foreign travel. At the time, in spite of Ayub Khan's 'decade of development', Pakistani migrants, particularly Mirpuris from Pakistan-administered Kashmir who had lost their agricultural lands on the completion of the Mangla Dam project, urban middle-class professionals and, in another wave, refugees from East Pakistan when Bangladesh was carved away, were streaming into the UK in search of better lives and jobs. The Bonus Voucher Scheme was in operation to support exports. It used a points-based voucher system in exchange for forex payments that could be redeemed by the exporter in any currency. It effectively introduced a system of multiple exchange rates, with values changing according to the premium quoted on the market for the voucher, meaning that forex was sold for inflated prices against the Pakistan rupee and was prohibitively expensive for most private travellers or students. Salahuddin's father provided the means for him to live in London but only just.

He maintains that he found student poverty liberating. He walked miles to save a bus or tube fare in order to spend his savings on the latest LP although, unlike one of his friends, a highly successful international lawyer based between Islamabad and London where he trained, he did not end up moonlighting as a barman. As the bar in question was Annabel's, the well-known nightclub in Berkeley Square, and he was prepared to work during Christmas and other holidays, the tips alone were often good enough to pay his fees. Thinking of the contrast with his grandfather and with earlier and later visits of his own to London, Salahuddin says that he rarely took a black cab but had to take the tube to distant Moorgate in the city for classes in statistics and finance and to Finsbury Circus for law. He rarely travelled out of London, the unexpected exception being trips to Kent to look at Labrador puppies, which were then taken home to Pakistan. His father paid for first-class return tickets on PIA once a year and the dogs were also booked seats on the flight from London to Karachi, resulting in occasional mishaps towards the end of the journey when their tranquillizers wore off.

He lodged in Kew, with the mother of his 'Jewish aunt', wife to one of his great-uncles. The Jewish aunt, the London great-uncle—Salahuddin's life has been littered with the offshoots of his grandfather's vast family. They crop up in conversation: the uncle or half-uncle who was a particular Bhutto supporter and organized the notorious rally in Bahawalpur. Another, or the son of another, or another again, who was a constant political thorn in his or his father's side from one or other of Pakistan's multiple rivalrous political parties. Then there were those uncles and cousins who have most damaged the fabric of Sadiq Khan's disputed inheritance, destroying family and national heritage, instead of preserving it. Always, in the shadows, there are the generations of nameless women, who drifted in and out of history and the zenana, and very occasionally pulled family strings and stamped until they were heard. One infuriated Sadiq Muhammad Khan. She was a jewel thief and a serial escaper who climbed out of the women's quarters. Who can blame her? As Salahuddin points out, these women were confined as much as any nun in an enclosed medieval convent. Their mothers were allowed to visit once a month, and no male visitor beyond their husband or the youngest child could penetrate their drearily luxurious prison.

Salahuddin recalls a few female relatives from his lifetime who stand out for their less hidden lives. Aunt Timmy, daughter of the English grandmother who chose Salahuddin's mother to be his father's wife, must have been remarkable. She had impressed Sadiq Muhammad Khan V enough to be allowed to qualify and practise as a psychologist in England. The Jewish aunt had come to London from Germany shortly before World War II and lived in Kew, apart from her husband. Salahuddin remembers her fondly and her personal cure all: not ubiquitous chicken soup but a tuna fish salad with apples and chives 'that would cheer me up immensely', he says. There were Saturday trips with her to the King's Road, with lunch at Peter Jones, the department store in Sloane Square, but Salahuddin only made a few friends in London. He lived far away from the centre of university life. Transient foreigners and British friends alike have been lost to time and change, leaving instead vague but shining memories of carefree youth, and a simple existence when there was time and energy for walks and tube journeys, passing friendships, pretty women, music, dogs, milk in gold-topped bottles and the small magic, in another place and time, of coins in a gas meter for hot water and a bath.

These days, in Pakistan, there are just a handful of close and long-standing friends. Few of them have negotiated the pitfalls of Pakistani politics except when politics impinge, as they tend to do, on every life and career in Pakistan. Salahuddin's friends have reached different goals through straightforward business acumen and hard work. They are a select few. So many other former friends or acquaintances, like those from his student days, have fallen by the wayside, sometimes due as much to time or lack of it as to any failings on either side. Salahuddin's duty has been all-consuming. He might fairly be said to have lived up to the heraldic implications of the pelicans on the Bahawalpur coat of arms; the pelican pecks her own breast to feed her young, just as a ruler must nurture his people with his lifeblood. Salahuddin maintains that he has retired from national politics and the fight for provincial status for Bahawalpur, but he sees a last battle to gain recognition of his son Bahawal as amir of Bahawalpur. He has seen the bottomless financial pit of his personal campaign for Bahawalpur's status consume his children's inheritance, but he wishes his title to be formally secured for the next generation. Just as he has remained nawab sahib to many, Bahawal may be perceived to be the next amir but that is not enough.

Heirs to titles formally recognized before 1964 have continued to hold them whether or not they amount to more than a piece of paper. Salahuddin himself had his recognition reconfirmed by Nawaz Sharif through the intercession of a close friend. He remembers Prince Aurangzeb of Swat, already married to Ayub Khan's daughter, asking advice as to his own recognition as Wali of Swat, which hinged on recognition pre-1964. Aurangzeb had been born in 1928, but remained Wali Ahad, heir to the Wali, throughout his life. Most Bahawalpur records may have been lost, but among those that remain is the letter from Sadiq Muhammad Khan V to Lord Wavell announcing the birth of his first grandson. Beyond that, Salahuddin says, his grandfather wrote to the Government of Pakistan after Partition, outlining his succession and ensuring his son's and grandson's legitimate claims to the throne of Bahawalpur while it existed, and to those titles that might remain after the state's merger into One Unit. Although the survival of these documents has been somewhat helpful during constant inheritance disputes, will high-level arm-twisting in the twenty-first century bring formal recognition for Bahawal and how much really does that rubber stamp matter? Salahuddin is certain that Benazir Bhutto's survival would have ensured the continuance of such niceties. Perhaps. For Bahawal, the practical idealist who would set the world and Bahawalpur to rights if he could but who has no illusions about the obstacles he faces, might such reminders of a different past be worth a fight? Or might his actions, like his father's, speak louder than any official paper and glean similar respect?

Both Salahuddin and his brother married unusually late, the years of their youth disappearing as they navigated the labyrinths of law and politics until shortly before Abbas Khan's death. Salahuddin was forty when he married Moniba, the cousin he had known all her life. Her family were his family too, and they were old friends. Moniba remembers how difficult life had become for Abbas Khan, pursued by rapacious relatives, by the time she married Salahuddin. Everything was slipping away, the amir's powers finally removed by Bhutto and under the sharia law implemented by Zia ul-Haq. The stress exacerbated his diabetes and led to renal failure. Moniba remembers him, in hospital in London or Karachi, during most of her first year of marriage and her sadness that a man who loved children never lived to see his grandchildren. Aneeza was born a few months after his death.

The huge family, Sadiq Muhammad's dependants and descendants, has shrunk, all those widows and wives of former generations and the troublous uncles, have gone. The nucleus is now Moniba, Aneeza, Bahawal, and, radiating outwards, a handful of Salahuddin and Moniba's immediate and extended family remain close, while others continue to make trouble and demands. In his older age, Salahuddin detests large gatherings: he is not part of the club or of any clique and does not entertain the Pakistani political rumour mill, whirling more than grinding since the advent of social media, and spitting out smaller and smaller grains of truth. Only In private is he happy enough to air his views of the 'idiots' who have mostly run his country since its birth and to tell a good story often prefaced with, 'you can't repeat this', but, as his family endorse, he never fully reveals himself.

Like his father and his grandfather, Salahuddin has also developed diabetes, happily for him as a disciplined but nonetheless dedicated lover of sweet things, the disease has become more easily and better managed than for former generations. Happily too, for a man who knows there may yet be battles to wage from behind the scenes in the political world regardless of retirement. Beyond that, he is a perfectionist, constantly changing, making better and changing again, which, combined with unusual skill with his hands and a desire to use them to create, makes him a restless companion at times. A lifelong nature lover and gardener, he is always improving, remaking a garden and remembering, regretting the failing populations of bird and animal life in Islamabad, or Bahawalpur, where his mother fed squadrons of striped squirrels outside the house. A conversation starts with Moniba at home in Islamabad where the house, surrounded by a garden, was designed by her husband: 'Those chairs are the wrong height, let's cut 6 inches off all the legs of those other ones and move the furniture from there to there.' He gestures round the drawing room. The ceiling, like the panelled walls of the dining room, was stitched together to his design from the jigsaw of pieces left when the family house in Karachi was demolished. He reconstructed and repaired the old chandeliers and designed new and beautiful engraved glass screens to divide a space where tables bear flamboyant nineteenth-century French marble busts and other European objects. Coco the Peke, her master's close companion, shares his breakfast scrambled eggs and then drapes herself along the top of a sofa with a good view across the garden down to the guard at the high front gate. Less favoured outside dogs loll in the shade waiting to ambush invaders. They are all bark and no bite.

In cupboards there are collections of beautiful glassware and porcelain pieces, sometimes carefully mended from myriad fragments, examples of spectacular hand-painted dinner services ordered in England by Sadiq Muhammad Khan V. A few numberless sets of plates survive, whole or in part, to be used and admired by dinner party guests. These are definitely plates to be picked up, turned over and examined, however unmannerly. Each one is unique, and individual plates, lost or looted from this or that palace, appear in London in dealers' catalogues at prices even more spectacular than they deserve. Only paintings somewhat defeat Salahuddin's instinct to restore: gloriously icy Himalayan landscapes by Edward Mary Joseph Molyneux, uncle of the better-known couturier; splendid family portraits and more recent, carefully chosen acquisitions, interspersed with Victorian quasi-orientalist canvases of tigers, which are full of holes. They were shot at, according to Salahuddin, by his grandfather. Salahuddin is immensely knowledgeable about these treasures and curiosities but the stresses of his efforts to salvage and restore family treasure, both tangible and intangible, show. Salahuddin can never relax even when apparently at ease, and then there is the constant cigarette, smoked, half-smoked, another lit from the first, seldom without one in his hand and an often emptied but still brimming ashtray at his elbow.

It is rare to find a person long involved in politics about whom voices are not quickly found to speak for or against. Salahuddin has retained respect because of his carefully maintained independence, only occasionally lending his support to other politicians and their parties where it might have brought improvements to Bahawalpur, never taking anything in exchange for a service or a helping hand other than a benefit for Bahawalpur. Anyone throwing stones might say, in spite of depredations on his personal inheritance and fortune, Salahuddin is not a poor man—he has not needed financial supplements from bribery and corruption. Existing wealth has not, however, discouraged the many Pakistani politicians from enlarging their fortunes. Salahuddin has avoided getting too close to anyone or any party, or being party to the mutating loyalties of traditional feudal leaders with whom he might have been expected to make expedient common cause. He has kept and continues to keep his own counsel and has gained an aura, or perhaps a carapace, of untouchable dignity that is only allowed to slip among close friends and family.

Diverging paths, failures and often death; Salahuddin is not yet an old man but he was alive when India divided. He knew, and could claim friendships with, earlier generations whose memories stretched back to the dawn of the twentieth century and before. Now they are part of the past, among them were those who would have chosen different leaders and a different future for Pakistan to the one it is living today. Salahuddin is cast to a far greater degree in their image than of others of closer contemporaneity. He is, above all, like his father had always wished to be, a very private man, keeping people at arm's length, however politely, difficult to know even for his family. Open with his opinions perhaps, but never with his feelings. He avoids publicity as much as possible. As he says, his family always has, insofar as such a thing was possible for those one-time jewelled princes who survived into the spotlit celebrity glare of the late twentieth century. He is unimpressed, actually offended, by the proliferation of any news story by social media if it should mention him or his family, and finds it hard to believe how much material on their lives and activities is readily available online. Most of it is, according to him, highly inaccurate. He might be happier to know that much of it is equally highly supportive of his initiatives for Bahawalpur's provincial status and for greater recognition of the lower Punjab region in Pakistan.

15

THE LAST AMIR

Salahuddin Abbasi knew Z.A. Bhutto for most of his younger life, spent time in his house, was very fond of his wife Begum Nusrat and liked his mother's friend, Zulfikar's second partner, Husna. In the early days when Salahuddin first plunged into politics, Bhutto took a fancy to a bright young man who was quite unafraid of saying what he thought or acting upon it. The young man in question was himself somewhat seduced by Bhutto's famous charisma, not least reflected against 'that bloody drunk', President Yahya Khan. General Agha Muhammad Yahya Khan, chief of army staff, had taken over the presidency from a sick and defeated Ayub Khan on 25 March 1969, largely at Ayub's own behest. Wearing his military hat in his dual role as chief martial law administrator and president, Yahya Khan spoke, in his first address to his nation, of the 'determination of the armed forces to bring back "sanity" and save the country from "utter destruction"'.[1] He spoke as the secessionist movement grew in East Pakistan and the general air of unrest in Pakistan since the war with India and the Tashkent Declaration rose to boiling point.

Recent historians have to some extent rehabilitated Yahya from a record wholly blackened by the 'catastrophic'[2] end of his regime in another war with India and the final loss of East Pakistan. The balance has been redressed by the view that he was a good general,[3] as even Salahuddin reluctantly agrees, with no real political ambition. He fell into a political role by virtue of his army command, and made a genuine effort to re-democratize as fast as possible. In that spirit, Yahya was responsible for 'the first truly free and fair elections held in Pakistan despite the allegations of official patronage of favoured political groups'[4] within a year of his takeover. That said, he was a disastrous politician whose misunderstanding and misplay of those elections and their aftermath led to the 'brutal military crackdown'[5] on East Pakistan, a new war with India, international condemnation, and the bloody end of the fiction of a united Pakistan.

Yahya was seen as a traitor, the 'murderer of the nation' in a Lahore newspaper headline,[6] or as the demon-faced personification of West Pakistan in an East Pakistani cartoon captioned 'Annihilate These Demons'. He has retained a similar image in Bahawalpur and in the last amir of Bahawalpur's memory. From the Bahawalpur point of view, Yahya was the perpetrator of an additional monumental crime, the effects of which have continued to echo down the years of marginalization of the former state and the south Punjab. Salahuddin's grim delight in unsavoury stories, rumour or not, of the president 'who should be written out of history', might be lessened if Yahya had not been responsible for ending Bahawalpuri expectations and hopes for provincial status. When he broke up the One Unit of West Pakistan into the provinces of Punjab, Sindh, Baluchistan and NWFP, Bahawalpur was absorbed yet again into a greater entity, Punjab. Beyond that, Yahya ushered Zulfikar Ali Bhutto over the threshold of a door long since kicked open by the new polymorphic embodiment of power in Pakistan.

Yahya was almost certainly an alcoholic whose drinking and womanizing were public enough to be embarrassing. In fact, all his predecessors and his immediate successor drank heavily, and Bhutto was probably the biggest and the most triumphant womanizer of them all. The officers of the Pakistan Army, including President Musharraf, have maintained their traditional taste for Scotch whisky, just as they and their civilian counterparts have retained their close ties with the USA. That long relationship, confirmed by President Eisenhower's development projects and the invasion of the Peace Corps, and later tangled with CIA involvement in Pakistan, is barely touched on in this book. Suffice it to say, Salahuddin Abbasi is not alone in laying many of the ills of his country at Washington's door. So much has been written, so much of that slewed by the swirl of rumour and counter-rumour, focused not least on the enduring enmity with India that has made their friends Pakistan's foes and vice versa, that the picking out of fact from gossip or fiction often seems impossible. The frowning face and withdrawal of American favour after the atrocities perpetrated in East Pakistan, combined with Z.A. Bhutto's efforts to promote his and his country's Islamic and socialist credentials through new flirtations and relationship-building with the Middle East, Russia and China, nevertheless did little more than stretch those strings.

Bhutto's wilfulness in American eyes, however, may in part have been the cause of his own downfall. Salahuddin suggests that Bhutto's new determination to unite the Muslim nations, their financial support for Pakistan, and the invention of modern Dubai that sidelined Karachi as a financial and commercial hub, was not likely to appeal to any American master. American interest in Pakistan more recently is undisputed, the American hand clearly discernible in efforts to defray threats to internal security that might upset the design of delicate balances. Salahuddin may think himself lucky that his efforts to rebuild regional autonomy in Bahawalpur were, in the tradition of his family, always political, negotiated and non-violent, unlike those previously mentioned of Nawab Akbar Bugti. Nawab Bugti's long political and ultimately armed struggle, in his own tradition and that of his Baluchi tribespeople, led him through the highest corridors of political power and finally to his violent death during the tenure of President Musharraf. According to more or less reliable sources, given the careful clearing of the attack site, the culprits were American special forces.

In the end, Pakistan has been and still is moulded by its allies or friends, each to suit his own geopolitical purpose, whatever the gifts as payment or bribe for convenient malleability. Salahuddin asks why his country has allowed it. If Pakistan had only learnt to live on what little resources it could generate, such outside influences would never have been so devastating. If the country's politicians had not been so busy enriching themselves and had cared for their people, things would have been different. That is to rise above Pakistan's poverty and strategic importance at a crossroads in the world shared by Afghanistan, the site of the nineteenth-century Great Game and, before that, the route of manifold invasions. Now China is the latest invader, as in so many other parts of the world, building roads across the backbone of Pakistan to their vast investment in the new port at Gwadar. Salahuddin gloomily recounts the story of Majuj and Yajuj[7] and the end of days according to the Koran, at the hands of a race previously identified with Central Asia, the Mongols, and conceivably with the Chinese.

In the preface to his memoirs of the 1970s,[8] Fakir Aijazuddin described the 'traumatic convulsions of change' wrought by Zulfikar Ali Bhutto and continues, 'even his detractors cannot deny that alive, he was one of the most enigmatic, charismatic, complex, paradoxical, and eventually suicidal of politicians the country has experienced. Dead, his legacy endures still with damaging potency.' That summation, with the vindictiveness and envy Aijazuddin later mentions, and the narcissism and self-delusion described by others, fits neatly both with the jigsaw character of the man Salahuddin knew and with his reaction to Bhutto's death. Regardless of what had gone before, Salahuddin considers the eventual unsafe charge, sentencing and hanging by his successor of a man who was a towering statesman, for all his manifest faults, to be horrific and barbaric acts. His later dealings with Benazir Bhutto grew from lifelong acquaintance, although he did not choose to trust or support her until he believed she had finally become the woman who had learnt the right way to lead her country. Unfortunately, it was too late for her and for Salahuddin's hopes for Bahawalpur which were vested in promises received from her had she been returned to power in 2008. If he had been horrified by her father's ignominious execution, he says Benazir's assassination, 'what a damn shame', made him 'rabid' to the extent that he plunged into the general election that should have brought her personal triumph, campaigning for her PPP in his former constituency with the rallying cry, 'You are not voting for Benazir Bhutto, you are voting for my dead sister.'

On his return from London, Salahuddin's earliest political excursions were made under the guise of social work in the Indian Social Organization, originally founded in the 1930s by the last nawab of Junagadh,[9] and were in part an exercise in pulling the ogre Zulfikar's beard. Salahuddin describes his work as a quest on a massive scale. He covered all three districts of Bahawalpur and further out into Baluchistan, cajoling private funding for services for the poor, the socialist prime minister's mythical *awam*, the ordinary people who continued to have no political voice.[10] Salahuddin calls those good days; he was a young man playing the game regardless of its hazards and the indignities suffered by his father and other former princes. As a favourite of the prime minister, he remembers how Bhutto 'used to send for me periodically and I'd go quite happily to

Islamabad. Nice trip there and I used to go through the back door to Begum Bhutto first.'

He was always in trouble, the naughty boy with his fingers in the sweet tin, and the begum, he says, was lovely in those days, only changing after her husband's arraignment. She would ask him what he had done this time before he was summoned to the Bhutto presence and a flurry of mild enough accusations. He had made anti-PPP statements in Bahawalpur; fomented trouble over the province movement or against his uncle, the Bhutto stooge; and he was being used as his father's troubleshooter. The charges were always denied or forgiven until the same thing happened all over again a few months later. During all the years he knew Bhutto, Salahuddin says, he only once asked, while wearing his social service hat, for a favour, a mobile unit for his TB clinic in Bahawalpur with an on-board X-ray unit to take into the rural areas. Bhutto gave him Rs 20 lakh (2 million) without batting an eye. 'The price of a good Rolls Royce,' Salahuddin says.

Salahuddin did not formally enter the political field until he stood for a National Assembly seat in 1977, not in this case for his home constituency of Ahmedpur, where he would have been standing against his uncle, but for Bahawalpur. He was pushed to stand, he says, by Bhutto, with the support in his case of his father, Abbas Khan. In theory, he stood on a PPP ticket while maintaining, as he always has, his determined independence. Salahuddin was duly elected by a huge majority, by some 98,000 to 3000 votes, after a door-to-door campaigning approach followed in all his later elections and owing more to European democracy than the standard mass-rally approach of South Asian political candidacy. He retired finally from an elected position when General Pervez Musharraf became chief executive of Pakistan prior to his presidency. He neither has served, nor would serve, under a military dictatorship, and had different battles to fight during the Zia years.

Then, soon after the 1977 elections, Bhutto was gone. He had opened Pandora's box for the army and the Islamists. If Zia ul-Haq's mannerly treatment of Abbas Khan Abbasi came as a surprise after Bhutto's overarching bullying, it did nothing to save the Bahawalpur inheritance from the new enforcement of *Nizam-e-Mustafa*, the Rule of Muhammad, or from the army. General Zia's rule was an interregnum in the national political process, so far as Salahuddin was concerned. Zia was personally less of an enemy than Bhutto had been, but the form of his rule caused far greater damage to Bahawalpur than had yet been achieved. Its repercussions remained unresolved until the early twenty-first century and the apportioning and rebalancing of the Bahawalpur inheritance. The family quarrels and envy continue to the present day, manifest in non-communication, backbiting, destruction or theft of remaining property. All the while the army has waited in the wings or camped in a palace garden waiting to add to the spectacular property portfolio manifest everywhere from agricultural land in Baluchistan to the square miles of the Defence Housing Authority holdings in Lahore, Karachi, Rawalpindi, Multan and other cities including, most lately, Bahawalpur.

Salahuddin can hardly bear to talk about the disastrous break-up of his grandfather's remaining estate, the sheer waste when good sense might have prevailed for the benefit of his immediate and wider family, as well as for Bahawalpur and Pakistan. Like the army, the press has picked over the bones, recounting a story that is a hotchpotch of rumour, fact and point scoring. When Bhutto had first put the seals on Sadiqgarh Palace and the palace museum, there seems to have been some sense of preserving its treasures in one place. All the silver and gold were moved into the palace, only the heavy elephant howdahs left where they were but it all disappeared. When the palace was resealed under General Zia in 1982 as claims on property were pursued through the courts by a multitude of heirs, the real destruction began. Treasures were progressively looted, furniture and interiors smashed. A flood in the palace cellar in the absence of any caretaker destroyed a priceless trove of antique books and manuscripts, their existence commemorated by the few ruined survivors whose leather bindings cover illuminated pages now glued together beyond restoration. The great wealth of family records was forcibly removed to the new Punjab Archives at Anarkali's Tomb in Lahore. Apart from the extraordinary social history they contained, everything from land jagir*s* to marriage settlements and lists of kitchen supplies, there were, more pertinently at the time, the wills and records of property ownership and inheritance of the nawabs. When Salahuddin got legal authority to search for the necessary documents to support or refute his own and his relatives' various claims, the files had gone missing from the new system, 'cleaned out by some bureaucrat'.

An online paper from 2015 refers to the Punjab Archives as a 'goldmine of information'[11] including on Bahawalpur, Kashmir and Patiala. It continues, 'unfortunately most of this information is inaccessible'. The paper mentions records kept in gunny sacks and a chaos of rooms, almirah*s* and files piled floor to ceiling, all 'consumed with dust'. The author of the paper believes the problems are largely due to lack of funds. The staff, he writes, are essentially helpful but helpless, and he mentions an 'ambitious digitization plan' in collaboration with Punjab Information Technology Board, and a similar project undertaken successfully in Baluchistan. Currently, the Baluchistan archive is unreachable online, from the UK at least. The Punjab Archive website has a tremendous opening page. It has been assuring readers, for at least the duration of the research for, and writing of, this book, that the requisites for the implementation of the digitization project are being 'finalized and readied'. There are other tales told of the records, manuscripts and books thrown into the old stables of the Lahore Secretariat to rot[12] and rumours of the Islamist bureaucrat now in charge of Punjab Archives who repels all comers, especially hopeful foreign researchers, regardless of any authority. Others, who know the archives well, suggest that access can be arranged but there appears to be small chance of reassembling the Bahawalpur records for a historical picture that stretches beyond the imperial view preserved in the India Office Records of the British Library. The picture suffers more from the colouration of recent history by the diaspora of endemically disputatious Abbasi kin and those long since distanced from lost Bahawalpur among the urban elite of Pakistan and elsewhere. No family history lacks its collateral versions. Nowhere is this more apparent than in a composite country where society thrives on rumour, counter-rumour and faith.

After battles fought in and out of the courts, the surviving movable royal property of Bahawalpur was dispersed among the '23 legal heirs and their 70 descendants'[13] of the last nawab on 10 May 2004 under the auspices of SAFRON. The cars were sold to the highest bidders and included the Jaguar still used by Salahuddin. A subcommittee of local revenue officials 'held the draws for the allotment of the lots of the palace remaining articles, including furniture (broken as well) and library books. Later, the legal heirs and descendants took their share of furniture and books by trucks and tractor-trollies to their residences.'[14]

There was a further distribution of property recovered from 'alleged thieves' the following day. The thought of the trucks and tractor-trollies piled high with broken furniture is too depressing for words and that was not all. In 2006, the courts were petitioned in a rerun of the 1982 and 2004 court cases brought, not by Sadiq Muhammad Khan V's so-called legal heirs, but by 'collaterals, successors of the predecessors of the said late Ameer'.[15]

They claimed descent from Haji Khan, that half-brother probably responsible for the poisoning of Bahawal Khan V at Aden, via his son Mohtasin Billah Abbasi and his wife, Princess Mehr-un-Nisa, a daughter of Bahawal Khan. Their claim insisted that the property left by Sadiq Muhammad Khan V had 'wrongly and illegally been distributed among the legal heirs' because it was not personal property but either 'common family property which had devolved on the entire family including the petitioners' or belonged to the 'Ameerate'. The petition was dismissed, but the judgment mentioned remaining cases pending and the possibility for the petitioners of 'availing any other remedy(s) under the law'. In order to avail themselves of such 'remedy(s)' petitioners have taken the law into their own hands to the extent on occasion of setting fire to that which they cannot own. The burnt-out shell of a small and once charming palace, Mubarak Manzil bears witness. The army has meanwhile encroached into the garden at Sadiqgarh as the Bahawalpur cantonment has expanded. The remaining contents of the palace have been looted or smashed; the broken shaft of its famous crystal fountain gleams faintly through the dust in the darkened durbar hall.

In the run-up to the 2004 sale, ever more bizarre claims from this or that family member were fed to the press including that of the British widow, daughter of the 'railway carter', who had married Haroon ur-Rashid Abbasi. He had been ambassador of Pakistan to Tunisia in London and, Salahuddin says, born of a different mother, was only three months younger than Abbas Khan. His pretensions to being the amir involved him calling himself amir of Bahawalpur. While ambassador, he was arrested for trafficking drugs between Tunis and Rome, and was imprisoned in Rome until pressure was brought to bear by President Yahya. He came to a sticky end due to another disputed will when his mother died and he had no intention of sharing her jewellery with other claimants. Salahuddin, quite charitably, says Haroon ur-Rashid had already gone mad after the Rome incident but lost control of his 'lovely Mercedes' while making good his escape with the contested jewels and went straight into a tree somewhere between Dera Nawab Sahib and Rahim Yar Khan. The package of jewellery was saved and returned to the heirs by the deputy commissioner, who had rushed to the scene of the accident and happened also to be a relative, one of unusual honesty. The widow and her son entered the Bahawalpur fray, complaining that they had not been paid their share of the pooled money from Sadiq Muhammad Khan's property already collected by the government over the past thirty-seven years and describing the coming auction at Sadiqgarh as illegal.[16] Curiously, she maintained that the only money she had received was her share of Rs 1.3 million (13 lakh) from the sale of Noor Mahal. Given its confiscation rather than purchase by the army, notwithstanding their disclaimer plaque in the durbar hall noting a sale, there must be some question as to the provenance of that windfall.

The effects of President Zia's policies over eleven years of rule, more or less under martial law, have haunted the Abbasi family and especially Salahuddin since his father's death in 1988. It was the same year the president died when his aeroplane crashed ten minutes after take-off from Bahawalpur, killing all on board. Rumours continue to abound; there were mangoes on board, if they exploded nobody knows but it made a good story.[17] The consequences of those years reverberated internationally and rebounded on Pakistan: they have been what Ian Talbot described as Zia's 'doleful inheritance'.[18] Not only Islamization, the medieval blueprint little modernized by succeeding democratic leaders, but an escalation of the enmity with India bred into generations of Pakistanis since Partition. Most dangerously, there were Bhutto's and Zia's efforts to add nuclear capability to both sides of that simmering pot. Those efforts came to fruition for Pakistan a decade after the latter's death. The 'flood of drugs and weapons'[19] into Pakistan has grown in tandem with the flood of jihad as the CIA worked with the Inter-Services Intelligence (ISI) to support and supply the mujahideen in Afghanistan in the fight against Russia during almost the whole of Zia's tenure. Little did the CIA realize what it was letting loose on the world and on Pakistan as the ISI burst out of its American bonds to follow its own agenda. ISI is responsible for the creation or greater unity of jihadi groups with roots in Afghanistan and ties to the Taliban and al-Qaeda that are intended to escalate the war against India in Kashmir. One of them, Jaish-e-Muhammad (JeM), has its headquarters in Bahawalpur.

Zia presided over 'mounting sectarian violence and increased ethnic conflict'[20] borne of Islamization, in the extreme Deobandi orthodoxy, that has forced the broader tradition of Barelvi adherence in Pakistan into retreat. Militarization and promotion of members of his own Punjabi Arain community to positions of power, by Zia, led to the increasing domination of Punjab over other provinces. Salahuddin cautions that the particular dominance of the upper Punjab came later, under Nawaz Sharif. If 'Talibanization proved to be the flip side of Zia's Islamisation programme',[21] it has been a seed cast on fertile ground in marginalized regions including south Punjab and Bahawalpur where extreme intolerance has manifested in violence against minorities, in particular the long-persecuted Ahmadis and Christians. The slogan 'Shias are Kafirs' has appeared on walls all over Pakistan during the last ten years.[22] In 2001 masked gunmen with AK-47s killed seventeen Christians attending a service at St Dominic's Church in Bahawalpur. Of all Pakistan's jihadist groups, JeM is most active in preaching jihad among students of school-going age.[23] Marginalization and poverty, lack of services, education and any sort of social care have always sent people back to religion—in Pakistan, the mosque and the madrasa. Lack of government interest has created a perfect breeding ground in areas outside the promised land of upper Punjab where poverty and alienation are compounded by lack of education to provide ready recruits for radicalization and extremism.

> These Madrassahs are not just the place of worship or education; they provide the rationale of their existence and goal for their lives. They indoctrinate them with the wishful thinking of changing the world in accordance with their plans. They provide food and shelter for them and nourish their thought and mind. They also ensure their future recruitment and allocate them in different cells of their organizations. In this way the bulk of rural youth is going to Madrassahs as they offer much better returns than government educational institutions. This trend is one of the biggest factors of radicalization of youth in Pakistan in general and Southern Punjab in particular which comes to be known as the area of Punjabi Taliban.[24]

16

IN THE LABYRINTH

Salahuddin Abbasi's foray into national politics during Z.A. Bhutto's final days in power did not give him broad experience of, or a noticeable taste for, close engagement in the political bear pit in Islamabad, to which he returned after his father's death in 1988. He says he started from a very weak position, but was impelled by the impossibility of failure in negotiating the political labyrinth to the best advantage for Bahawalpur and his immediate family. With his nine uncles ranged against him, he had always to be on guard, metaphorically and literally: in the melodrama of Pakistan, the knives are often real. Moniba, his wife, says the husband she had only recently married never spoke to the press about the family matters that also have so often played out on the Islamabad stage. He has never allied himself with any party beyond support for policies of benefit primarily for Bahawalpur, albeit they might additionally profit other areas of Pakistan. His position was both isolated and exposed but he had once been Zulfikar Ali Bhutto's blue-eyed boy, for all the damage done to his family by that quixotic paladin, and he learnt fast how best to play the game.

Salahuddin was on every possible parliamentary committee: from the environment, of extraordinary importance in Cholistan, where environmental efforts have been singularly unsuccessful in the face of the vested interests of one after another governments, to public accounts. He discovered which committee bureaucrats were answerable to whom and for what, notwithstanding the 'you scratch my back and I'll scratch yours' culture throughout the system. Salahuddin could hardly be other than well versed in the facts of corruption at all levels of Pakistani society, particularly under Nawaz Sharif. He says, 'I can't even think of a single honest businessman here who takes pride in paying his taxes. No, everybody cuts corners, wants a quick boost to the next level of society, the next level of wealth.' He must have been a disappointing dead end for politicians attempting to curry favour on the basis of Salahuddin's personal power to sway the vote in the Bahawalpur region. The only real bargaining chip for his support, as important since his retirement as during his elected political life, remains the restitution of provincial status for Bahawalpur. Beyond that, possibly also recognition, in practical terms, of his efforts to lead a renaissance of the former state to place Sadiqgarh Palace and, most of all, Derawar, among the major sights of the world.

Hopes for Bahawalpur have been the sole reason for his and other leaders and supporters of the province movement nominally to support different parties at different times, based on promises that were always broken. The parties have included Nawaz Sharif's Muslim League (N) in 1993 and 1997. Nawaz Sharif had at least the good sense not to offer other softeners for Bahawalpur support beyond attempts to acquire new '*turki* topis' for Salahuddin and his staff through the Pakistani ambassador in Morocco. He had noticed Salahuddin wear his cap into the assembly chamber and then remove it on to his desk better to preserve it. The gift almost literally fell flat as the Moroccan and Tunisian fez have a lower crown than the Turkish model used in Bahawalpur. On these grounds, the offending caps were returned to the aggrieved ambassador who later assured Salahuddin he had been pursued by prime-ministerial demands as he personally searched high and low for the correct hats.

Day-to-day life in the National Assembly for Salahuddin meant dutiful attendance every day of the sitting, intense frustration, that habitual state of mind of the people's elected backbench representative who is unable to further his constituents' needs, and unutterable boredom. The main discipline was avoidance, to avoid contributing to the 'bullshit', the temptation always to engage with pointless rhetorical argument. Benazir Bhutto, intent on changing her country, attended the house much more often than most prime ministers of Pakistan. Most likely she was the only one after her father who could think on her feet. 'What do they think with? They haven't got brains,' Salahuddin sniffs. He swears the only worthwhile moments were spectator sport, when scuffles leading to fisticuffs broke out on the floor of the chamber. He used to take constituents to visit the assembly, arranging passes, seats and the attention of a minister for their particular concern. He admits that little was done immediately for such petitioners, but that was seldom the point. Cynically, the ordinary constituent driven from Ahmedpur in his MNA's own car with its diplomatic plates, to meet a government minister and be treated as someone who mattered, was perfectly happy to wait for a solution to his original problem. Attention was always the key. Most practical and effective efforts to achieve improvements were implemented locally, breaking the chain of vested interests from the centre and bypassing provincial corruption. Once sworn in as an MNA, Salahuddin was able to gather together the best and most honest, generally meaning better-educated, members of the police force and civil administration in his constituency to work with him without the usual sweeteners. He says that such measures were not popular initially with a public more used to the snakes and ladders of bribery and favour. After his first two parliamentary terms, his constituents woke up to the advantages of a system that actually dealt with problems on merit.

Major infrastructure projects required bargaining at the centre, or, in the constant battle for better water rights for Bahawalpur, at Punjab legislative level. To his surprise, Salahuddin found Shahbaz Sharif, brother of Nawaz and three times chief minister of Punjab, both cooperative and quick to grasp the issues. Multan, through the city's highly influential pir-descended politician and other landlords and bureaucrats, controlled the flow of precious water to Bahawalpur. Salahuddin's success in respect of water rights has not maintained the necessary water supply to forgotten Bahawalpur in the longer term, although the Sharifs proved themselves almost obsessive infrastructure builders. Questions over costs and contracts are too tangled to explore here, and there is no need; the Panama Papers have opened that door to the eyes of the world. If Nawaz Sharif's major road-building projects can be seen as a success story for upper Punjab, they have been less so for the rest of the country including Bahawalpur as always. The journey time from Lahore to Islamabad has been shortened, partly because the new motorway is so little used. The old, crowded Grand Trunk Road is shorter in actual distance and, with no tolls, remains the people's choice. The economic boom in Pakistan, regardless of the new housing complexes and golf courses under construction outside Islamabad and the holiday complexes spread over the Murree Hills, has not yet materialized in a country seen as unstable.[1] The motorway purportedly to lead eventually from Lahore to Karachi, that should at last serve Bahawalpur on the way, presently stops dead, close to Multan and to Sharif landholdings.[2]

Argument over other infrastructure construction, seen as Sharif vanity projects, has raged in recent years. The first phase of the planned Lahore Metro, the Orange Line, threatens the integrity of the Shalimar Gardens and has already seen numerous other historical sites bulldozed. The chairman of the government's steering committee for the project said, 'The provincial administration's obligation to protect heritage sites comes only after its duty to provide a transport facility to the public.'[3] The metro is also part of President Xi Jinping of China's buyout of Pakistan, to be rewarded by emblazoning his name on the new Islamabad Airport, just as it is set to be on other projects from Lhasa to London. Like the Sharifs, it is unlikely the Chinese value the glorious history and heritage of Pakistan. If anything of the ancient past survives the bulldozers, it should, after so many centuries in existence, easily outlive the Orange Line and similar projects. UNESCO archaeologists have reported the cement being used for the above-ground sections of the mass transit system has a maximum lifespan of 100 years. That there is need of proper public transport in Lahore nobody denies; that the Orange Line is the best way forward is doubted by most Lahoris and confirmed by the International Council on Monuments and Sites (ICOMOS) and the UNESCO World Heritage Committee.

Benazir Bhutto, according to her PPP 2008 Election Manifesto, had infrastructure ambitions focused on the needs of the 'Pakistani peasant, mired in poverty and debt'.[4] They included 'aggressive agriculture and rural development'[5] through provision of farm-to-market roads, water and energy security, better transport infrastructure, universal primary education and improved opportunity for secondary and tertiary education. She proposed madrasa reforms, to stop the alienation of another generation of young people bred on 'hate and paranoia', and put a stop to the role of the madrasas 'not as schools, but as 'irregular army recruitment centres for militants'.[6] In Salahuddin's case, there is no question that he found Benazir and her ministers easier to deal with than any other government and more invested in the real needs of the country, but the political game still had to be played if anything concrete was to be achieved.

When Salahuddin re-entered Parliament in 1988, 'floated into it', and into the intense rivalry between Benazir and Nawaz Sharif, it was also his father-in-law, Malik Muhammad Aslam's first term. He was a PPP, Benazir, man and quietly pressured his son-in-law to support her in the December 1989 vote of confidence that allowed her fragile government to limp on until the following August. The PPP had won 105 of 237 parliamentary seats in the general election, making it the largest party, but it needed alliances with an assortment of minor parties 'that did not necessarily have the same ideologies or policy programmes'[7] for an overall majority. The most important among them was the Muttahida Qaumi Movement (MQM), formerly the All-Pakistan Muhajir Student Organization, founded by Altaf Hussain. It had swept the board in urban Sindh and, in 1989, changed allegiance to support Nawaz Sharif. It later became notorious for its violence. Nawaz Sharif, then chief minister Punjab, the embodiment of heavily represented Punjabi interests, played on existing issues of regional identity and gender to undermine 'the Sindhi woman'.

Benazir was not her father; she was a thirty-five-year-old woman whose political instincts were nowhere near as natural or as honed. The PPP agenda was changing in her hands, and Zulfikar's old cohort of PPP supporters were not hers. Beyond her domestic lack of confidence and the enervating vendetta with Sharif, she was opposed or handicapped by formidable forces who neither trusted nor understood their untried, dynastically entitled, female prime minister. They included the army, the CIA-led intelligence forces and the president, Ishaq Khan, who, under the Eighth Amendment, had the power to dismiss her government and dissolve the assembly. Benazir won her 1989 vote of confidence by twelve votes but her government was dismissed eight months later by the president, whose powers she had fought to repeal. The lobbying was fierce, confrontational, threatening and vicious as both sides of the vote of confidence harvested support from unaffiliated independents who might be persuaded or coerced. Nawaz Sharif's men were more or less camped outside Salahuddin's gates in Lahore, as gentler pressure on Benazir's behalf was applied within the family. Finally, Salahuddin says, he sent for a loyal Bahawalpuri to drive him to Islamabad in the middle of the night when the whole household was asleep. He did not tell anyone, including Moniba, where he was going.

He remembers arriving at the house of an apolitical and recently divorced friend, having dinner with him and his mother, and then retiring to a room where he remained hidden until he decided what to do. Finally, he telephoned a furious Moniba, who had no idea where he was in the days before mobile communications, to inform her, as her father's daughter, that he had not been prepared to commit to the PPP on grounds of family pressure or to Nawaz Sharif under more overt threat. His decision ultimately to vote for Benazir won him a lady's favour in that joust of the political tournament. When the result was confirmed, Farooq Leghari, later the president who dismissed Benazir's second government in 1996 and known for his honesty in the den of thieves, came over to Salahuddin's seat on the floor of the assembly to offer Salahuddin a reward. The messenger was met with an uncompromising, 'What do you mean by that?' Leghari suggested taking a textile mill paid for by the government to provide a steady income, an offer countered by outrage, still apparent as Salahuddin tells the story. 'You go and tell Bibi to bribe someone else, she has offered nothing to Bahawalpur and I have supported her, I do not want anything else.'

In the end, an accommodation was reached, between two people who had known each other most of their lives, with agreement for the provision of miles of pipeline to bring gas from the Sui gas field to Ahmedpur and nearby Uch Sharif. As the pipeline was a federal project, Nawaz Sharif later made attempts to stop it, but funding had already been designated and the cogs of bureaucracy turn inexorably slow, for good on rare occasions. Salahuddin remains gleeful about his success, 'It must have cost at least as much as three textile mills in those days and I was able to tell my constituents that my house was the last one to get gas.'

Those constituents were never far from Salahuddin's mind. They were his people. They, in return, learnt to expect the full attention of their elected representative. He never dared stay an extra day in Islamabad at the end of a parliamentary sitting in case of constituency grumbling and local press gossip. He continued to haggle for improved services, including electricity, throughout his constituency and neighbouring areas of the former state. Breakthroughs did not always involve drama. Ministers, Salahuddin says, were often sensible people, especially if they came from Baluchistan rather than Punjab. His enormous constituency, when he was first elected, included the whole of the Cholistan Desert. It was the largest constituency in Pakistan, only shrinking when Cholistan was separated in 1990 at the same time as Mubarakpur, the oldest town in Bahawalpur, at its opposite end. Although he was somewhat offended to no longer represent all his people, it was a huge relief for Salahuddin to lose Cholistan. Its nomadic tribes made logistically difficult constituents in conjunction with an Abadkar settler population, originally brought in to cultivate new canal lands, and a numerous settled urban population.

Salahuddin never forgot the durbars, when any of his grandfather's subjects could petition their ruler in person. He made himself regularly available to constituents and was both seen and known, just as he campaigned with a far more personal approach than is usual in South Asia. Visits to Parliament; visibility and access in the constituency and election campaigns, which in the early days included travel from end to end of the desert, and which were fought village to village and face-to-face. There were more standard giant rallies in urban areas but they too were attended by rural populations, who poured in on tractors and carts. At night, starting as late as 10 p.m., when most people were home and in bed, there was door-to-door canvassing, waking inhabitants who, while rubbing their eyes, apparently took such extraordinary interruptions as an honour. As a rule, political candidates in Pakistan, so many former feudal overlords among them, are not known for wearing out their own shoe leather.

Salahuddin's steadfast independence, never toeing the line of a major political party, has broken on rare occasions when he has seen a glimmer of hope for a bargain based on delivery of some service to Bahawalpur, or for the dreamed of provincial status. In 2008, after Benazir's assassination, he fought for the PPP more from a sense of outrage than from any expectation that promises made in her lifetime would be kept after her death. In 1977, under pressure from her father, he had stood on a PPP ticket. In 1990, he stood for the second and last occasion on a party ticket for the Islami Jamhoori Ittehad (IJI), an alliance of nine conservative parties founded by Ghulam Mustafa Jatoi to fight the PPP in 1988. Jatoi, a major Sindhi landlord, had been chief minister of Sindh under Z.A. Bhutto, was married to Salahuddin's aunt and was a dear friend of his family. A 'thorough gentleman' in Salahuddin's estimation, he had continued to support PPP under Zia, then founded the NPP or National People's Party and had been twice imprisoned, in 1983 and 1985. He had been appointed caretaker prime minister after Benazir's dismissal in 1989. The IJI alliance brought Nawaz Sharif, Zia's chief minister of Punjab and leader of the alliance party, PML, to the forefront of national politics. After Benazir's government was dismissed for corruption, IJI swept the board in the 1990 elections amid accusations of rigging by the intelligence service. The ISI had tipped huge amounts of money into the campaign against the PPP. The NPP later joined Benazir in fighting the Nawaz Sharif autocracy in the 1993 election.

As Benazir Bhutto and Nawaz Sharif fought for political supremacy over more than a decade of chaotic democracy and at great ongoing cost to their country, there were always deals to be made. A comprehensible battle of left and right is so great an oversimplification of the Byzantine political game played out in Pakistan in this period that, for most participants, any real political conviction was a handicap. Loyalties changed by the day, based on promises, threats, bribes, family or ethnic ties and who had last dripped poison or attar into an ear over dinner the night before. There was little time for proper governance as the atmosphere encouraged a marketplace of favour bought and sold until in 1999, the army marched in once again, under General Pervez Musharraf, to fill the vacuum and govern the country. Members of important political families have often continued to keep a foot in several camps, through brothers, sons or daughters, and the wider extended family of blood or tribal allegiance. The political hurly-burly of the 1990s never settled into the calm of convinced and convincing government. Parties, and even the most independent MNAs, were on a permanent battle footing as elections came thick and fast and no government survived for a full term.

Salahuddin remembers working all year round, the campaigning never ending, to get the highest vote in Pakistan without any party support and from a population swayed this way and that by hollow promises. His voters decided, he says, at the last minute, to support the independent candidate who had been seen in their village, had kept promises, and, for what it was worth, was their amir. Salahuddin managed to retain his independence until after his retirement from elected politics after a five-year extension of Musharraf's rule was confirmed in a dubious referendum in 2002. Only later, with the return of Nawaz Sharif and a changed Benazir Bhutto to Pakistan and to power, could he see a chance for Bahawalpur through alliance with one or the other.

He saw Benazir as a reformed character, divested of her publicly detested husband, Asif Ali Zardari, 'Mr ten per cent', whom she had abandoned to his own pursuits in Dubai, and one worthy of his support. In retrospect, Salahuddin believes the promises she made to him, a man she had known all her life, would have redeemed his lifelong mission for Bahawalpur province, and ensured Bahawal's future right to hold the title of amir of Bahawalpur. 'Anyway,' he says, 'I would only have had to wave Bahawal in front of her, she would not have said no.' Nobody can say what might have been, but the importance of Salahuddin Abbasi's support in the matter of forming governments is illustrated by the story of his penultimate meeting with Mohtarma, meaning 'the respected lady', Bhutto, in London during the summer before her last return to Pakistan in October 2007. She was using the house of a supporter near the Water Gardens development in Bayswater, west London, where a crowd of 2000 or 3000 aspiring to PPP party tickets were waiting hopefully, and far from silently, in the private gardens as Salahuddin strode past.

Salahuddin remembers Benazir, always ready to dissolve into expedient tears, telling him through her sobs that no one really supported the PPP, and her old allies had been knifing her in the back. No longer contesting his own seat, Salahuddin found himself, to his astonishment he says, requesting the list of aspirants for constituencies in Bahawalpur so that he could provide her with the names of genuine PPP supporters who were also genuinely likely to win their seat. In the end, a copy of the list was found and, on the proviso that his name was not mentioned, he was able to approve about 90 per cent of the candidates before Benazir left for Dubai. He was increasingly sucked into the campaign, like it or not, in more telephone conversations from Dubai asking for information and names of candidates at provincial as well as national levels. His last meeting with the prospective prime minister was during her visit to Bahawalpur after her return to Pakistan, when he refused to confirm rumours of any alliance, food for damaging political gossip, by joining her on a rally platform. When a questioner described Salahuddin as a *jehla,* a slightly pejorative term for an old party hack or diehard, and inquired as to his authority regarding tickets for the election, Benazir 'lit into him' from the platform. 'Don't you dare to speak like that about Nawab Sahib in front of me; if necessary, I will disqualify you from the party!'

After that she left for Lahore and on to Rawalpindi. The controversy and questions over the responsibility for her assassination have never abated, for absence of any clear evidence. There was an almost instant clean-up of the crime scene, no autopsy and constant accusations of a deliberate police botch-up of the investigation. Everyone from General Musharraf to Asif Ali Zardari, or any number of terrorist groups, has been accused. Several investigations, including one requested by Musharraf himself and undertaken by Scotland Yard, another, led by Chilean diplomat Heraldo Muñoz, who was delegated by UN Secretary General Ban Ki-moon, have been inconclusive. A 'final investigation report' by the Pakistan Federal Investigation Agency in 2012 named twenty-seven different terrorist groups for involvement in the assassination.[8] Salahuddin has his own opinion. He maintains to some extent his original view of 'Mr ten per cent', who was swept to power on a wave of sympathy after his wife's murder. He remembers Benazir's high-handedness until she needed his help, in contrast to her husband's good manners; he recalls being ignored as he stood to greet Benazir at her wedding, but being embraced by Zardari who had noticed the insult. He continues to say that the gentleman was at least a better thing than the 'shopkeeper', Nawaz Sharif.

17

THE BAHAWALPUR PROVINCE MOVEMENT

Redemption of the broken promise of provincial status for Bahawalpur has, as we have seen, been the overriding goal and dream of Salahuddin Abbasi. Where others have willingly gathered the textile mills and other valuable fruits of their political versatility, that dream has informed the brief alliances made with holders of power in Pakistan, and has been consistently broken as they failed to deliver. Straightforward corruption for financial gain, being part of the club, as the majority of Pakistan politicians have long since discovered, is so much easier than standing alone on the hard rock of principle. The Bahawalpur province movement explored in this chapter and usually bracketed with other movements for regional autonomy, is the odd man out in the politics of language and ethnicity in Pakistan that is a large piece in the geopolitical jigsaw of the national map.

In its earliest incarnation, the Bahawalpur movement appeared coterminous with Saraiki nationalist movements; several of its earliest initiators and leaders were one and the same. The Bahawalpur movement, however, was and remains mainly focused on the economic and administrative injustice of Bahawalpur's situation as part of Punjab. It need not be emphasized that the full value of its unique culture and shared Saraiki-belt language would also be realized with the restitution of province status. The Bahawalpur movement itself has divided and subdivided, died and revived, been fiercely separate in some incarnations or absorbed in others into the Saraiki movements that demand recognition of a Saraikistan which includes Bahawalpur. Salahuddin Abbasi has always held to the clear message simply represented by Dr Umbreen Javaid, a former lecturer at the Islamia University, Bahawalpur.

> It is a historic fact that before One Unit, Bahawalpur had provincial status and Bahawalpur merged with the status of a province with West Pakistan at the time of One Unit. But when One Unit was broken on 30 March, 1970, Bahawalpur was made a part of Punjab Province although, at the time of the merger, an understanding was given to the Ameer of Bahawalpur that whenever One Unit will be broken, Bahawalpur will be restored as a separate Province.[1]

There is more of course, the list of grievances on the effects of One Unit on Bahawalpur dating back to the 1960s still continues to grow. They have been a running thread through Salahuddin's public life and through the second half of this book as well as various studies on the Bahawalpur movement. 'While One Unit countered Bengali domination in the legislature, it also brought small and culturally diverse provinces under the centralized control of Punjab. Bahawalpur State faced the same fate which bore serious consequences in the long run.'[2] The grievances have stood, substantially the same through nearly half a century since absorption into Punjab, but every complaint has been magnified. Former wealth and confidence have slipped away under the Punjabi hegemony that has ruled Pakistan and has also given rise to unrest in other marginalized regions. Bahawalpur is, however, or Bahawalpur state was, unique. It was far wealthier and more properly governed, for all the vicissitudes and eccentricities of some of its rulers. It had greater potential to play an equal or more than equal part in a federal Pakistan as a fifth province than smaller, more rugged and more tribal fiefdoms and princely states in other parts of the country. Before Partition, 'with a population of 2 million and 83 per cent majority of Muslims, Bahawalpur was considered one of the few rich states of the Sub-Continent'.[3]

Calls for a more representative government in the early 1950s led to elections to a newly instituted Bahawalpur provincial assembly on similar lines to every other provincial assembly. In constitutional drafts of 1952 and 1954, Bahawalpur was given provincial status and, furthermore, as was claimed by Makhdoom Noor Muhammad Hashmi, elected as an independent MNA in Bahawalpur in 1970, the Government of Pakistan published a Gazette notification where Bahawalpur was termed a province.[4] Like other provincial assemblies, the Bahawalpur assembly voted against One Unit. It was Sadiq Muhammad Khan who agreed to the merger, after a proclamation of his assumption of the powers of the Bahawalpur legislative assembly in order to do so. The battle for provincial status hinges not on the inception of One Unit and apparently unavoidable merger of Bahawalpur but on its break-up. Nevertheless, the nawab's actions resulted in a case brought against him in the Lahore High Court in 1956 by a thirty-year-old Bahawalpuri lawyer, Riaz Hashmi, later himself a high court judge in Lahore. In 1956, he was the Bahawalpur member of the Anti-One-Unit Front that included representatives of all provinces except Punjab. His case rested on grounds of the deprivation 'of his civil rights and franchise', and, 'that the act of the Constituent Assembly of Pakistan in respect of the State of Bahawalpur and its representation in the West Pakistan Assembly and the merger of Bahawalpur with the West Pakistan u/s 74 of the Interim Constitution of Bahawalpur were both *ultra vires*',[5] (literally beyond powers—beyond the legal powers of the person or illegitimate). According to Hashmi, constitutional history and law made it possible to say that the merger of Bahawalpur into the province of West Pakistan was altogether illegal.[6]

It hardly matters now, after the broken promises of the break-up of One Unit, whose name was appended to or who signed the Merger Agreement and whether or not it was countersigned by democratically elected members of the Bahawalpur legislative assembly. That there was no real choice is confirmed by the equal inability of any other province or state of the time, however ruled, to stand against the turn of that tide. The princes had already seen their powers leached away since Independence; Sadiq Muhammad Khan V may have seen the institution of the legislative assembly as the challenge it was to an autocratic prince. Its actions were likely to lead to a further loss of status and security for himself and his descendants, albeit not necessarily for Bahawalpur, within a federal Pakistan.

It had not been long, after all, since the Public Societies Act of 1942 banning the establishment of political parties in Bahawalpur had been enforced to quell participation in imported nationalist movements that also threatened the Bahawalpur status quo. As Umbreen Javaid points out, the majority in Bahawalpur was Muslim, led by a Muslim prince, and generally politically unaware. The nawab's people expected his word to be law. His own hopes for fulfilment of promises made by the government must have weighed on the side of agreement with the greater power. Beyond that, however, the ageing man who had already lost the greater part of the dignities, settings, traditions and decisions of his existence and those of his forefathers, knew he must accede when there was no viable alternative. The assurances of future change given to him by the government at least kept some hope in the air to hand on to the next generation.

When Bahawalpur merged into West Pakistan, it handed over Rs 100 million of revenue. After that, published figures show a steady impoverishment of the region during the 1960s as an annual income of Rs 200–220 million poured into West Pakistan's coffers from Bahawalpur. Bahawalpur received in return a development budget of Rs 30 million, rising to Rs 40–50 million after a campaign by Bahawalpur MNAs in 1970. Other regions fared better, receiving more funds than they paid to the Centre. The revenue of Baluchistan was about Rs 5.63 million, it received some Rs 90 million; and a revenue of Rs 70 million in NWFP was balanced against their expenditure of Rs 350 million.[7] Forced spending cuts in Bahawalpur meant proposals for setting up new technical colleges and a new university were dropped, free education ended and the quota for Bahawalpur students at colleges outside the state was stopped, although it continued for students from Karachi, Hyderabad, Quetta, Kalat and other centres in Sindh, Baluchistan and Khyber Pakhtunkhwa.

Effectively Bahawalpur was already absorbed, not only into West Pakistan but vanishingly into Punjab. All local institutions ceased to exist, meaning Bahawalpuri bureaucrats had to leave to find employment in other areas while quotas on new government jobs included Bahawalpur in Punjab, reducing the numbers actually from Bahawalpur almost to zero. As the administration filled with bureaucrats from everywhere except Bahawalpur and nepotism ruled appointments, institutions, industry and finance, Bahawalpur no longer had a voice and could be sidelined or forgotten. The region's resources were diverted elsewhere, successful industries abandoned and Bahawalpur was starved of cash that went to promote projects and industry in more favoured regions.

During the 1960s, the yearning for autonomy in Bahawalpur gathered impetus. It also fostered an additional emphasis on the Saraiki language. Saraiki was originally the language spoken by those who navigated the rivers of north India for trade. By the 1960s, it was effectively a conglomeration of local languages, Uchi, Derewali, Multani, Hindko and other dialects used across south Punjab and Sindh and previously seen as discrete. Thus, the purely Bahawalpur issue was broadened and confused. Efforts to promote Saraiki included translation of the Koran into Saraiki, and a biannual festival, *Jash-e-Farid*, of music and mushaira (poetry reading) was organized by the energetic Riaz Hashmi, who was himself an Urdu poet. He also founded *Razm-i-Saqafat*, a cultural group for the dissemination and preservation of local culture, in particular through translation of the mystic poetry of Khwaja Ghulam Farid into Bengali, English and Urdu. If these initiatives lost their guiding spirit when Hashmi moved to Lahore, there were others. The Saraiki movement continued to grow throughout the 1970s and 1980s, and onwards, in opposition to Punjabi and the all-powerful province.

The Saraiki Adabi Majlis (Saraiki Literary Society) had been founded by the author of the *Sadiqnamah*, Brigadier Nazeer Ali Shah, in the mid-1960s to focus more particularly on Bahawalpur as opposed to the wider Saraiki movement. The Bahawalpur movement was reinforced by the immigrant Abadkar and Muhajir communities, who had been encouraged to come to work in the state by the nawab. They had suffered particularly from the loss of industry as well as the departure of the bureaucracy in which many of these well-educated Urdu speakers were employed, forcing them once more to migrate for employment. Fearful of a movement less interested in economic and regional growth than imposing a culture and language they do not share, they have remained a mainstay of the periodically resurgent Bahawalpur province movement over forty years, as opposed to the Saraiki movements that hoovered up much of the Bahawalpur movement's support after it first fizzled out in 1971.

Alternately smouldering or flaring throughout the 1960s, the early surge of popular feeling and positive action for Bahawalpur reached its twin apogees in violence and election success in 1970.[8] As unrest grew during 1969, Makhdoom Gilani, a member of the Punjab assembly, issued a press release demanding separate province status for Bahawalpur. Prince Said ur-Rashid Abbasi, Salahuddin's uncle who had accepted that despised parliamentary secretaryship, supported by his brother, the amir, appealed for peaceful action towards separate provincial status. When a subcommittee under Justice Fazal-e-Akbar, later Chief Justice of Pakistan, came to Bahawalpur to explore the effects of One Unit, the only notable voice raised against a separate province was that of Makhdoom Hassan Mahmood. He was from a powerful Bahawalpuri pir family who had, in due course, become major landowners in Jamal Din Wali near Rahim Yar Khan and who caused trouble for Sadiq Muhammad Khan V and for Abbas Khan. Hassan Mahmood's sister was married to the seventh Pir Pagara; his son, Makhdoom Ahmed Mahmood, who was briefly governor of Punjab under President Zardari, is a friend of Salahuddin's and has been active in more recent incarnations of the Bahawalpur province movement. Other delegations beat the path towards Bahawalpur during 1969 led by Air Marshal Noor Khan, governor of West Pakistan at the time and previously best known for turning PIA into an internationally successful airline. As a dedicated reformer, he had fallen out with President Yahya Khan, and, as one of the main architects of the dissolution of One Unit, may have been sympathetic to Bahawalpur's situation.

In late November 1969, the expected end to One Unit was reported in the press, with confirmation of the restitution of former provinces and the amalgamation of Bahawalpur with Punjab. Various groupings from a range of political parties and important professional organizations, such as the Chamber of Commerce and Bar Association, began to muster. The foremost among them became the Bahawalpur Muttahida Mahaz (BMM—Bahawalpur United Front). Religious parties were attracted by an emphasis on restoring not only Bahawalpur province but also the traditions of the region, including a return to sharia law. They were contrastingly and inevitably against the policies of parties characterized as leftist, and were fighting for regional autonomy based on language such as the Saraiki movement,[9] believing 'Pakistan was liberated in the name of Islam with the only solution of all problems of the country lying in the enforcement of Sharia'.[10] Makhdoom Noor Muhammad Hashmi, elected to the National Assembly on an independent, (read province) ticket in the 1970 general election, wrote the following:

> One Unit not only paralysed our political and economic set-up and but also engulfed our social and religious purity. Before the merger of Bahawalpur into One Unit, there were neither unveiled women nor co-education. Following the traditions of Islam, there was a holiday on every Friday . . . the holy remove month of Ramadan was held in great esteem. There was a ban on selling wine and the preaching of Christianity was prohibited within the boundaries of the State. There was not even a single Church or missionary school . . . All the criminal and civil cases were decided according to Shariah . . . but after the merger of Bahawalpur, all these religious characteristics vanished.[11]

The traditionalist/religious aspect of the BMM and involvement of the former ruling family in the Bahawalpur movement led all too obviously to suggestions that the additional intention of restitution of provincial status for Bahawalpur was a reinvention of princely rule. It is worth dissecting this far-fetched conjecture to consider the number of cases where close attachment to, and connection between, former princes and their former states in independent India have brought rewards to their region through their efforts and hard work for their former people, as well as through the lure of royal stardust to the lucrative tourist trade.

From February 1970, the BMM organized large-scale protest marches and public meetings in support of Bahawalpur's demands. The leadership included Tahira Masood, daughter of Khawaja Nazimuddin, the former prime minister of Bahawalpur, who led separate women's protest marches for twenty-two days running and later spoke out against Z.A. Bhutto's handling of East Pakistan, her father's ancestral home. Hussain Ahmad Khan notes her remarkably inappropriate nickname, Joan of Arc.[12] On 24 April the government retaliated. The police opened fire, killing several, after marchers started throwing bricks, and the army was brought in to impose a curfew. Seventy or more leaders of the BMM were arrested, including Tahira Masood, who was expelled from Bahawalpur for a month, as against the prison sentences passed on the men. Most sentences were later remitted. The end of One Unit was officially enacted by President Yahya Khan on 1 July 1970.

In the run-up to the general election that December, it was not only Mujibur Rahman who talked the talk so far as resolving the province issue: the huge support for Bahawalpur province was demonstrated by its candidates, whether standing as independents or on whichever party ticket, sweeping the board with 80 per cent of the votes. Thereafter, as noted earlier, the machinations of

Zulfikar Ali Bhutto and the shock of the loss of East Pakistan in 1971 put an end to the dream. Prince Said ur-Rashid is quoted on his abandonment of the Bahawalpur cause, saying, 'a new province was no longer a priority issue'.[13] Others who entered Parliament on the hidden Bahawalpur ticket were strangely passive. Ghulam Mustafa Khar, governor of Punjab, announced BMM leaders had 'reached an agreement with his party (PPP) and would no longer insist on their demands',[14] and others among them were accused of using the opportunity afforded to accumulate personal wealth, as opposed to credit for the Bahawalpur movement. In other words, everyone had sold out or been bought.

Those who still had energy and determination to go forward carried both into the Saraiki movement. It has never gained the popularity within the boundaries of the former Bahawalpur state that it has found, albeit without real electoral success, in other Saraiki-speaking areas. In a paper published in 2009, as the Bahawalpur province movement once again achieved popular interest, Dr Umbreen Javaid wrote:

> The people strongly feel that the problems of Bahawalpur region can be solved if it is made a separate province rather than a part of Punjab. While comparing the level of development of Bahawalpur region with that of other areas of Punjab, the difference can be seen and felt immediately. The people of the region are not wrong in feeling left out of the mainstream. At the moment there is no political party or platform working towards the Bahawalpur Province demand but during national and provincial elections, the people are only like[ly] to vote for those candidates who support the cause. In Bahawalpur region it is very difficult for a candidate to win no matter from which political party, if he does not support a separate province for Bahawalpur. The demand for

> a separate province is popular amongst all sections of people. The masses of the region seem to be very touchy on this issue, it is still very fresh in their minds that this region, when a State was a flourishing one.[15]

The 'what might have been' of provincial status for Bahawalpur at that stage is something that Salahuddin lived with throughout his political career and it weighs on him until today: the development that might have happened, the revenue raised spent within the province; educational foundations; reduction of poverty; improved agriculture through direct negotiation with India for a return of the Sutlej waters; and Cholistan greening instead of being dredged dry to the brackish bottom of every borehole. Bahawalpur, a wealthy province founded on the principles that established Pakistan—a Muslim state but not an Islamized one on the model promoted by Zia, whatever Makhdoom Hashmi's pronouncement—might have been a wealthy and secure region for its inhabitants and for incomers and tourists to the magnificent palaces of Dera Nawab Sahib and the desert forts. For the Bhutto and Zia years there were other political and family battles to fight, and the growing marginalization of south Punjab and Bahawalpur under those leaders sapped the spirit of the generally peaceable Bahawalpuris. The power of the mosque grew to provide solace and alternative meaning for life or, alluringly, for a life to come. During the complicated decade of failed democracy and the swinging door of Benazir/Nawaz ascendancy, there were practical improvements to be negotiated and bargained for Bahawalpur, the demands of constituents to be attended, and almost continual campaigning. For Salahuddin, semi-retirement when the military once again grabbed power under General Musharraf, 'a decent man who made the right moves except when he felt he wanted to perpetuate his regime and picked corrupt people to back him', allowed a breathing space by 2004 to start a new movement for Bahawalpur province.

The popular desire for provincial status in Bahawalpur had in no way abated, but it was countered by the apathy of a largely forgotten population suffering under the yoke of a burgeoning upper Punjab. If it is as true today as in 1970 that 'the majority of masses of the region aspire for a separate province for Bahawalpur region, this strong feeling may turn into a political movement, if the grievances of the region are not seriously looked upon'.[16] The truth is that the masses have not yet summoned the energy to rise en masse to challenge the federal and Punjab governments. They may choose quietly to keep the peace when the guardians of the status quo, the Pakistan Army, sits not only in the garden of Sadiqgarh Palace but has its Southern Command HQ in Bahawalpur and the approximately 60,000 troops of XXXI Corps. It is unlikely the army would take 'an active movement, which will have a negative impact on the integration of Pakistan'[17] sitting down, should such an eventuality arise.

If Salahuddin's revived Bahawalpur province movement, embodied in his Bahawalpur National Awami Party (BNAP), kindled popular imagination and press interest, it failed to energize the powerful people's movement it needed among the second and third generations of a Bahawalpur population who remembered nothing of a different past. Thus, while provincial status remains the hope, there are few prepared to hazard more than their electoral vote in its practical support, and, although Salahuddin's party has lent its own support judiciously to those once again making suitable promises, it has been unable to stand alone. He found himself pumping personal funds into the movement, funds that he could no longer generate, thus eating into his descendants' inheritance, but unable to build on success, or challenge the expensive games of transferable loyalties and rigged election results of the leaders of his country.

In 2008, after Benazir Bhutto's assassination and as a result of those promises made by her to Salahuddin and his campaign on her behalf, PPP had a historic victory in Bahawalpur. Reward was not forthcoming from her party under her husband's leadership. As ever, promises, including those for cuts in interest on agricultural loans and plans for new communication and water infrastructure projects, both highly relevant to south Punjab, were ignored. Worse still for Bahawalpur was the announcement by Prime Minister Yousaf Raza Gillani in March 2009 of a planned division of Punjab for the creation of a new Saraiki province. This was considered to be a PPP ploy to make Bahawalpuri ambitions unachievable.[18] In July 2009, district assemblies in Bahawalpur, Bahawalnagar, Rahim Yar Khan and Lodhran passed resolutions in favour of demands to the federal government for a separate province. There were reports of a cross-party alliance of Bahawalpur MNAs and MPAs (member of provincial assembly) purely on the question of provincial status, although the prime minister ruled out any possibility of its creation.[19] By September that year, *Dawn* was reporting the involvement of influential members of PPP and PML(N) and meetings between Salahuddin, Makhdoom Ahmed Mahmood, son of Makhdoom Hassan, and Senator Muhammad Ali Durrani, one of the most energetic, active and vociferous supporters of the Bahawalpur movement, to discuss an active relaunch of the province movement.[20] The launch of BNAP, the 'Bahawalpur Declaration' took place in front of enormous crowds at a public meeting at Sadiqgarh in April 2011.

A breathless report in the *Nation*[21] described 22,000 people spread over 6 acres of land, and traffic jams on all roads leading to the palace from the three districts of Bahawalpur, Bahawalnagar and Rahim Yar Khan. The district bar associations and high court bar associations came out on strike 'to express their solidarity', and all the markets and bazaars were closed. National and provincial leaders from all parties attended the meeting to listen to Salahuddin, as the sole speaker, delivered his straightforward and essentially apolitical appeal for all the communities of Bahawalpur—Saraiki, Muhajir and Abadkar—to come together as Bahawalpuris alone, to unite in their efforts to see their province restored and bring an end to the plunder of its wealth by successive governments. Salahuddin made it quite clear that PML(N) could look for no more support in Bahawalpur than PPP since there was no longer any room in Bahawalpur for those who did not support the restoration of the province.

Not unexpectedly, a revival of the linguistic/ethnic political debate opened a can of worms for PPP and PML(N). Every separatist group or troublemaker in Pakistan jumped on the bandwagon in favour of one or other regional aspirant. In 2012, after President Zardari had announced the creation of a Saraiki province while touring the country, Muhammad Ali Durrani warned him in a speech of taking a 'voyage of hatred on linguistic basis'. He accused Prime Minister Gillani, of 'hatching conspiracies against South Punjab as they have failed to control the law and order situation in Gilgit-Baltistan, Balochistan, Sindh, Khyber-Pakhtunkhwa and in northern areas'.[22] In addition to damning the nation's leaders' countrywide policies, he alleged the PM had used Rs 120 billion on roads leading to his residence that had been allocated for the development of south Punjab and called for a referendum in Bahawalpur. He ended by thanking Nawaz Sharif for his promise to restore Bahawalpur.[23]

In August 2012, there were rumours of deals struck between Zardari and PPP and Salahuddin. Potential blandishments were aired, including a promise of the governorship of a new south Punjab province. This was denied at the time by both PML(N) and a BNAP spokesman. More accurately, during discussion of the history of the province movement, Salahuddin confirmed the offers to him of the governorship on more than one occasion but no deal was ever made. PML(N) continued during 2012-13 to uphold its promises of a new province, to be carved out of Punjab even before the coming general elections. In January 2013, as the May elections approached, Shahbaz Sharif, chief minister of Punjab, bizarrely enhanced his restated promise to Bahawalpur during a ceremony at Islamia University, by issuing free solar lamps to students of the region's schools and colleges. In his speech he condemned President Zardari's policies and character and finished by saying: 'Darkness, which President Asif has spread during his last five years, will be transformed into light by me. Asif has given darkness to agriculture and industrial sectors, schools, colleges and hospitals in the country and destroyed them through loot and plunder.'[24] In March 2013, the relatively new boy on the block, the leader of Pakistani Tehreek-i-Insaf, (PTI), Imran Khan, came calling. He requested a meeting with Salahuddin in Bahawalpur. It took place, for convenience, in Islamabad, where a joint announcement of their support for each other's candidates in Bahawalpur was made. Salahuddin once again drew attention to his straightforward, one-point agenda. Election results in the general election in the Bahawalpur division support his allegation of serious vote rigging as PML(N) won all except one seat in the National Assembly and all but three, of which one was BNAP, in the Punjab Assembly.

In the lead-up to another general election, in July 2018, Salahuddin was adamant he could not be enticed to try the process again. In the end, he says, Benazir was the only leader, with real stature in both international and domestic arenas, who could dilute the overweening power of Punjab in Pakistan. Moniba and her parental relatives have high hopes for Imran Khan and PTI as the wheel turns again. Salahuddin, however, considers that nothing really changes, and, swapping cynicism for faith, in hope or disappointment, announces that the Almighty has made it clear He will give people the leader they want. If they want corruption that is what they will get, regardless of changing faces. Nothing, he says, is likely to change very soon but, if or when it did, the widely cast and entrepreneurial Pakistani diaspora might return to its roots and then perhaps there would be transformation.

> The problem of Bahawalpur is one that has been awaiting a solution for a long time. The adversaries had shed a false light on it and violently opposed the demand on the ground that those who want to turn the former Bahawalpur State into a Province in reality desire to revive the princely state. These adversaries are equally frightened of the linguistic province of Siraikistan because in the reorganization of the provinces in West Pakistan on the generally recognized principles, the adversaries are going to be the losers. I have placed before the reader both sides of the picture. Time is on our side and it is only a matter of time until Bahawalpur Province is formed.
>
> Riaz Hashmi, 1972.

POSTSCRIPT

The last paragraphs of this book are not by any stretch conclusive but are merely final remarks. *Bahawalpur: The Kingdom That Vanished* was conceived and written in the hope that any evaluation of pieces of the past may add some small extra knowledge to support and inform the future. That is especially the case where the primary source of information has lived his life in tandem with that of his young country and shared in its vicissitudes. More particularly, he has shared the troubles of south Punjab of which Bahawalpur is a part. This postscript is just that, the last remembered snippets left over at the end of conversations with Salahuddin, with others, and of odds and ends of reading and research; the postscript to bring the picture as up to date as possible at the completion of this book.

It is too soon to look for conclusions to a history that, for all its long roots, has still barely begun. Pakistan is so young that the travails of its nativity will be in living memory for some years to come. Its future is still muddied by its well-remembered beginnings, not only in independence from colonial rule but a rending of its cultural, historical, ethnic and religious narrative. That is the macrocosm, past and present, against which the microcosm of the story of Bahawalpur and its Abbasi rulers is set. Hopes for a transformed and successful future for the greater part are shared with the lesser, but in Bahawalpur and other marginalized regions of Pakistan the hope has leached away like the river waters and the wealth. Hopes have been replaced by the broken promises of politicians and the panacea of extreme religion, peddled by opportunistic missionaries. Pakistan's unforgettably magnificent past, from distant extremes of antiquity through the metamorphoses generated during centuries of conquest and change, is fully discernible within the confines of the former Bahawalpur state. Added to that are the relics of its own unique and separate identity as a princely state and estate.

The future for Bahawalpur could, and should, include its important, conservable, and to an extent restorable, history and its extraordinary past. Pakistan, however, in its relative youth, is no place for old age, in particular under the progressive/regressive influence of recent regimes where high-speed forward motion and short-term financial gain have allowed no consideration for the gilded past to get in their way. The overriding dream of power holders in Pakistan in the twenty-first century, torn between conservative religious imperative and futuristic aspiration, has been almost as destructive, if less dramatic or overtly violent, as the iconoclastic wrecking of Syria, Iraq and Afghanistan by one or another Islamic extremist group.

Destruction of the past has always been part of war and often also of peace. Not everything can or should be preserved, but this is the twenty-first century, when people understand better what they are losing and what it is important to save. For a younger generation, as heedless as the young are meant to be, wedded to electronic images and the selfie stick as they tear blindly round the Lok Virsa Museum in Islamabad or the Victoria and Albert in London, the hold on images, words and the solid stone of historic and cultural roots must be maintained. Without them the foundations on which, in their future lives, they will build the future of their countries, will be weakened. There are already plenty of people in the world, and in Pakistan, who have forgotten how to value their past. They are 'out with the old', like the successful woman (or perhaps she was the wife of a successful man) who visited Moniba Abbasi at home. 'Yes,' she said, 'very nice,' as she looked round the antique-filled room, 'but don't you have anything new in your house?'

Pakistan is a democracy but its elected leaders follow their own agendas quite regardless of powerless public concern that can be bought, denied or diverted. Optimists may sense a change in the air but, if the present rates of progress and destruction are allowed to continue, there will be little left of the past for later generations. In forgotten south Punjab, the historic secular-built environment is already collapsing into architectural salvage. Only the saintly shrines may survive, although they too are threatened by the rise of the puritanical Deobandi radicalism. Perhaps the only thing left to provide religious solace and promises of heavenly reward for an immiserated population will be the innumerable mosques, old and new, spectacularly beautiful or made of lavatory brick on a garage forecourt. Their walls echo to the messages of an aggressive Islam, barely heard by past generations with hearing more attuned to devotional music and lives lived within the precepts of a simpler and kinder daily faith.

> South Punjab has emerged as a leading centre of Deobandi activity. Deobandi activities even in the colonial era were centred in this region because they wished to challenge its strong Sufi influence. Partition saw a number of Deobandi organisations re-established from Jullundur and Ludhiana in the region including Multan and Bahawalpur. In recent years there has been both a proliferation of

> Deobandi religious institutions and considerable recruitment for the Afghan and Kashmir jihads from this region of Pakistan.[1]

In a 2010 research paper for the Centre for Peace and Development Initiatives, an NGO based in Islamabad, Zubair Faisal Abbasi states the tragically obvious,

> that the areas in Southern Punjab, which are being called under the influence of violent conflict and are recruitment grounds for militants, have higher levels of poverty. Poverty can be taken as a proxy indicator of deprivation and socio-political exclusion from mainstream development. This deprivation has a connection with identity formation and politics of violence.[2]

Radical Islam is providing for poor people while the government ignores them. It may be educating their children only in a medieval form of their faith but that is a fine fit with devout and conservative poverty. The poor are further encouraged to divert or convert to different forms of their faith by free healthcare or even cash handouts from the mullahs of wealthy hard-line sects funded by Saudi Arabia.[3] The government buries its collective head in the sand or takes its own fat fee under cover of charitable donation, infrastructure funding or lucrative joint venture initiatives. Someone pays someone else for the shooting parties, organized for the princes of friendly Arab countries, that have accelerated the decimation of the once abundant wildlife of the reserved shikar lands round Derawar Fort and the 18,852 sq. km of the Greater Cholistan Desert.

Today there is hardly a wild bird or beast to be seen between Derawar and the crumbled remains of seventeen other desert forts built approximately 29 kilometres apart[4] that date from eighteenth-century rebuilding on much older structures. They may date back, like the remains of Bijnot Fort, to the eighth century CE. Beyond forts, 410 archaeological sites were identified by Mohammed Rafique Mughal, emeritus professor of archaeology at Pennsylvania University, in his 1997 book *Ancient Cholistan, Archaeology and Architecture,*[5] the great majority within the borders of the former Bahawalpur state. At that time, Professor Mughal remarked on the ruination of the forts due to neglect, vandalism and natural erosion. Today, only Derawar, the starting point for this book, stands, neglected and disputed but still magnificent, for now. If Salahuddin Abbasi and his immediate family could do anything to preserve that magnificence and the place where their ancestors are buried, they would.

Professor Robin Coningham, holder of the UNESCO chair in Archaeological Ethics and Practice in Cultural Heritage, and the UK's leading South Asian archaeologist, visited Derawar in 2017. He was with a UNESCO team engaged in updating the listings for possible World Heritage status for important Pakistani sites. The chance to penetrate the walls of Derawar came as a surprise, and Professor Coningham remains somewhat vague about the circumstances or under whose auspices the visit happened. It may have been clearer who was in charge of what when he visited Jehangir's tomb in Lahore. At Derawar, where the amir's authority to enter the fort is maintained but is constantly overseen by army and government eyes, the changing dynamics of responsibility or ownership further complicate designations of status on an internationally important cultural asset. There is a bigger picture of the issues of conservation in a country where nothing old or new is fully secure or necessarily valued by its theoretical caretakers.

The putative tourist to Pakistan might look at the treasures of the rest of the subcontinent and say who cares? I don't need Pakistan; I can go to India. India is indeed easier, but India's record on conservation has not always been perfect; destruction of history one way or another goes on as neglect, progress or money demands. Leaving aside seventy years of simmering enmity, the legacy of the religious divide at Partition has had effects on individual estates in India that are closer to the Bahawalpur experience. The son of the last Muslim raja of Mahmudabad, in the erstwhile kingdom of Oudh, who was four years old at the time of Partition, has fought the Indian government through the courts for restitution of the Mahmudabad properties originally confiscated at Independence under the 'Enemy Property Order'. The last raja took Pakistani citizenship, although his son remained in India and is an Indian citizen. The properties have been sealed, returned and retaken over the years under changing rulings. The Muslim population in India is set to become the largest in the world in the next few years. In 2017, Narendra Modi's Hindu nationalist government amended the Enemy Property Act to include Pakistani citizens and their legal heirs even if they are Indian citizens.[6] The properties were confiscated once again and, like Bahawalpur, the long-disputed built heritage of Mahmudabad crumbles.

All the same, who cares about a palace more or less in a place I have never heard of, the tourist asks. They can go to the Taj Mahal, to the forts of Jaisalmer and Jodhpur, they can see tigers in Rajasthan, watch birds in Himachal Pradesh, see elephants in Tamil Nadu and perhaps still a rhinoceros in Assam. They can shop for shawls from Mumbai to Ladakh, they can wear a bikini on the beach in Kerala or Goa, they can stay in luxury hotels from Kanyakumari to Kolkata and on a houseboat in Kashmir. Should they choose, they can tip whisky down their throats almost all the time in almost every state. They will be unlucky if they get shot or blown up, just as they will be if the same happens in London or New York and, in truth, in Lahore. But why should they go to Pakistan, it sounds more dangerous, more uncomfortable, and isn't it all the same stuff anyway? Well, yes and no. It is a major part of the same, more and the same and different, beautiful, fascinating, difficult and extraordinary.

Of course, the tourist should go, as should anyone who is curious or who loves the subcontinent. The vast panoply of cultures, religions and unvisited treasures to be rediscovered. Old walled Lahore, the Badshahi Mosque, and Kim's wonder house. The major remains of the cities of the Indus Valley Civilization. Gilgit and Chitral, evocative of the dangers and larger-than-life characters of the Great Game, and the famously beautiful Swat Valley. Karachi and the sea, once another Bombay. Baluchistan and Kalat, names of wild imaginings in Edwardian diaries. The great and gloriously tiled shrines of Sindh and Multan and Uch Sharif; and then Bahawalpur, encompassing ancient history and all the princely glamour and byzantine drama of nineteenth-century expectation that haunt tourist-filled Indian palaces today. The relics and remains of populations; Hindu, Buddhist, Greek, Mughal, Sikh, and British, not to mention the traditional hospitality of today's population in a region that cherishes the guest with unparalleled warmth.

But all that is for tomorrow, and tomorrow, and tomorrow. In the meantime, if Pakistan wishes to hold on to hope as it looks to the future, the outsider looking in can only hope too that its competing rulers will do their best to preserve their country's marvellous historical heritage, 'to remind the present generation that we can profit by our past errors and failures, and that we have the capacity to repair old defects and the power of reascending and attaining by new paths the heights which we failed to reach in the course of our previous efforts'.[7]

BIBLIOGRAPHY

Zubair Faisal Abbasi, *Federalism, Provincial Autonomy and Conflicts* (Islamabad: CPDI, 2010).

Rafique Afzal (ed.), *Selected Speeches of Quaid-i-Azam Muhammad Ali Jinnah, 1911-34 and 1947-48* (Lahore: Research Society of Pakistan, 1976).

F.S. Aijazuddin, *The Fickle Seventies: Memoirs 1972-79* (Lahore: Sang-e-Meel Publications, 2016).

Shahamet Ali, *The History of Bahawalpur, with Notices of the Adjacent Countries of Sindh, Afghanistan, Multan and the West of India* (London: James Madden, 1848).

Brooke Allen, *Benazir Bhutto, Favored Daughter*, Icons Series (New York: Amazon Publishing, 2016).

Yaqoob Khan Bangash, *A Princely Affair: The Accession and Integration of the Princely States of Pakistan, 1947-1955* (Karachi: OUP, 2015).

Mountstuart Elphinstone, *An Account of the Kingdom of Caubul and Its Dependencies in Persia, Tartary and India*, New and Revised Edition (London: Richard Bentley, 1839).

Benazir Bhutto, *Daughter of the East* (New York: Simon & Schuster, 1989).

Pir Soomro Bukhsh, 'Politics of Accession in the Undivided India: A Case Study of Nawab Mushtaq Gurmani's Role in the Accession of the Bahawalpur State to Pakistan', *Pakistan Journal of History & Culture*, vol. XXV, no. 2, 2004.

Alexander Burnes, *Travels into Bokhara, Narrative of a Voyage by the River Indus. Memoir of the Indus and Its Tributary Rivers in the Punjab,* vol. 111 (London: John Murray, 1834).

Henry Manners Chichester, *Dictionary of National Biography, 1835-1900,* vol. 35 (London: Smith, Elder & Co., 1893).

Lord Curzon, *Lord Curzon in India, Being a Selection of His Speeches as Viceroy and Governor-General 1898-1905* (London: Macmillan & Co., 1906).

William Dalrymple and Anita Anand, *Koh-i-Noor: The History of the World's Most Infamous Diamond* (New Delhi: Juggernaut Books, 2016).

Mahmood Khan Durrani, G.C., *The Sixth Column* (London: Cassell & Co. Ltd, 1955).

The Economist, Asia, January 2017.

Tarek Fatah, *Chasing a Mirage: The Tragic Illusion of the Islamic State* (Ontario: John Wiley & Sons Canada Ltd, 2008).

Almas Fatima and Aftab Hussain Gillani, *Impact of Measures of Defense Strategy Adopted by Bahawalpur State* (Saarbrucken, Germany: Lambert Academic Publishing, 2015).

Altaf Gauhar, *Ayub Khan: Pakistan's First Military Ruler* (OUP: Karachi, 2000) (reprinted, Lahore: Sang-e-Meel Publications, 2011).

Aftab Hussain Gillani, 'History of Bahawalpur State and Its Culture', *Pakistan Journal of Social Sciences* (PJSS), vol. 34, no. 2, 2014, pp. 463–71.

Rehana Saeed Hashmi and Gulshan Majeed, 'Saraiki Ethnic Identity: Genesis of Conflict with State', *Journal of Political Studies*, vol. 21, no. 1, 2014, pp. 79–101.

Riaz Hashmi, *Brief for Bahawalpur Province* (Bahawalpur : Bahawalpur Suba Mahaz, 1972).

Daniel R. Headrick, *The Tentacles of Progress, Technology Transfer in the Age of Imperialism, 1850-1940* (New York: Oxford University Press, 1988).

Ahmad Khan Hussain, *Re-Thinking Punjab: The Construction of Siraiki Identity* (Lahore: Research and Publication Centre [RPC], National College of Arts, 2004).

Yasir Hussain, *The Assassination of Benazir Bhutto* (New Delhi: Epitome Books, 2008).

Zahid Hussain, *Frontline Pakistan: The Path to Catastrophe and the Killing of Benazir Bhutto* (London: I.B. Tauris, 2008).

Professor Shaikh Inayatullah, 'Bahawalpur', in P. Bearman, Th. Bianquis, C.E. Bosworth, E. Van Donzel and W.P. Heinrichs (eds), *Encyclopaedia of Islam,* 2nd ed.(Leiden: Brill, 1960–2007).

Professor Shaikh Inayatullah, Presidential Address delivered at the Pakistan History Conference, 7th Session, February 1957.

Lawrence James, *Raj: The Making and Unmaking of British India* (London: Little, Brown & Co., 1997).

Dr Umbreen Javaid, *Politics of Bahawalpur: From State to Region (1947-2000)* (Lahore: Classic, 2004).

Amy Kazmin, 'The 70-Year Property War', *Financial Times*, London, 11 June 2017.

John Keay, *India: A History from the Earliest Civilisations to the Boom of the Twenty-First Century* (London: Harper Press, 2010).

Iram Khalid and Mina Ehsan Leghari, 'Radicalization of Youth in Southern Punjab', *Journal of South Asian Studies*, vol. 29, July–December 2014.

Imran Khan, *Pakistan: A Personal History* (London: Bantam Press, 2011).

Muhammad Ayub Khan, *Friends Not Masters: A Political Autobiography* (Karachi: OUP, 1967).

Surendra Nath Kaushik, *Zulfikar Ali Bhutto: Pakistan under Bhutto's Leadership* (reproduced by Sani Hussain Panhwar, Member Sindh Council PPP, 1985).

Surendra Nath Kaushik, *Politics in Pakistan* (reproduced by Sani Hussain Panhwar, Member Sindh Council PPP, 1984).

Anatol Lieven, *Pakistan: A Hard Country* (London: Penguin, 2012).

R.D. Mackenzie, 'At the Court of an Indian Prince', *Century Magazine,* vol. LVII, no. 5, March 1899.

Shahamet Ali, *The History of Bahawalpur, with Notices of the Adjacent Countries of Sindh, Afghanistan, Multan and the West of India* (London: James Madden, 1848).

Iftikhar H. Malik, *State and Civil Society in Pakistan: Politics of Authority, Ideology and Ethnicity* (Basingstoke, Hampshire: Macmillan Press Ltd, 1997).

Muhammad Akbar Malik, 'Elite Politics in the States: A Study of Bahawalpur Muslim League (1925-1947)', *Pakistaniaat: A Journal of Pakistan Studies,* vol. 4, no. 1, 2012.

Muhammad Din Malik, *Gazetteer of the Bahawalpur State with Map, 1904* (Lahore: Sang-e-Meel Publications, 2001).

Ahmed Asif Manan, 'Advent of Islam in South Asia', in Roger D. Long (ed.), *A History of Pakistan* (Karachi: OUP, 2015).

Charles Masson, *Narrative of Various Journeys in Balochistan, Afghanistan and the Panjab*, Vol. 1, (London: Richard Bentley, 1838).

Mary Minto, *Vicereine: The Indian Journal of Mary Minto,* edited by Anabel Loyd (Ghaziabad: Academic Foundation, 2015).

Satish Chandra Mittal, *Freedom Movement in Punjab, 1905–29* (Delhi: Concept Publishing).

Sir Penderel Moon, *Divide and Quit* (London: Chatto & Windus, 1962).

———, *The British Conquest and Dominion of India* (London: Duckworth, 1989).

Mariam Mufti, 'The Years of a Failed Democratic Transition', in Roger D. Long (ed.), *A History of Pakistan* (Karachi: OUP, 2015).

M. Rafique Mughal, *Ancient Cholistan, Archaeology and Architecture* (Lahore: Ferozsons (Pvt.) Ltd, 1997), quoted in Sajida Haider Vandal, *Cultural Expressions of South Punjab* (Lahore: THAAP, 2011).

Craig Murray, *Sikunder Burnes, Master of the Great Game* (Edinburgh: Birlinn Ltd, 2016).

Prof. Dr Razia Musarrat, 'Terrorism and Politico-Religious Extremism in Pakistan Post 9/11', *Journal of Public Administration and Governance,* ISSN 2161-7104 2014, vol. 4, no. 1, Macrothink Institute.

V.S. Naipaul, *Beyond Belief: Islamic Excursions among the Converted Peoples* (London: Picador, 2010).

Tariq Rahman, *Language and Politics in Pakistan* (Karachi: OUP, 1997).

Dr Atiq ur Rehman and Dr Zia ur Rehman, *Influence of Fatwa on the Judicial System of the State of Bahawalpur* (Al-Idah, 26 June 2013).

Saeed Shafqat, 'From Official Islam to Islamism', in Christophe Jaffrelot (ed.), *Pakistan, Nationalism without a Nation*, (New Delhi: Manohar, 2002).

Brigadier Nazeer Ali Shah, *Sadiqnamah, The History of Bahawalpur State* (Lahore: Maktaba Jadeed, 1959).

Masud Hassan Shahab, 'Bahawalpur Ki Siyasi Tarikh', (Urdu), Bahawalpur, 1978 quoted in Muhammad Akbar Malik, 'Elite Politics in the States: A Study of Bahawalpur Muslim League (1925-1947)', *Pakistaniaat: A Journal of Pakistan Studies*, vol. 4, no. 1, 2012.

Ayesha Siddiqa, *Military Inc., Inside Pakistan's Military Economy* (London: Pluto Press, 2007).

Ian Talbot, Introduction, in Roger D. Long, Gurharpal Singh, Yunas Samad and Ian Talbot (eds), *State and Nation-Building in Pakistan: Beyond Islam and Security,* (Abingdon, Oxon: Routledge, 2015).

———, *Pakistan: A New History, Revised and Updated* (London: G. Hurst & Co. [Publishers] Ltd, 2012).

Salmaan Taseer, *Bhutto: A Political Biography* (Ithaca, New York: Ithaca Press, 1979).

G.P. Tate, 'The Kingdom of Afghanistan: A Historical Sketch', *The Times of India*, Bombay and Calcutta, 1911.

Romila Thapar, *A History of India* (London: Penguin, 1990).

Ahmad Tufail, *The Next Decade of Jihadism in Pakistan, Current Trends in Islamist Ideology* (Hudson Institute, 20 June 2013).

Wayne Ayres Wilcox, *Pakistan: The Consolidation of a Nation* (New York: Columbia University Press, 1963).

Stanley Wolpert, *Zulfi Bhutto of Pakistan: His Life and Times* (New York: OUP, 1993).

Ron Wood, *The God Given Kingdom of Bahawalpur* (Hampshire: R. & J.L. Wood, Petersfield, date unknown).

Syed Muhammad Zulqurnain Zaidi, 'The Assassination of the Prime Minister Liaquat Ali Khan: The Fateful Journey', *Pakistan Journal of History and Culture,* vol. XXXI, no. 1, 2010.

Mahmood Zaman, *State Vandalism of History in Pakistan* (Lahore: Vanguard Books, 2011).

Lawrence Ziring, 'The Zia ul-Haq Era', in Roger D. Long (ed.), *A History of Pakistan* (Karachi: OUP, 2015).

Websites

1911 Imperial Durbar Album, https://bit.ly/2Ri6217

Aijazuddin, F.S., *The Potohari Bonaparte, A Short Bio of Ayub Khan on Pakistan's 70th Anniversary,* https://bit.ly/2rNMcjL

Encyclopaedia of Islam, https://bit.ly/2RipbAk

'Three Archives in Pakistan', https://bit.ly/2sJJooj

Ehsan Ahmed Sehar, 'Nawab Abbasi launches 'Bahawalpur Awami Party', *The Nation*, 5 April 2011, https://bit.ly/34OkyBV

Asif Javed, 'Nawab of Kalabagh: The Man Who Knew Too Much', *The Nation*, 29 June 2014, https://bit.ly/33InM8J

Text of the Punjab Waqf Properties Ordinance, 1979, https://bit.ly/34N3qwj

'Martial Law Under Field Marshal Ayub Khan', Story of Pakistan, 1 June 2003, https://bit.ly/34LP9jj

'Cultural Expression of South Punjab', UNESCO, https://bit.ly/2LlWuOV

A brief history of the Abbasi Dynasty, https://bit.ly/2RkqBds

A blog article on Bahawalpur, https://bit.ly/2LkiOIU

'Pakistan up against terror', Sutlej News, 21 December 2019, https://bit.ly/34PfqgL

Salman Rashid, 'The treasure of Derawar Fort', *The Express Tribune*, 17 July 2011, https://bit.ly/2ONUu4j

Abdul Manan, 'Durrani warns PPP against creation of Seraiki province', *The Express Tribune*, 16 April 2012, https://bit.ly/2LhVICr

———, 'Covert understanding: Nawab drops demand for Bahawalpur province', *The Express Tribune*, 2 August 2012, https://bit.ly/34N13tx

'Poverty in Pakistan: Issues, Causes And Institutional Responses', Asian Development Bank, July 2002, https://bit.ly/2rbtCCb

Majid Sheikh, 'How Our Entire History Was Dumped in a Horse Stable', *Dawn*, 6 October 2013, https://bit.ly/2Rj9VDg

Nadeem F. Paracha, 'Smokers' corner: Who was Yahya Khan?', *Dawn*, 19 March 2017, https://bit.ly/33OAkLw

'BAHAWALPUR: Prince Abbasi's widow terms auction unlawful: Sadiqgarh Palace', 14 February 2004, *Dawn*, https://bit.ly/2RdmRdM

'BAHAWALPUR: Auction of Nawab's cars fetches Rs10m', *Dawn*, 10 May 2004, https://bit.ly/2Pe9bfI

'Movement for Bahawalpur province under study', *Dawn*, 28 September 2009, https://bit.ly/2PaisFV

'Origins of poverty in south Punjab', *Dawn*, 2 August 2010, https://bit.ly/34PlvtB

Zoltan Barany, 'Authoritarianism in Pakistan', Hoover Institute, University of Stanford, https://hvr.co/2PfSNeK

Shahid Hussain Raja, 'Political Economy of Pakistan Under Zulfiqar Ali Bhutto', Scribd, https://bit.ly/2ONdDDm

Jon Boone, 'The saints go marching out as the face of Islam hardens in Pakistan', *Guardian*, 15 January 2014, https://bit.ly/2rfvlX0

'Is Bahawalpur province a pipe dream after all?', *The News International*, 14 July 2009, https://bit.ly/2P8Jj5b

'Bahawalpur, South Punjab to be separate provinces: Shahbaz', *The News International*, 30 January 2013, https://bit.ly/2PaYwTb

Full text of *The Golden Book Of India: A Genealogical and Biographical Dictionary of the Ruling Princes, Chiefs, Nobles, and Other Personages, Titled or Decorated, of The Indian Empire, with an Appendix for Ceylon*, https://bit.ly/37XxAyO

British Library, India Office Records

IOR/F/4/1401/55487 June 1831–December 1832.

IOR/F/4/1523/60136 May 1833–March 1835.

IOR/L/PS/6/538 Coll. 86/1 and 86/2 1865.

IOR/L/PS/6/532.

IOR/L/PS/6/516/543 Coll. 48/1 and Coll. 48/2 1866.

IOR/L/PS/6/545 Coll. 69/3 Report of William Ford on his mission to Bahawalpur.

IOR/R/1/1/189 1897.

IOR/R/1/1/207 1898.

IOR/l/PS/11/202 P4734/1921 29 September 1921–1 November 1921.

IOR/1/1/1498 1925–26.

IOR/R/1/1/1767 1926.

IOR/R/1/1/1901 1929–30.

IOR/R/1/1/3077 1938.

IOR/R/1/1/3683 1941.

IOR/R/4028 1943.

IOR/R/1/4/31 1931.

IOR/R/1/1/4279 1945.

IOR/P(S) 1933 File 324.

IOR/R/1/1/2740 1935.

IOR/R/1/1/3190 1938–39.

IOR/P(S) 1936 File 574, Correspondence between Lt Col. Wilberforce-Bell, Resident, Punjab States, and Khan Bahadur Nabi Bakhsh Hussain, Prime Minister, Bahawalpur, 1928–43.

IOR/R/1/4/42 1925–26.
IOR/P(S)/1922 File 1056 Pt. 2
IOR/R/1/1/3226 1939.
IOR/R/1/1/3455 1940.
IOR/P(S)/1945 File 100.
IOR/R/1/1/2735.

NOTES

Foreword

1. *The Royal Visit to India, 1911-12* by the Hon. John Fortescue (London: Macmillan and Co., 1912). After the durbar, the king went shooting in Nepal for ten days over Christmas. The total bag for his party was thirty-nine tigers, eighteen rhinoceroses and four bears.

Introduction

1. Dr Shaikh Inayatullah, Professor of Arabic, University of the Punjab, 1957, and later used by Arthur M. Schlesinger Jr.
2. Acquired by the royal family of Jammu and Kashmir in 1951, it was renamed Taragarh in honour of the dowager maharani who lived there. It is now a hotel.
3. Tarek Fatah, *Chasing a Mirage: The Tragic Illusion of the Islamic State* (Ontario: John Wiley & Sons Canada Ltd, 2008).
4. The Great Leader.
5. Pakistan Movement for Justice.
6. Anatol Lieven, *Pakistan: A Hard Country* (London: Penguin, 2012).
7. Yaqoob Khan Bangash, *A Princely Affair* (Karachi: OUP, 2015).
8. Nazeer Ali Shah, *Sadiqnamah: The History of Bahawalpur State* (Lahore: Maktaba Jadeed, 1959).

9. Penderel Moon, *Divide and Quit* (London: Chatto & Windus, 1962).

Part 1: The Wide Sweep of History

Chapter 1: Dynasty

1. Shahamet Ali, *The History of Bahawalpur, with Notices of the Adjacent Countries of Sindh, Afghanistan, Multan and the West of India* (London: James Madden, 1848).
2. One of the first students to join the first English class at the Persian College, Delhi, founded in 1792. He became munshi to Captain Claude Martin Wade during the negotiations between the Sikhs and Shah Shuja of Afghanistan and, later, prime minister of Indore.
3. *Tabarrukat*—Islamic holy relics.
4. Some historians and archaeologists believe that the term Saraiki is a corruption of Savistan, of interest in this case because Bahawalpur is a Saraiki-speaking region and one among several areas in Pakistan with specific non-Urdu linguistic identities which continue to fight for greater autonomy based on those groupings. The movement for provincial status for the Saraiki region clashes with the movement for provincial status for Bahawalpur alone based on promises made at Independence.
5. Brigadier Nazeer Ali Shah, *Sadiqnamah: The History of Bahawalpur State* (Lahore: Maktaba Jadeed, 1959).
6. V.S. Naipaul, *Beyond Belief: Islamic Excursions among the Converted Peoples* (London: Picador, 2010).
7. Shaikh Inayatullah, 'Bahāwalpūr', in, *Encyclopaedia of Islam*, Second Edition, edited by P. Bearman, Th. Bianquis, C.E. Bosworth, E. Van Donzel and W.P. Heinrichs, 1960–2007.
8. *Sadiqnamah.*
9. 'Cultural Expression of South Punjab', UNESCO, https://bit.ly/2LlWuOV
10. Manan Ahmed Asif, 'The Advent of Islam in South Asia', in *A History of Pakistan,* edited by Roger D. Long (Karachi: OUP, 2015).
11. Tarek Fatah, *Chasing a Mirage* (Toronto: Wiley, 2008).

Chapter 2: The Family Line

1. Shahamet Ali, *The History of Bahawalpur, with Notices of the Adjacent Countries of Sindh, Afghanistan, Multan and the West of India* (London: James Madden, 1848), p. 17.
2. William Dalrymple and Anita Anand, *Koh-i-Noor: The History of the World's Most Infamous Diamond* (New Delhi: Juggernaut Books, 2016).
3. BL/EUR/MSS/B/28/f.40 quoted in Craig Murray, *Sikunder Burnes, Master of the Great Game* (Edinburgh: Birlinn Ltd, 2016).
4. Pillar of the State, Victorious in War, Keeper of the Kingdom.
5. G.P. Tate, 'The Kingdom of Afghanistan: A Historical Sketch', *The Times of India*, Bombay and Calcutta, 1911.
6. *Gazetteer of the Bahawalpur State,* 1904.
7. *The History of Bahawalpur*, p. 130.
8. Ibid., p. 137.
9. Mountstuart Elphinstone, *An Account of the Kingdom of Caubul, and Its Dependencies in Persia, Tartary and India,* New and Revised Edition (London: Richard Bentley, 1839).
10. Ibid., p. 502.

Chapter 3: Anglophile Princes

1. John Keay, *India: A History from the Earliest Civilisations to the Boom of the Twenty-First Century* (London: Harper Press, 2010); and Sir Penderel Moon, *The British Conquest and Dominion of India* (London: Duckworth, 1989).
2. Charles Masson, *Narrative of Various Journeys in Balochistan, Afghanistan and the Panjab,* vol. I (London: Richard Bentley, 1844).
3. Charles Masson was the pseudonym of James Lewis, an inveterate army deserter and the first European to see the ruins of the pre-Indus city of Harappa.
4. Arthur Conolly, *Journey to the North of India, through Russia, Persia and Afghanistan* (London: Richard Bentley, 1838).
5. IOR/F/4/1401/55487 June 1831–December 1832.
6. IOR/F/4/1523/60136 May 1833–March 1835.

7. Alexander Burnes, *Travels into Bokhara, Narrative of a Voyage by the River Indus. Memoir of the Indus and Its Tributary Rivers in the Punjab*, vol. III (London: John Murray, 1834); and Lawrence James, *Raj: The Making and Unmaking of British India* (London: Little, Brown & Co., 1997).
8. Sydney Cotton, *Dictionary of National Biography, 1885–1900*, vol. 35, Henry Manners, Chichester.
9. *Gazetteer of the Bahawalpur State*, 1904.
10. Lawrence James, *Raj*.
11. Sir Penderel Moon, *The British Conquest and Dominion of India*.
12. Feudal system of land grants whereby the *jagirdar* managed and received income from the landholding of which part was due to the state in addition to military support when required.
13. *Gazetteer of the Bahawalpur State*, 1904.

Chapter 4: Family Matters

1. The Doctrine of Lapse enabled the British annexation of princely states where there was no direct male heir to the ruler or the ruler was deemed incompetent.
2. Michael Pakenham Edgeworth was the youngest of the siblings of Maria Edgeworth, the novelist. Being commissioner was a sideline to his career as a botanist and he was also known as a pioneer of photography.
3. Administrator in India, writer and revenue minister in Bahawalpur during Partition.
4. IOR/L/PS/6/538 Coll. 86/1 and 86/2 1865.
5. IOR/L/PS/6/532; and IOR/L/PS/6/516/543.
6. Ibid., Coll. 48/1 and Coll. 48/2 1866.
7. IOR/L/PS/6/545 Coll. 69/1 June 1866–July 1866 and Coll. 69/2 and Coll 81/2 August 1866.
8. IOR/L/PS/6/545 Coll. 69/3 Report of William Ford on his mission to Bahawalpur.

Chapter 5: Trappings of Modernity

1. 'The Effect of Travel on Indian Princes,' *The Spectator*, 2 July 1888.

2. R.D. Mackenzie, 'At the Court of an Indian Prince', *Century Magazine*, vol. LVII, no. 5, March 1899.
3. IOR/R/1/1/1053 1896–97.
4. L.J.H. Grey, *Tales of Our Grandfather: or, India since 1865*, edited by F. & C. Grey (London: Smith, Elder & Co., 1912).
5. IOR/R/1/1/189 1897.
6. IOR/R/1/1/207 1898.
7. In the 1930s, Arthur Evill was headmaster of Ashdown House prep school in the UK where 'he wielded a 3 ft cane on the boys'. The school was more recently attended by Prime Minister Boris Johnson among other well-known names.
8. Quoted in Almas Fatima and Aftab Hussain Gillani, *Impact of Measures of Defense Strategy Adopted by Bahawalpur State* (Saarbrucken: Lambert Academic Publishing, 2015).
9. *Vicereine: The Indian Journal of Mary Minto,* edited by Anabel Loyd (Ghaziabad: Academic Foundation, 2015).

Chapter 6: Another Century

1. *Lord Curzon in India, Being a Selection of His Speeches as Viceroy and Governor-General 1898-1905* (London: Macmillan & Co., 1906).
2. IOR/L/PS/11/202 P4734/1921 29 September 1921–1 November 1921.
3. Satish Chandra Mittal, *Freedom Movement in Punjab, 1905–29* (Delhi: Concept Publishing, p. 93).
4. Ibid., p. 110.
5. Masud Hasan Shahab, *Bahawalpur Ki Siyasi Tarikh* (Urdu) (Bahawalpur, 1978), pp. 56–57, quoted in Muhammad Akbar Malik, 'Elite Politics in the States: A Study of Bahawalpur Muslim League (1925-1947)', *Pakistaniaat: A Journal of Pakistan Studies*, vol. 4, no. 1, 2012.
6. Penderel Moon, *Divide and Quit* (London: Chatto & Windus, 1962).
7. Daniel R. Headrick, *The Tentacles of Progress, Technology Transfer in the Age of Imperialism, 1850-1940* (New York: Oxford University Press, 1988).
8. Ibid.

9. IOR/1/1/1498 1925–26.
10. Penderel Moon, *Divide and Quit.*
11. Ibid.

Chapter 7: The Last Nawab

1. R/1/1/1498 1925-6 1920s.
2. Ibid.
3. Ibid.
4. IOR/R/1/1/1751.
5. Ibid.
6. Ibid.
7. Ibid.
8. R/1/1/1498 1925–6 1920s.
9. IOR/R/1/1/1767 1926.
10. IOR/R/1/1/1901 1929–30.
11. Ibid.
12. IOR/R/1/1/3077 1938.
13. Ibid.

Chapter 8: The Exercise of Power

1. IOR/R1/1/3683 1941.
2. IOR/R/4028 1943.
3. A brief history of the Abbasi Dynasty, https://bit.ly/2RkqBds
4. IOR/R/1/4/31 1931.
5. Ron Wood, *The God Given Kingdom of Bahawalpur*, R. & J.L. Wood, Petersfield, Hampshire, date unknown.
6. IOR/R/1/1/4279 1945.
7. IOR/P(S) 1933 File 324.
8. This was for sale in London in 2016.
9. The waiting period after divorce or widowhood in Islam when the woman may not marry again.
10. IOR/P(S)/1933 File 324.
11. IOR/R/1/1/2740 1935.
12. IOR/R/1/1/3190 1938–39.

13. IOR/P(S)/1936 File 574, Correspondence between Lt Col. H. Wilberforce-Bell, Resident, Punjab States, and Khan Bahadur Nabi Bakhsh Mohammed Hussain, Prime Minister, Bahawalpur, 1928–43.
14. IOR/R/1/4/42 1925–26.
15. IOR/P(S)/1922 File 1056 Pt. 2.
16. IOR/R/1/1/3226 1939.
17. IOR/R/1/1/3455: 1940.
18. IOR/P(S)/1945 File 100.

Part 2: A New Country

Chapter 9: Division and State

1. Mahmood Khan Durrani, *The Sixth Column* (London: Cassell & Co. Ltd, 1955).
2. Rafique Afzal (ed.), *Selected Speeches of Quaid-i-Azam Muhammad Ali Jinnah, 1911-34 and 1947-48* (Lahore: Research Society of Pakistan, 1976), pp. 415–17, quoted in Pir Bukhsh Soomro, 'Politics of Accession in the Undivided India: A Case Study of Nawab Mushtaq Gurmani's Role in the Accession of the Bahawalpur State to Pakistan', *Pakistan Journal of History & Culture*, vol. XXV, no. 2, 2004.
3. Wayne Ayres Wilcox, *The Consolidation of a Nation.*
4. Ibid., quoted in *Dawn.*
5. Letter from M.A. Gurmani to Mr Ikramullah, 14 August 1947, from *Dawn,* 22 May 1958, quoted in Pir Bukhsh Soomro, 'Politics of Accession in the Undivided India: A Case Study of Nawab Mushtaq Gurmani's Role in the Accession of the Bahawalpur State to Pakistan', *Pakistan Journal of History & Culture*, vol. XXV, no. 2, 2004.
6. *Dawn*, 25 August 1947, quoted in Wilcox, *The Consolidation of a Nation.*
7. Wayne Ayres Wilcox, *The Consolidation of a Nation* (Columbia University Press: New York, 1963).
8. Pir Bukhsh Soomro, 'Politics of Accession in the Undivided India: A Case Study of Nawab Mushtaq Gurmani's Role in the Accession of the Bahawalpur State to Pakistan', *Pakistan Journal of History & Culture*, vol. XXV, no. 2, 2004.

9. Later General J.M. Marden, utterly loyal to the nawab, died after retirement in Bahawalpur and is buried at Derawar.
10. Outlaw followers of the Pir Pagara of Sindh.

Chapter 10: Pakistan

1. Yaqoob Khan Bangash, *A Princely Affair: The Accession and Integration of the Princely States of Pakistan 1947-1955* (OUP, 2015).
2. On a recent visit to Sir John's retirement home in Waterlooville, near Portsmouth, with his great-niece, the author met his neighbour who remembered that Sir John had been known locally in his old age as Sir John Gin.
3. British Library Mss Eur 226/8.
4. The rank, titles and honours of the nawabs of Bahawalpur were stripped from Amir Abbas Khan under Zulfikar Ali Bhutto in 1972.
5. Dr Umbreen Javaid, *Politics of Bahawalpur: From State to Region (1947-2000)* (Lahore: Classic, 2004).
6. Ibid.

Chapter 11: Childhood and Memory

1. Roger D. Long, *A History of Pakistan* (Karachi: OUP, 2015).
2. Muhammad Ayub Khan, *Friends Not Masters: A Political Autobiography* (Karachi: Oxford University Press, 1967), p. 41.
3. IOR/R/1/1/2735.

Chapter 12: Public Lives

1. Between veil and four walls.
2. Roger D. Long, *A History of Pakistan* (Karachi: OUP, 2015).
3. President Ayub Khan quoted in *President Mohammad Ayub Khan, A profile* (Karachi: Pakistan Publications, 1962).
4. F.S. Aijazuddin, 'The Potohari Bonaparte', 17 August 2017, https://bit.ly/34R4z63
5. Mohammad Ayub Khan, *Pakistan Perspective*, Embassy of Pakistan, USA.

6. Iftikhar H. Malik, *State and Civil Society in Pakistan: Politics of Authority, Ideology and Ethnicity* (Basingstoke: Macmillan Press Ltd, 1997).
7. Altaf Gauhar, *Ayub Khan: Pakistan's First Military Ruler* (Karachi: OUP, 2000) (Lahore: Meel Publications, 2011), p. 481.
8. Saeed Shafqat, 'From Official Islam to Islamism', in Christophe Jaffrelot (ed.), *Pakistan, Nationalism without a Nation* (New Delhi: Manohar, 2002).
9. Refer the text of the Punjab Waqf Properties Ordinance, 1979, https://bit.ly/34N3qwj
10. Altaf Gauhar, *Ayub Khan*.
11. Asif Javed, 'Nawab of Kalabagh: The Man Who Knew Too Much', 29 June 2014, https://bit.ly/33InM8J
12. Altaf Gauhar, *Ayub Khan*, p. 474.
13. Ibid.
14. Ian Talbot, *Pakistan: A New History, Revised and Updated* (London: G. Hurst & Co. [Publishers] Ltd, 2012).
15. Ayesha Siddiqa, *Military Inc., Inside Pakistan's Military Economy* (London: Pluto Press, 2007).
16. 'bread, clothing, shelter'.
17. Dr Umbreen Javaid, *Movement for Bahawalpur Province* (Lahore: Political Science Department, University of the Punjab, 2000).

Chapter 13: The Abuse of Greatness

1. Stanley Wolpert, *Zulfi Bhutto of Pakistan: His Life and Times* (New York: OUP, 1993).
2. This book was written in major part on Islay, a centre of malt whisky distilling where the author spent much of her childhood. She had never heard of Black Dog in Scotland or in India. It was first blended and bottled in Scotland in 1883 by James MacKinlay to meet an order placed by Herbert Musgrave Phipson, owner of Phipson & Co. Wine Merchants from Bombay. It is named after a salmon fly. Black Dog had been sold in Pakistan during the British Raj, prior to Partition and presumably thereafter. According to Google, it remains highly popular in India today, https://en.wikipedia.org/wiki/Black_Dog_Scotch_Whisky
3. Salmaan Taseer, *Bhutto: A Political Biography* (New York: Ithaca Press, 1979).

4. Ibid.
5. Surendra Nath Kaushik, *Zulfikar Ali Bhutto: Pakistan under Bhutto's Leadership*, 1985, reproduced by Sani Hussain Panhwar, member, Sindh Council, PPP, copyright www.bhutto.org
6. Almas Fatima and Aftab Hussain Gillani, *Impact of Measures of Defense Strategy Adopted by Bahawalpur State* (Saarbrucken: Lambert Academic Publishing, 2015), p. 104.
7. Ibid.
8. Under the 1975 Act, an ancient building was defined as one completed more than seventy-five years earlier.
9. Mahmood Zaman, *State Vandalism of History in Pakistan* (Lahore: Vanguard Books, 2011).
10. Salmaan Taseer, *Bhutto: A Political Biography*.
11. Stanley Wolpert, *Zulfi Bhutto of Pakistan*, p. 210.
12. Ibid.
13. Surendra Nath Kaushik, *Zulfikar Ali Bhutto*, p. 108.
14. Ibid., p. 110.
15. Salahuddin Abbasi interview.
16. Ibid.
17. Mumtaz Ali Bhutto quoted in Stanley Wolpert, *Zulfi Bhutto of Pakistan*, p. 7. *His Life and Times* (New York: OUP, 1993), p. 7.
18. Ibid, p. 19.
19. Salman Rashid, 'The treasure of Derawar Fort', *The Express Tribune*, 17 July 2011, https://bit.ly/2ONUu4j

Chapter 14: Salahuddin

1. Zahid Hussain, *Frontline Pakistan: The Path to Catastrophe and the Killing of Benazir Bhutto*, I.B. Tauris, London, 2008, p. 18.
2. Ian Talbot, *Pakistan: A New History*, OUP, Karachi, 2012, p. 105.

Chapter 15: The Last Amir

1. Roger D. Long, *A History of Pakistan* (Karachi: OUP, 2015), p. 515.
2. Ibid.

3. Described by Field Marshal Sam Manekshaw, who led the Indian Army against Pakistan in 1971 and Yahya's superior in 1947, as 'an excellent, hard-working officer who had a logical mind and could think clearly'.
4. Ibid., p. 521.
5. Ian Talbot, *Pakistan: A New History* (Karachi: OUP, 2012).
6. Ibid., p. 25.
7. The Gog and Magog of the Books of Genesis, Ezekiel and Revelations and thus all the People of the Book.
8. F.S. Aijazuddin, *The Fickle Seventies: Memoirs 1972-79* (Lahore: Sang-e-Meel Publications, 2016).
9. Research has not unearthed details of the organization founded by a man better known for his love of dogs and his conservation work for the Asian lion.
10. Iftikhar H. Malik, *State and Civil Society in Pakistan: Politics of Authority, Ideology and Ethnicity* Macmillan Press Ltd, in association with St Anthony's College (Basingstoke: Oxford, 1997).
11. 'Three Archives in Pakistan', https://bit.ly/2sJJooj
12. Majid Sheikh, 'How Our Entire History Was Dumped in a Horse Stable', *Dawn*, 6 October 2013, https://bit.ly/2Rj9VDg
13. 'BAHAWALPUR: Auction of Nawab's cars fetches Rs10m', *Dawn*, 10 May 2004, https://bit.ly/2Pe9bfI
14. Ibid.
15. Supreme Court of Pakistan, Civil Petitions No. 500 and 1539-L of 2004.
16. 'BAHAWALPUR: Prince Abbasi's widow terms auction unlawful: Sadiqgarh Palace', 14 February 2004, *Dawn*, https://bit.ly/2RdmRdM
17. *A Case of Exploding Mangoes*, the comic novel by Mohammed Hanif.
18. Ian Talbot, *Pakistan: A New History*, p. 140.
19. Ibid.
20. Ibid.
21. Lawrence Ziring, 'The Zia ul-Haq Era', in Roger D. Long (ed.), *A History of Pakistan*, p. 629.
22. Prof. Dr Razia Musarrat, Chairperson, Department of Political Science, Islamia University of Bahawalpur, 'Terrorism and Politico-Religious

Extremism in Pakistan post 9/11', *Journal of Public Administration and Governance,* ISSN 2161-7104 2014, vol. 4, no. 1, Macrothink Institute.
23. Tufail Ahmad, *The Next Decade of Jihadism in Pakistan, Current Trends in Islamist Ideology* (Hudson Institute, 20 June 2013).
24. Iram Khalid and Mina Ehsan Leghari, 'Radicalization of Youth in Southern Punjab', *Journal of South Asian Studies*, vol. 29, no. 2, July–December 2014, pp. 537–51.

Chapter 16: In the Labyrinth

1. *The Economist*, Asia, January 2017.
2. Since this book was completed, Nawaz Sharif has been found guilty of corruption and is presently serving a prison sentence. His brother Shahbaz is the present leader of the PML(N) and leader of the Opposition.
3. Sher Ali Khan in *Herald*, 23 April 2018.
4. PPP 2008 Election Manifesto quoted in Yasir Hussain, *The Assassination of Benazir Bhutto* (New Delhi: Epitome Books, 2008).
5. Ibid.
6. Ibid.
7. Mariam Mufti, 'The Years of Failed Democratic Transition', in Roger D. Long (ed.), *A History of Pakistan* (Karachi: OUP, 2015), p. 63.
8. Brooke Allen, *Benazir Bhutto, Favored Daughter*, Icons Series (New York: Amazon Publishing, 2016).

Chapter 17: The Bahawalpur Province Movement

1. Dr Umbreen Javaid, *Politics of Bahawalpur: From State to Region (1947-2000)* (Lahore: Classic, 2004), p. 133.
2. Hussain Ahmad Khan, *Re-Thinking Punjab: The Construction of Siraiki Identity*, Research and Publication Centre (RPC) (Lahore: National College of Arts, 2004), p. 66.
3. Ibid.
4. Ibid.
5. Riaz Hashmi, *Brief for Bahawalpur*, Bahawalpur Suba Mahaz, Bahawalpur, 1972, p. 164.

6. Ibid.
7. Ibid., p. 67.
8. Hussain Ahmad Khan, *Re-Thinking Punjab*.
9. Dr Umbreen Javaid, *Politics of Bahawalpur*, p. 167.
10. Hussain Ahmad Khan, *Re-Thinking Punjab*, p. 116.
11. Ibid., p. 108.
12. Ibid.
13. Tariq Rahman, *Language and Politics in Pakistan*, Karachi, OUP, 1997, p. 182.
14. Hussain Ahmad Khan, *Re-Thinking Punjab*, p. 109.
15. Dr Umbreen Javaid, 'Movement for Bahawalpur Province', *Journal of Political Studies*, Vol. XV, pp: 41–57, Summer 2009, University of Punjab.
16. Ibid.
17. Ibid.
18. Refer this blog article on Bahawalpur, https://bit.ly/2LkiOIU
19. 'Is Bahawalpur province a pipe dream after all?', *The News International*, 14 July 2009, https://bit.ly/2P8Jj5b
20. 'Movement for Bahawalpur province under study', *Dawn*, 28 September 2009, https://bit.ly/2PaisFV
21. Ehsan Ahmed Sehar, 'Nawab Abbasi launches 'Bahawalpur Awami Party', *The Nation*, 5 April 2011, https://bit.ly/34OkyBV
22. Abdul Manan, 'Durrani warns PPP against creation of Seraiki province', *The Express Tribune*, 16 April 2012, https://bit.ly/2LhVICr
23. Ibid.
24. 'Bahawalpur, South Punjab to be separate provinces: Shahbaz', *The News International*, 30 January 2013, https://bit.ly/2PaYwTb

Postscript

1. Introduction, Roger D. Long, Gurharpal Singh, Yunas Samad and Ian Talbot (eds), *State and Nation-Building in Pakistan: Beyond Islam and Security* (Abingdon, Oxon: Routledge, 2015).
2. Zubair Faisal Abbasi, *Federalism, Provincial Autonomy and Conflicts* (Islamabad: CPDI, 2010).
3. Jon Boone, 'The saints go marching out as the face of Islam hardens in Pakistan', *Guardian*, 15 January 2014, https://bit.ly/2rfvlX0

4. Sajida Haider Vandal, *Cultural Expressions of South Punjab* (Lahore: THAAP, 2011).
5. M. Rafique Mughal, *Ancient Cholistan, Archaeology and Architecture*, Ferozsons (Pvt.) Ltd, Lahore, 1997, quoted in Sajida Haider Vandal, *Cultural Expressions of South Punjab*.
6. Amy Kazmin, *Financial Times*, London, June 2017.
7. Dr Shaikh Inayatullah, Professor of Arabic, Presidential Address Pakistan History Conference, 7th Session, University of the Punjab, 1957.

ACKNOWLEDGEMENTS

My great thanks are due first to Salahuddin, Moniba, Aneeza and Bahawal Abbasi for my initial visit to Derawar and for prompting me to write this book. Subsequently I basked in their hospitality for weeks on end in Islamabad and Lahore while I questioned them, from a starting position of extreme ignorance about the past in Bahawalpur and the present in Pakistan.

Back in the UK, I would like to thank Barbara Schwepcke and Harry Hall of Haus Publishing, who helped push me and this book along. Without them it would not have made it into print. I owe many thanks to Sir Nicholas Barrington, former British high commissioner in Pakistan, who gave me an insight into the great Pakistani families whom he knew well and has carefully documented. Visiting him in Cambridge also involved an excellent lunch and a first-ever visit to glorious Ely Cathedral. Thanks also to Shama Husain for her kindness and patience in helping me with unfamiliar Pakistani names; to other friends for their help in reading, re-reading and suggesting improvements and corrections in the manuscript; and, as ever, to the wonderful people in the Asian and African Collections of the British Library.

Finally, special thanks are due to Gurveen Chadha and Penguin Random House India. Gurveen enthusiastically took on a book about a forgotten part of Pakistan, which was not necessarily going to be a popular project under present circumstances. Since then she has also had to put up with my foibles as she helped the story of the Abbasis and Bahawalpur along the path to publication.

Any mistakes in the complicated history of the state of Bahawalpur, in spite of, or especially after, so much expert advice, must be laid at the door of the author. Opinions expressed by her of the situation in present-day Pakistan and particularly in the Bahawalpur region, gleaned from too-brief-observation and broad reading of contemporary sources, are also those of the author. They do not necessarily reflect those of Salahuddin Abbasi or members of his family.

INDEX